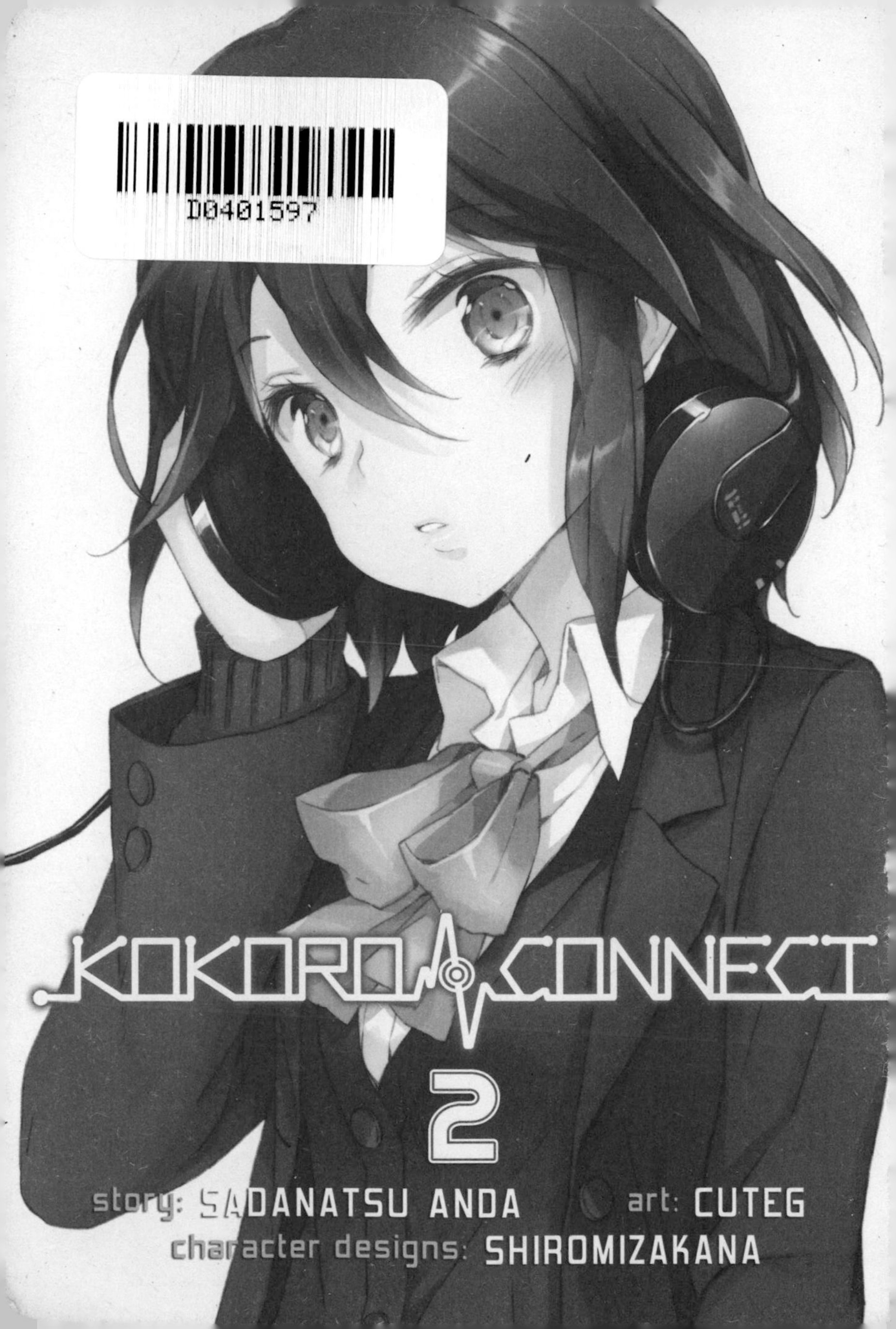

KOKORO CONNECT

2

story: SADANATSU ANDA art: CUTEG

character designs: SHIROMIZAKANA

SEVEN SEAS ENTERTAINMENT PRESENTS

KOKORO CONNECT

VOLUME 2

Story: **SADANATSU ANDA** / Character Designs: **SHIROMIZAKANA** / Art: **CUTEG**

TRANSLATION
Nan Rymer

ADAPTATION
Shannon Fay

COPY EDITOR
Lee Otter

LETTERING AND LAYOUT
Mia Chiresa

COVER DESIGN
Nicky Lim

PROOFREADER
Shanti Whitesides

MANAGING EDITOR
Adam Arnold

PUBLISHER
Jason DeAngelis

KOKORO CONNECT VOL. 2

First published in Japan in 2011 by KADOKAWA CORPORATION ENTERBRAIN. English translation rights arranged with KADOKAWA CORPORATION ENTERBRAIN through TOHAN CORPORATION, Tokyo.

ISBN: 978-1-626920-73-6

Printed Canada

First Printing: November 2014

10 9 8 7 6 5 4 3 2 1

FOLLOW US ONLINE: ***www.gomanga.com***

READING DIRECTIONS

This book reads from ***right to left***, Japanese style. If this is your first time reading manga, you start reading from the top right panel on each page and take it from there. If you get lost, just follow the numbered diagram here. It may seem backwards at first, but you'll get the hang of it! Have fun!!

1
2
3
4
5
6
7
8
9

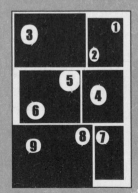

KOKORO CONNECT

Chapter 7

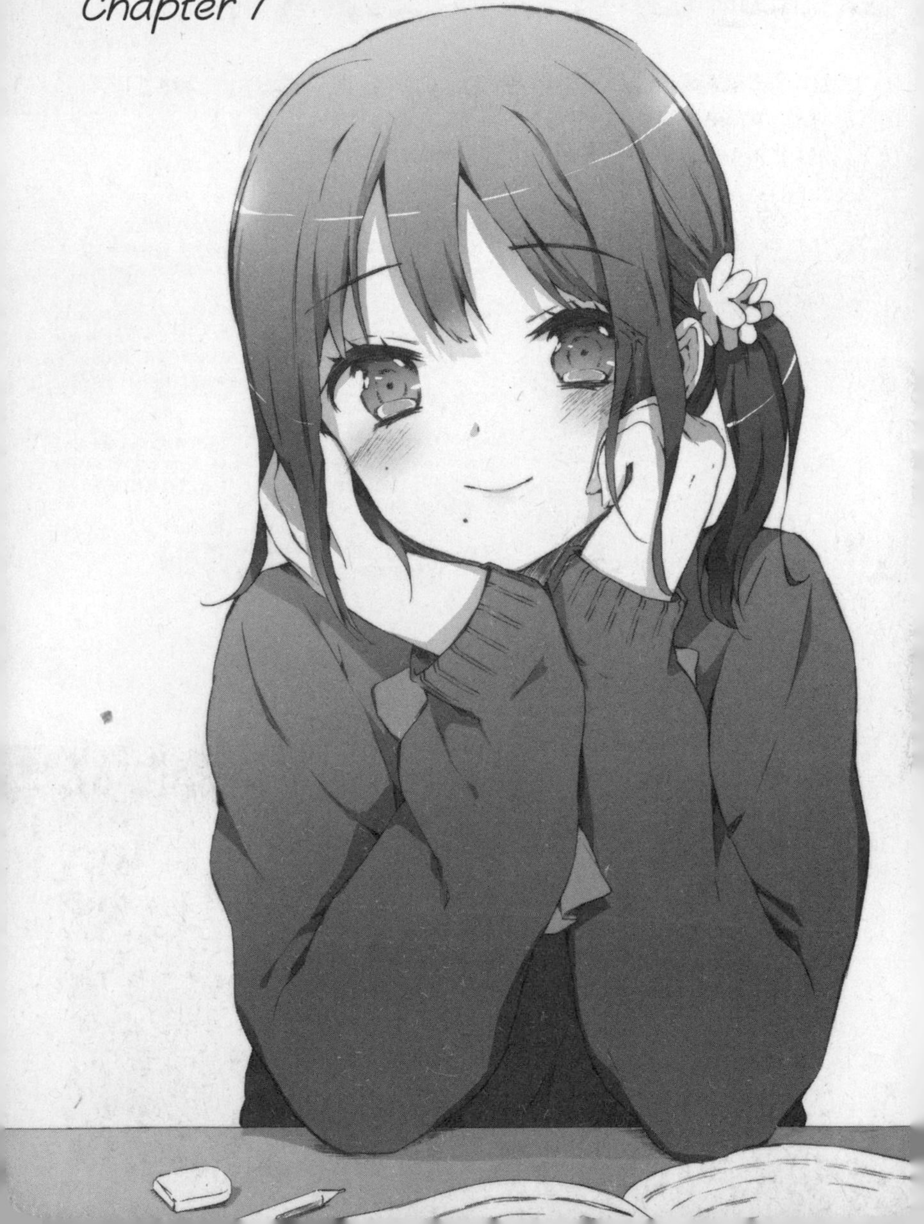

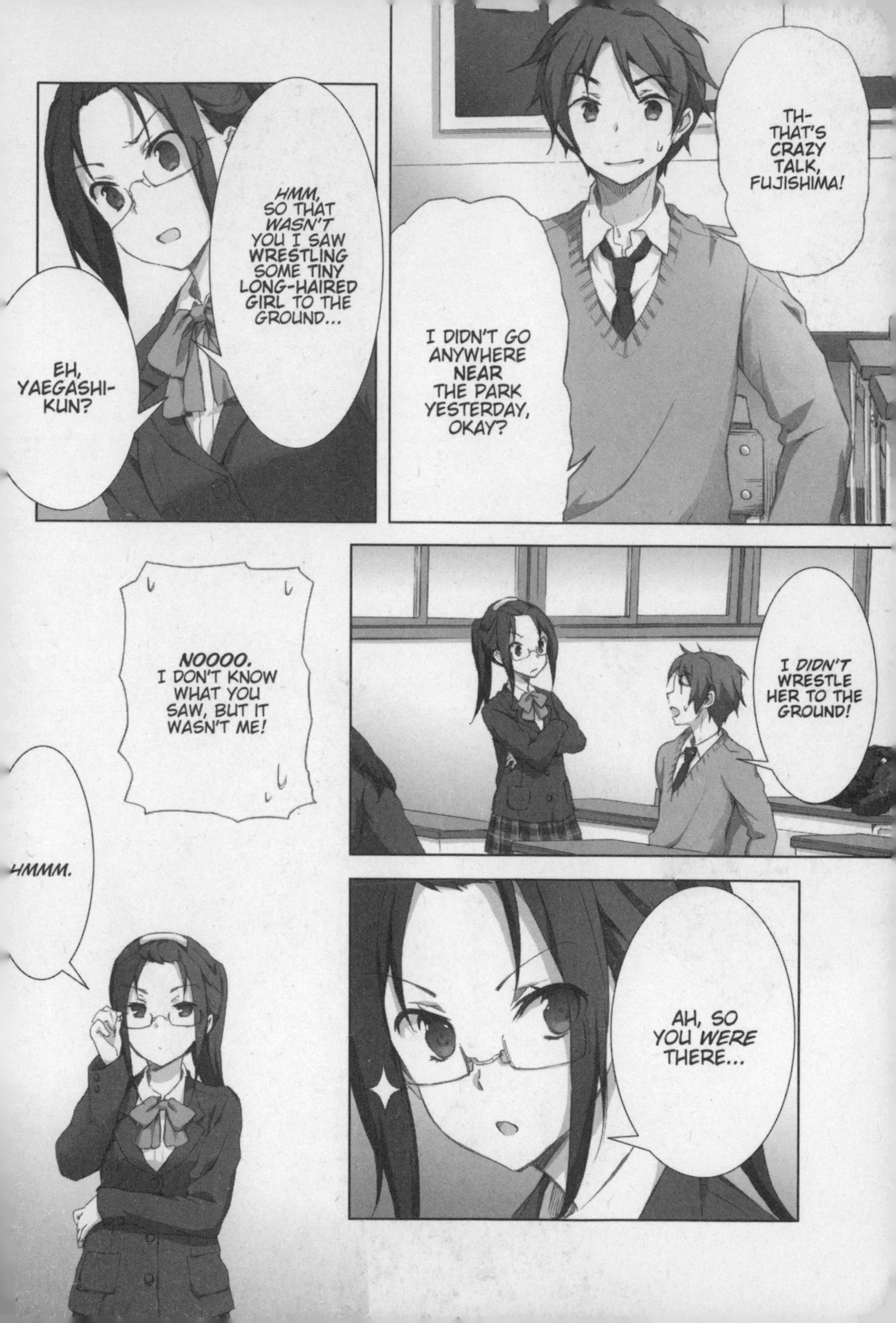
TH-THAT'S CRAZY TALK, FUJISHIMA!
I DIDN'T GO ANYWHERE NEAR THE PARK YESTERDAY, OKAY?
HMM, SO THAT *WASN'T* YOU I SAW WRESTLING SOME TINY LONG-HAIRED GIRL TO THE GROUND...
EH, YAEGASHI-KUN?
NOOOO. I DON'T KNOW WHAT YOU SAW, BUT IT WASN'T ME!
HMMM.
I *DIDN'T* WRESTLE HER TO THE GROUND!
AH, SO YOU *WERE* THERE...

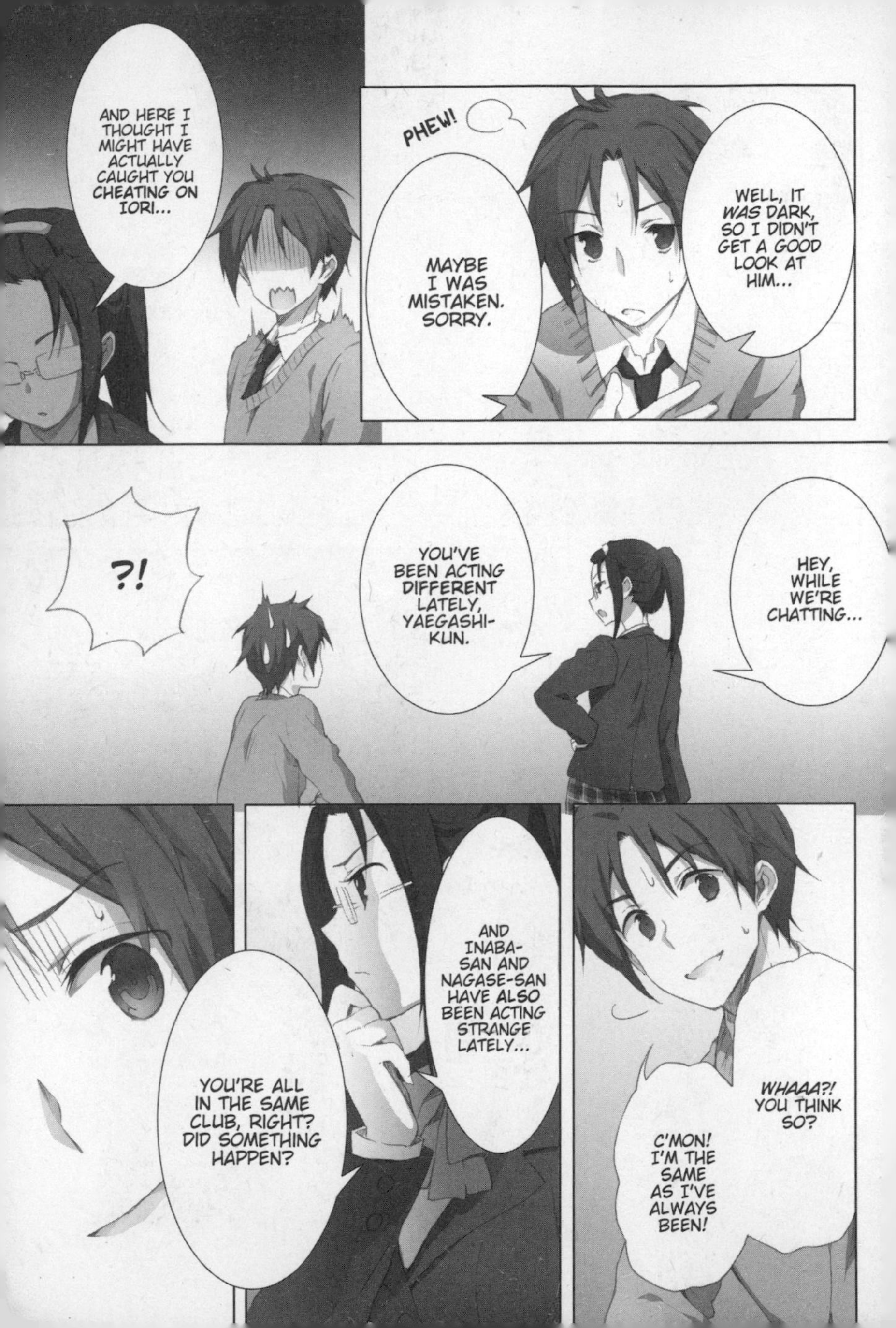
WELL, IT WAS DARK, SO I DIDN'T GET A GOOD LOOK AT HIM...
PHEW!
MAYBE I WAS MISTAKEN. SORRY.
AND HERE I THOUGHT I MIGHT HAVE ACTUALLY CAUGHT YOU CHEATING ON IORI...
HEY, WHILE WE'RE CHATTING...
YOU'VE BEEN ACTING DIFFERENT LATELY, YAEGASHI-KUN.
?!
WHAAA?! YOU THINK SO?
C'MON! I'M THE SAME AS I'VE ALWAYS BEEN!
AND INABA-SAN AND NAGASE-SAN HAVE ALSO BEEN ACTING STRANGE LATELY...
YOU'RE ALL IN THE SAME CLUB, RIGHT? DID SOMETHING HAPPEN?

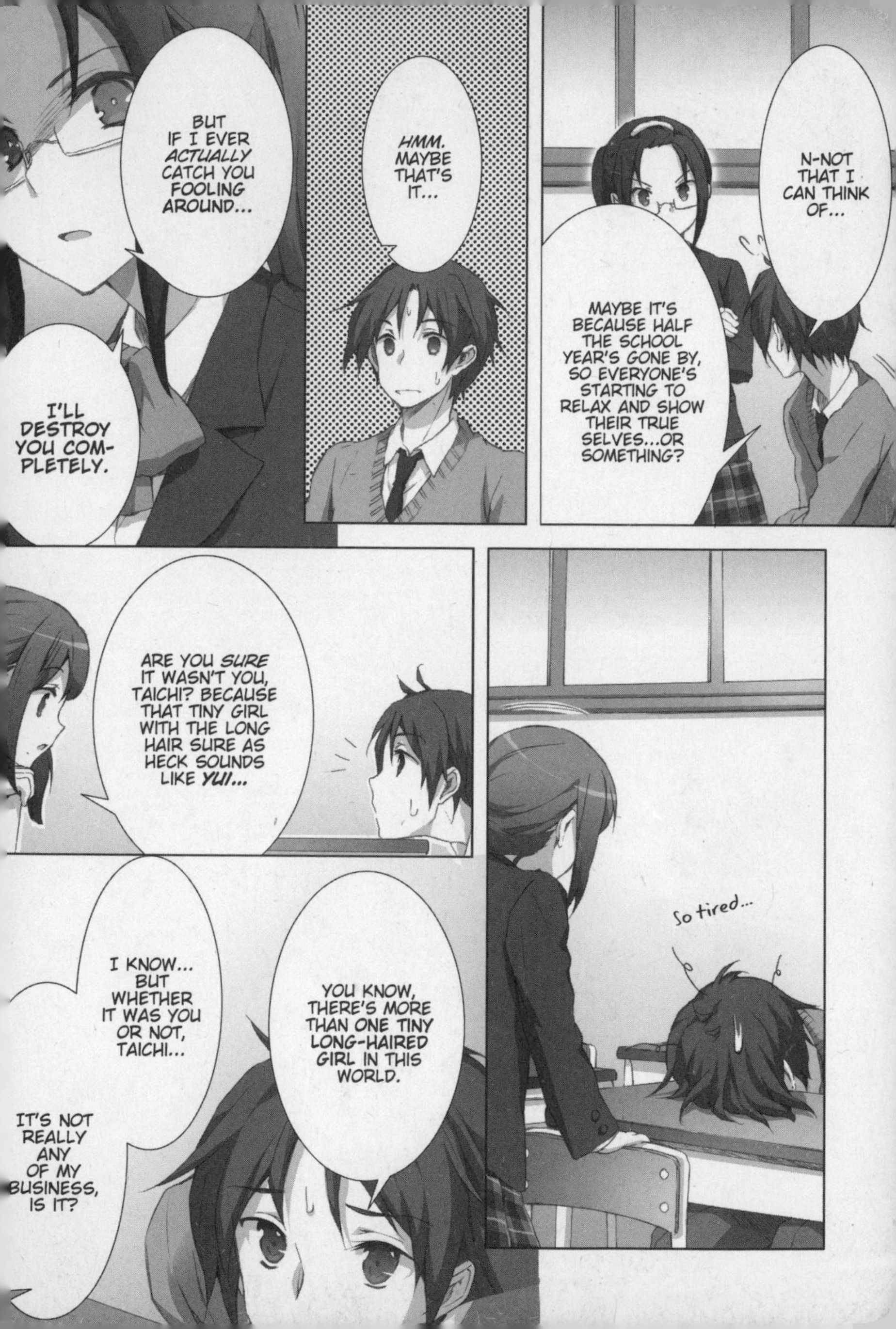
N-NOT THAT I CAN THINK OF...
MAYBE IT'S BECAUSE HALF THE SCHOOL YEAR'S GONE BY, SO EVERYONE'S STARTING TO RELAX AND SHOW THEIR TRUE SELVES...OR SOMETHING?
HMM. MAYBE THAT'S IT...
BUT IF I EVER *ACTUALLY* CATCH YOU FOOLING AROUND...
I'LL DESTROY YOU COMPLETELY.
So tired...
ARE YOU *SURE* IT WASN'T YOU, TAICHI? BECAUSE THAT TINY GIRL WITH THE LONG HAIR SURE AS HECK SOUNDS LIKE ***YUI...***
YOU KNOW, THERE'S MORE THAN ONE TINY LONG-HAIRED GIRL IN THIS WORLD.
I KNOW... BUT WHETHER IT WAS YOU OR NOT, TAICHI...
IT'S NOT REALLY ANY OF MY BUSINESS, IS IT?

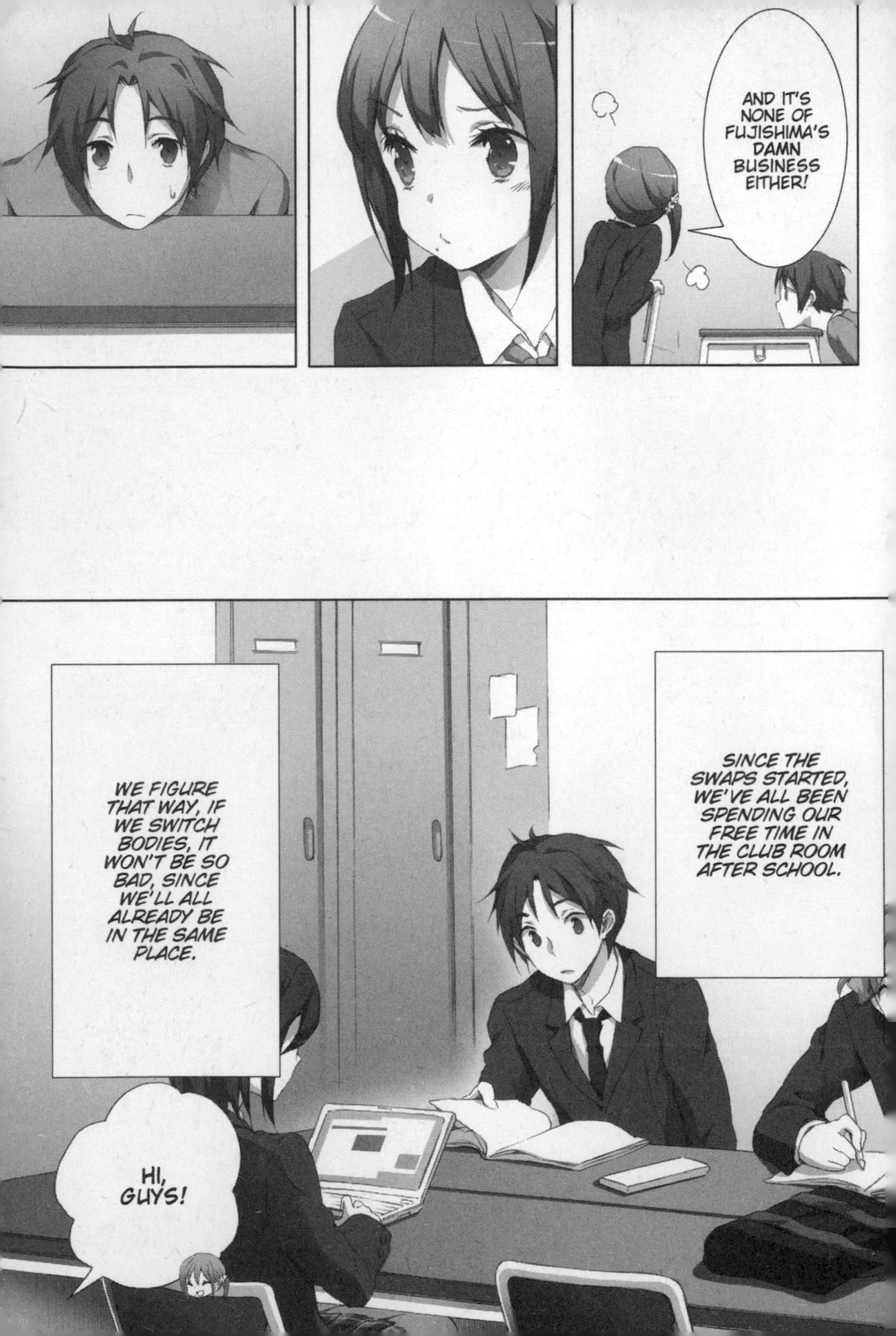
AND IT'S NONE OF FUJISHIMA'S DAMN BUSINESS EITHER!
SINCE THE SWAPS STARTED, WE'VE ALL BEEN SPENDING OUR FREE TIME IN THE CLUB ROOM AFTER SCHOOL.
WE FIGURE THAT WAY, IF WE SWITCH BODIES, IT WON'T BE SO BAD, SINCE WE'LL ALL ALREADY BE IN THE SAME PLACE.
HI, GUYS!

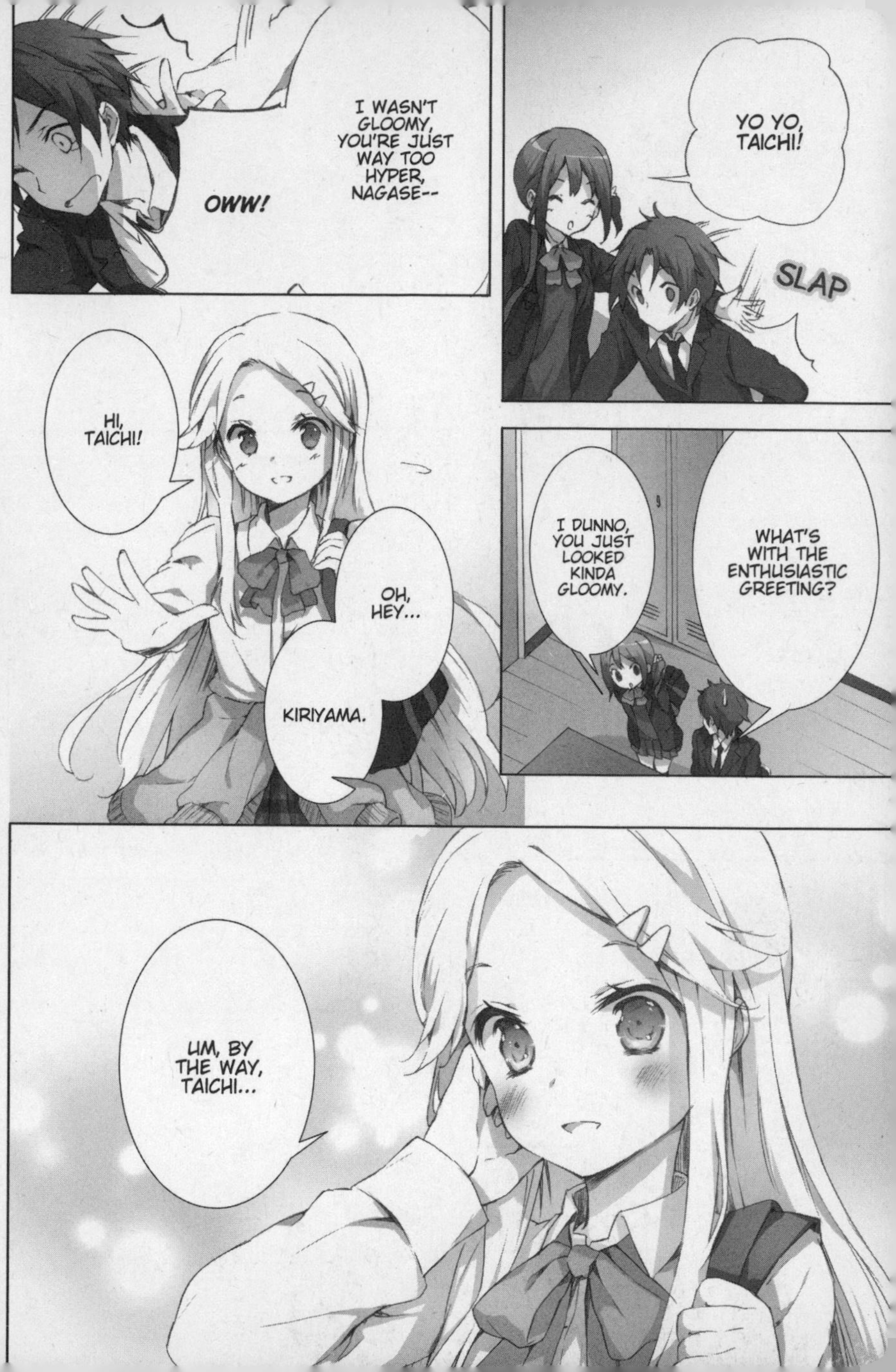
YO YO, TAICHI!
SLAP
WHAT'S WITH THE ENTHUSIASTIC GREETING?
I DUNNO, YOU JUST LOOKED KINDA GLOOMY.
I WASN'T GLOOMY, YOU'RE JUST WAY TOO HYPER, NAGASE--
OWW!
HI, TAICHI!
OH, HEY...
KIRIYAMA.
UM, BY THE WAY, TAICHI...

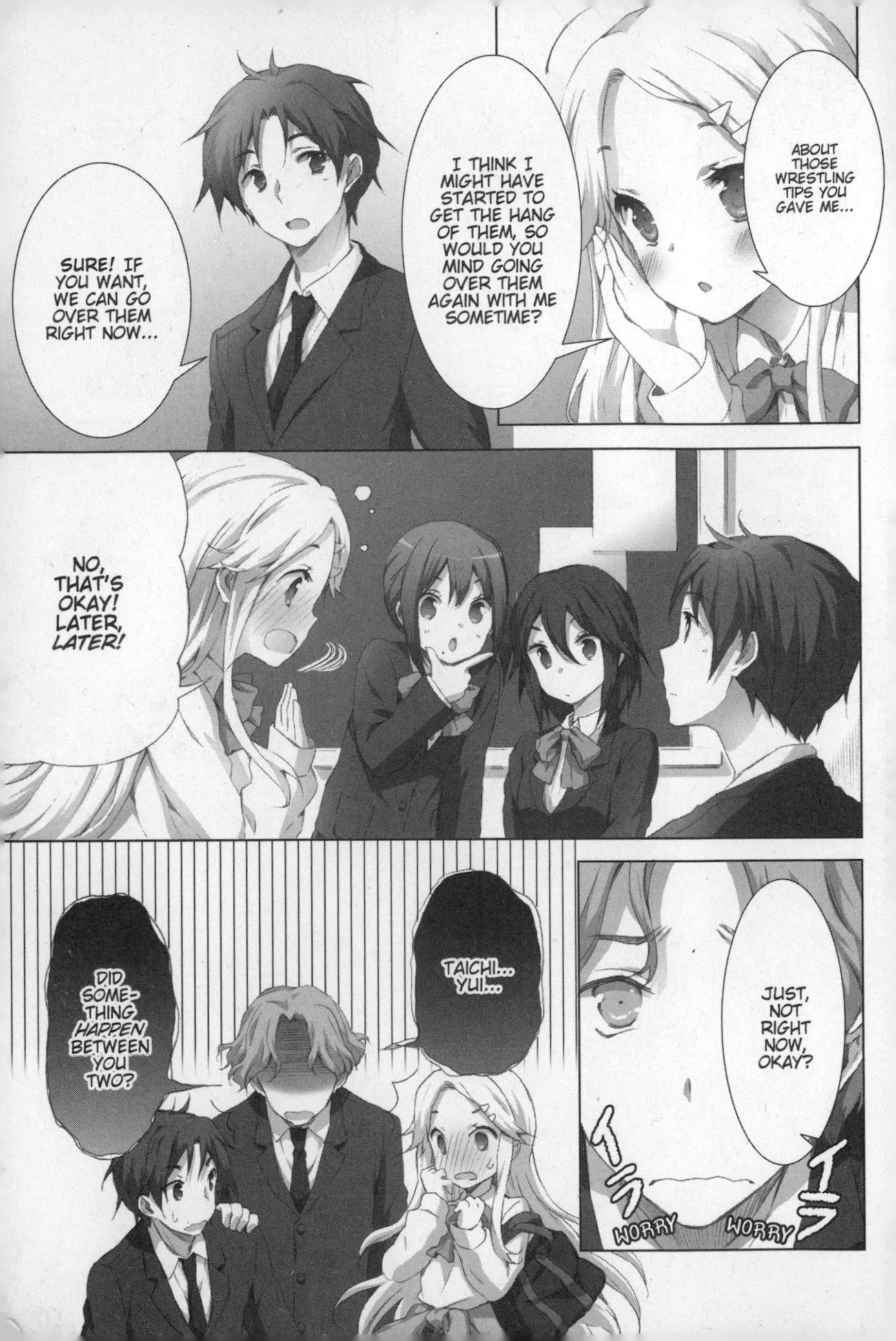
ABOUT THOSE WRESTLING TIPS YOU GAVE ME...
I THINK I MIGHT HAVE STARTED TO GET THE HANG OF THEM, SO WOULD YOU MIND GOING OVER THEM AGAIN WITH ME SOMETIME?
SURE! IF YOU WANT, WE CAN GO OVER THEM RIGHT NOW...
NO, THAT'S OKAY! LATER, *LATER!*
JUST, NOT RIGHT NOW, OKAY?
イラ WORRY
イラ WORRY
TAICHI... YUI...
DID SOMETHING *HAPPEN* BETWEEN YOU TWO?

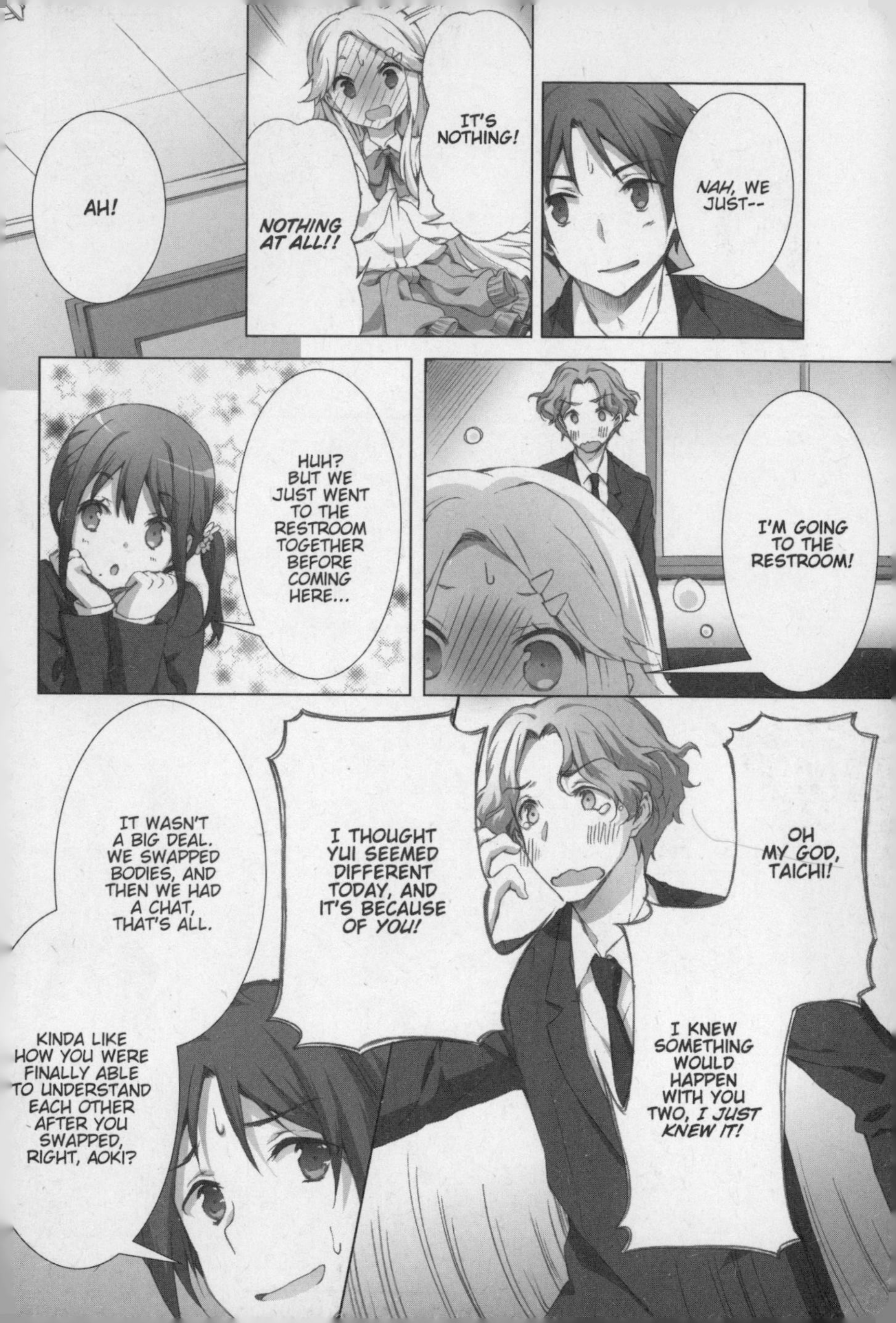
NAH, WE JUST--
IT'S NOTHING!
NOTHING AT ALL!!
AH!
I'M GOING TO THE RESTROOM!
HUH? BUT WE JUST WENT TO THE RESTROOM TOGETHER BEFORE COMING HERE...
OH MY GOD, TAICHI!
I THOUGHT YUI SEEMED DIFFERENT TODAY, AND IT'S BECAUSE OF YOU!
I KNEW SOMETHING WOULD HAPPEN WITH YOU TWO, I JUST KNEW IT!
IT WASN'T A BIG DEAL. WE SWAPPED BODIES, AND THEN WE HAD A CHAT, THAT'S ALL.
KINDA LIKE HOW YOU WERE FINALLY ABLE TO UNDERSTAND EACH OTHER AFTER YOU SWAPPED, RIGHT, AOKI?

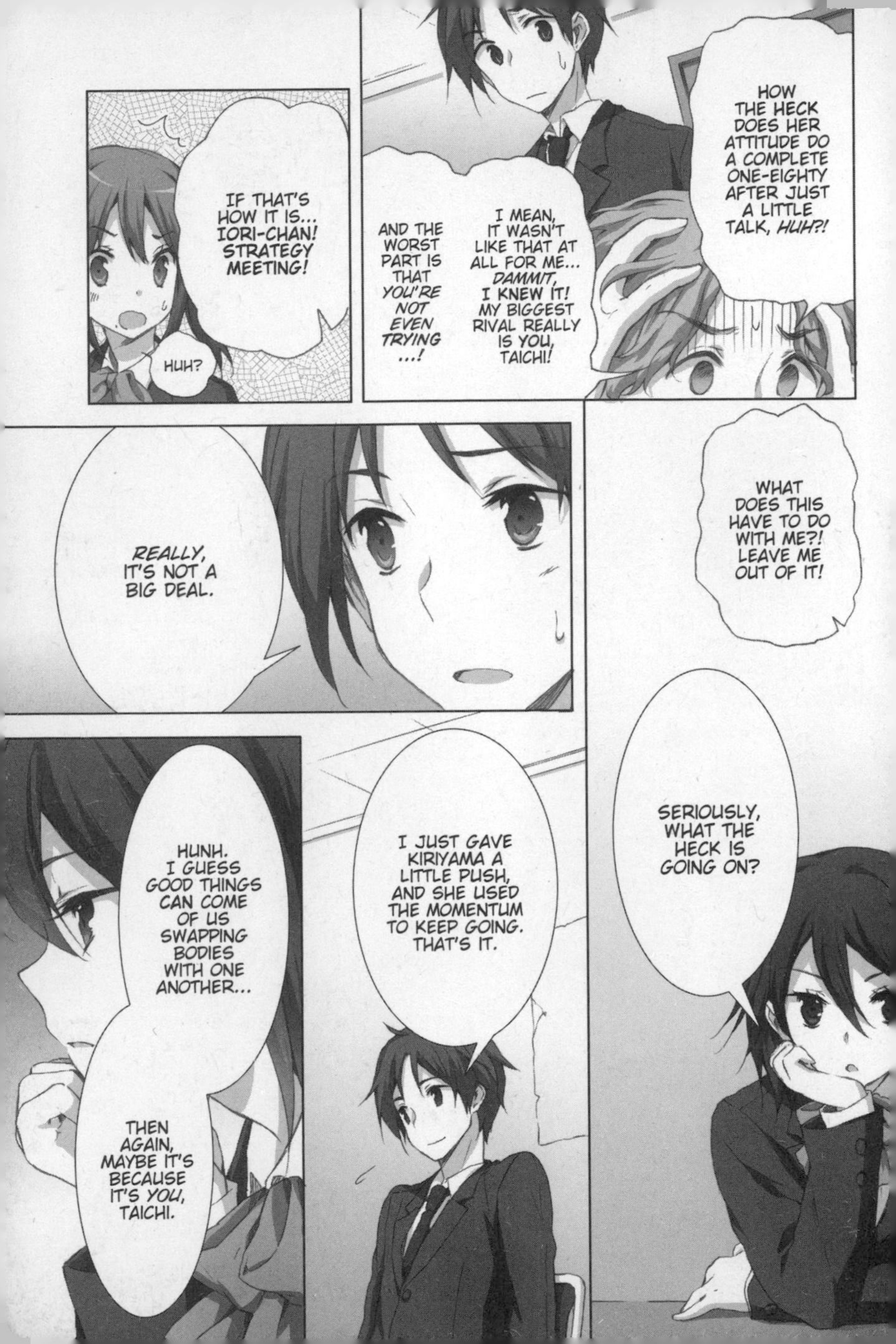
HOW THE HECK DOES HER ATTITUDE DO A COMPLETE ONE-EIGHTY AFTER JUST A LITTLE TALK, *HUH?!*
I MEAN, IT WASN'T LIKE THAT AT ALL FOR ME... *DAMMIT,* I KNEW IT! MY BIGGEST RIVAL REALLY IS YOU, TAICHI!
AND THE WORST PART IS THAT *YOU'RE NOT EVEN TRYING...!*
IF THAT'S HOW IT IS... IORI-CHAN! STRATEGY MEETING!
HUH?
WHAT DOES THIS HAVE TO DO WITH ME?! LEAVE ME OUT OF IT!
SERIOUSLY, WHAT THE HECK IS GOING ON?
REALLY, IT'S NOT A BIG DEAL.
I JUST GAVE KIRIYAMA A LITTLE PUSH, AND SHE USED THE MOMENTUM TO KEEP GOING. THAT'S IT.
HUNH. I GUESS GOOD THINGS CAN COME OF US SWAPPING BODIES WITH ONE ANOTHER...
THEN AGAIN, MAYBE IT'S BECAUSE IT'S *YOU,* TAICHI.

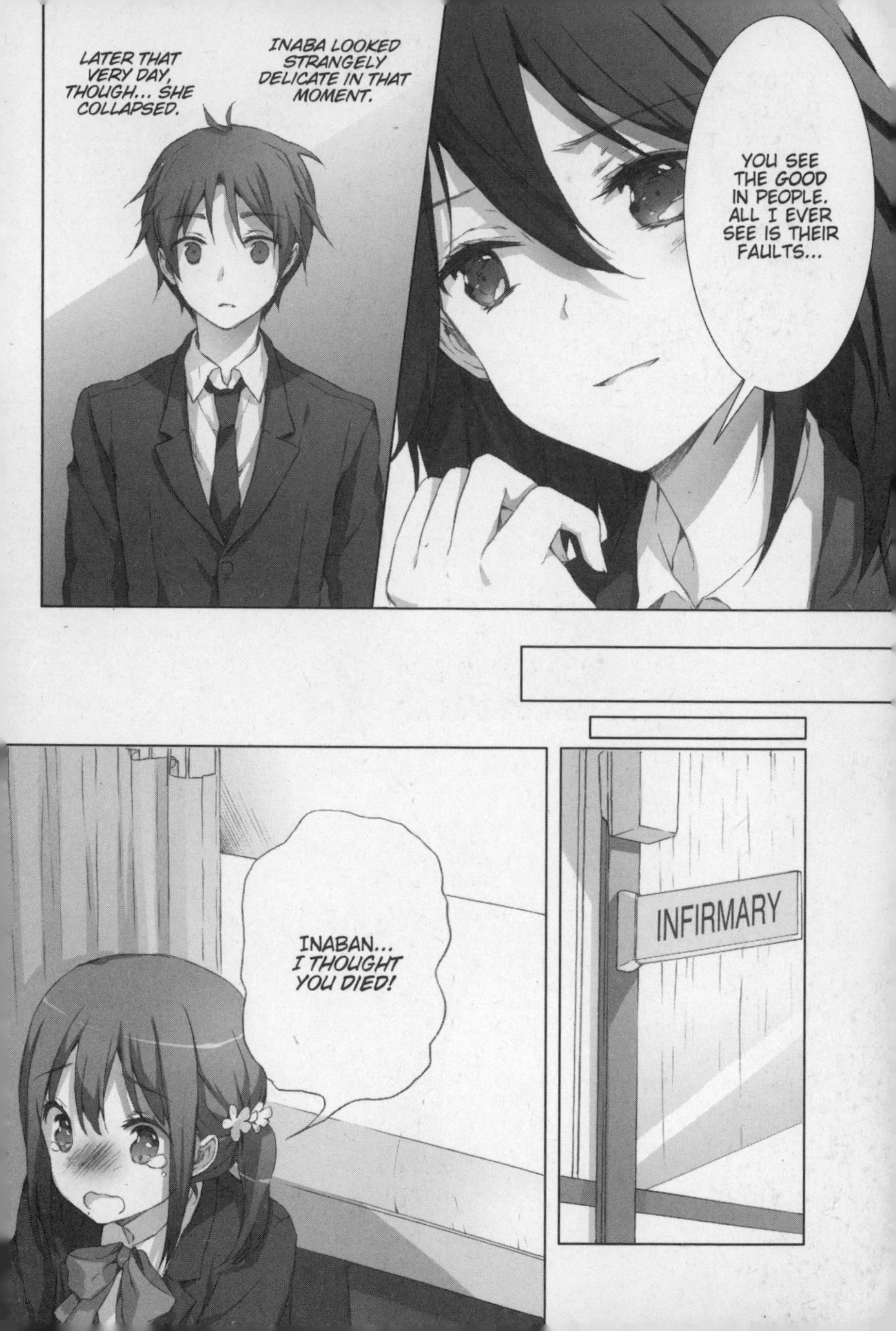
YOU SEE THE GOOD IN PEOPLE. ALL I EVER SEE IS THEIR FAULTS...
INABA LOOKED STRANGELY DELICATE IN THAT MOMENT.
LATER THAT VERY DAY, THOUGH... SHE COLLAPSED.
INFIRMARY
INABAN... I THOUGHT YOU DIED!

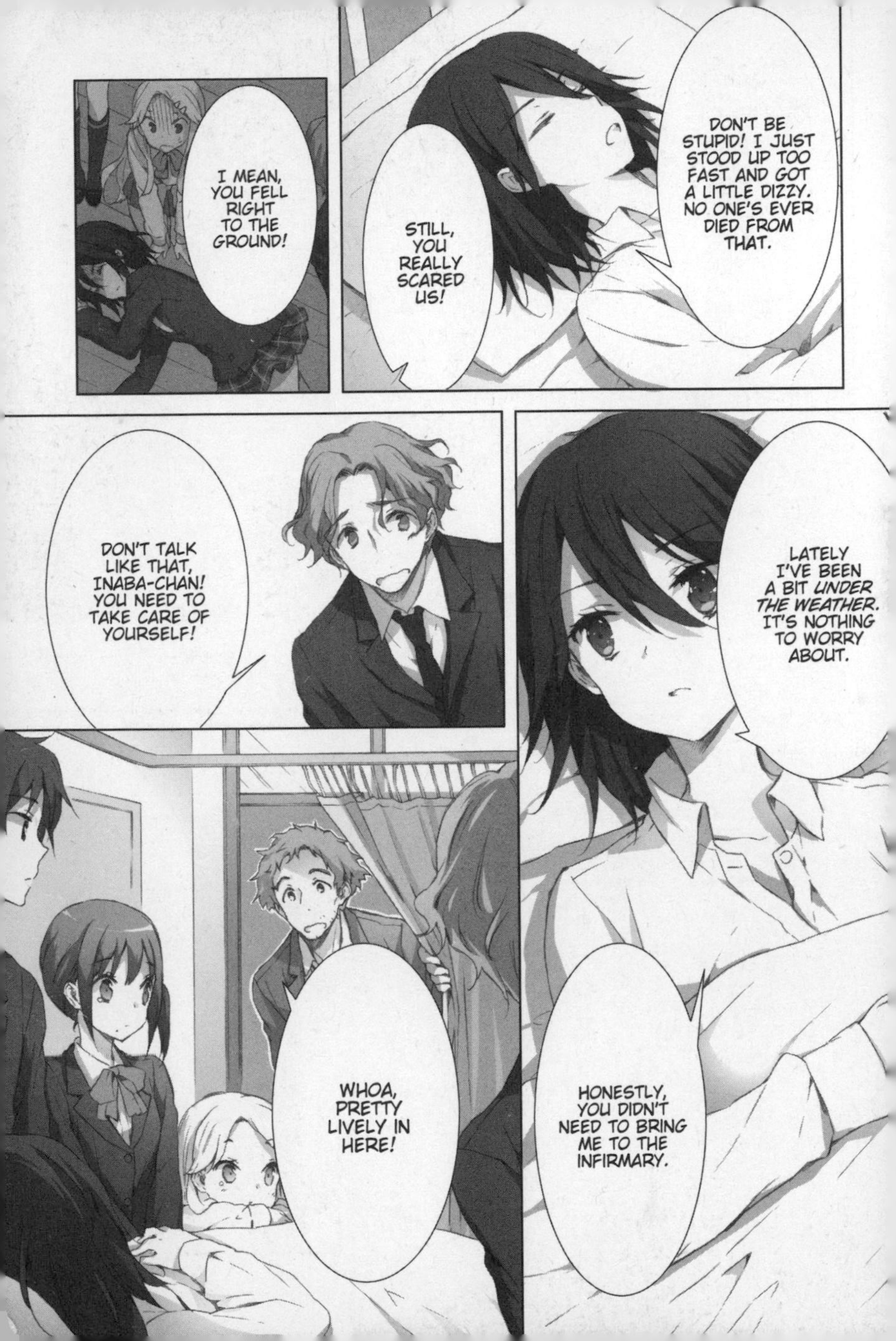
DON'T BE STUPID! I JUST STOOD UP TOO FAST AND GOT A LITTLE DIZZY. NO ONE'S EVER DIED FROM THAT.
STILL, YOU REALLY SCARED US!
I MEAN, YOU FELL RIGHT TO THE GROUND!
LATELY I'VE BEEN A BIT *UNDER THE WEATHER*. IT'S NOTHING TO WORRY ABOUT.
HONESTLY, YOU DIDN'T NEED TO BRING ME TO THE INFIRMARY.
DON'T TALK LIKE THAT, INABA-CHAN! YOU NEED TO TAKE CARE OF YOURSELF!
WHOA, PRETTY LIVELY IN HERE!

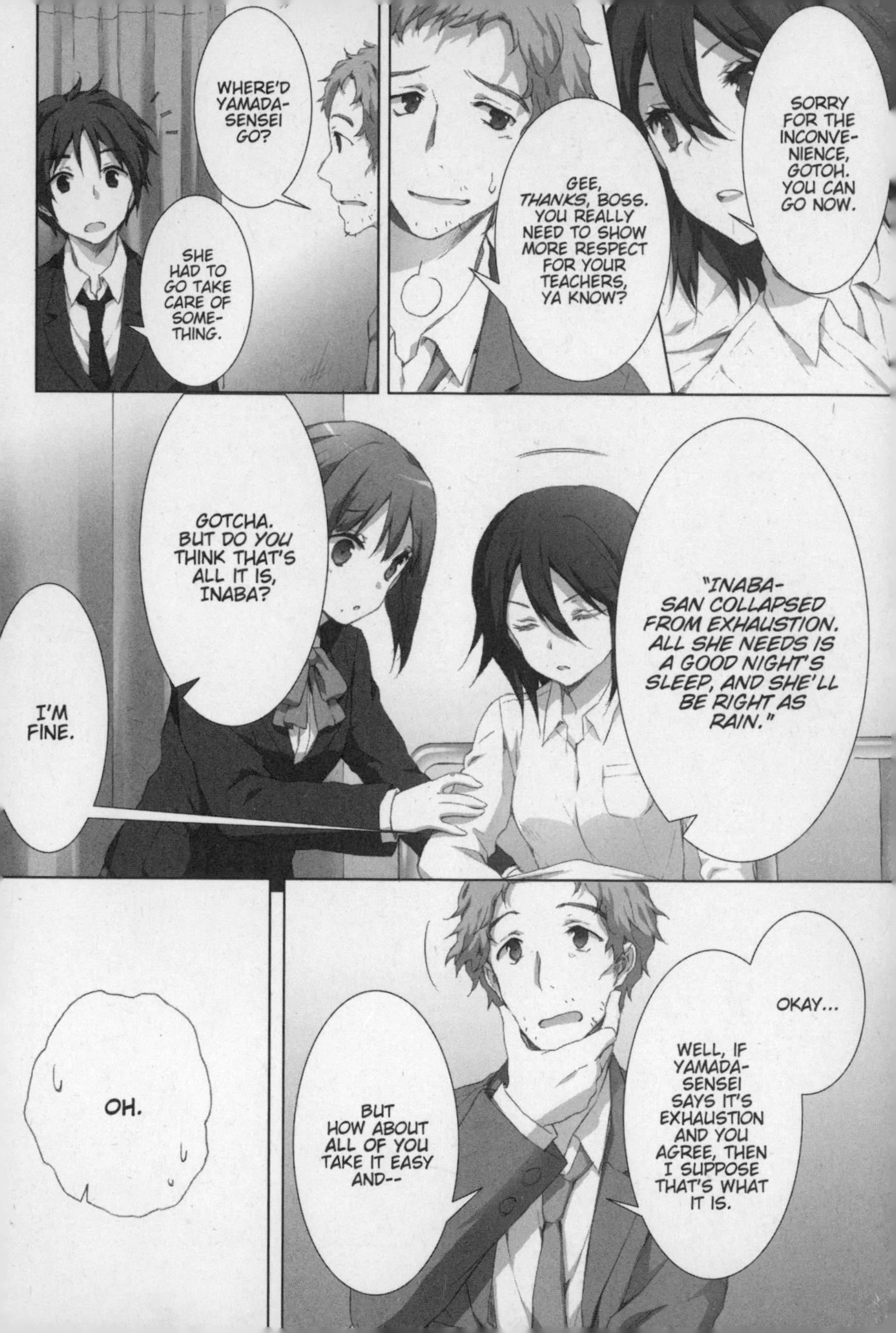
SORRY FOR THE INCONVENIENCE, GOTOH. YOU CAN GO NOW.
GEE, *THANKS*, BOSS. YOU REALLY NEED TO SHOW MORE RESPECT FOR YOUR TEACHERS, YA KNOW?
WHERE'D YAMADA-SENSEI GO?
SHE HAD TO GO TAKE CARE OF SOMETHING.
"INABA-SAN COLLAPSED FROM EXHAUSTION. ALL SHE NEEDS IS A GOOD NIGHT'S SLEEP, AND SHE'LL BE RIGHT AS RAIN."
GOTCHA. BUT DO *YOU* THINK THAT'S ALL IT IS, INABA?
I'M FINE.
OKAY...
WELL, IF YAMADA-SENSEI SAYS IT'S EXHAUSTION AND YOU AGREE, THEN I SUPPOSE THAT'S WHAT IT IS.
BUT HOW ABOUT ALL OF YOU TAKE IT EASY AND--
OH.

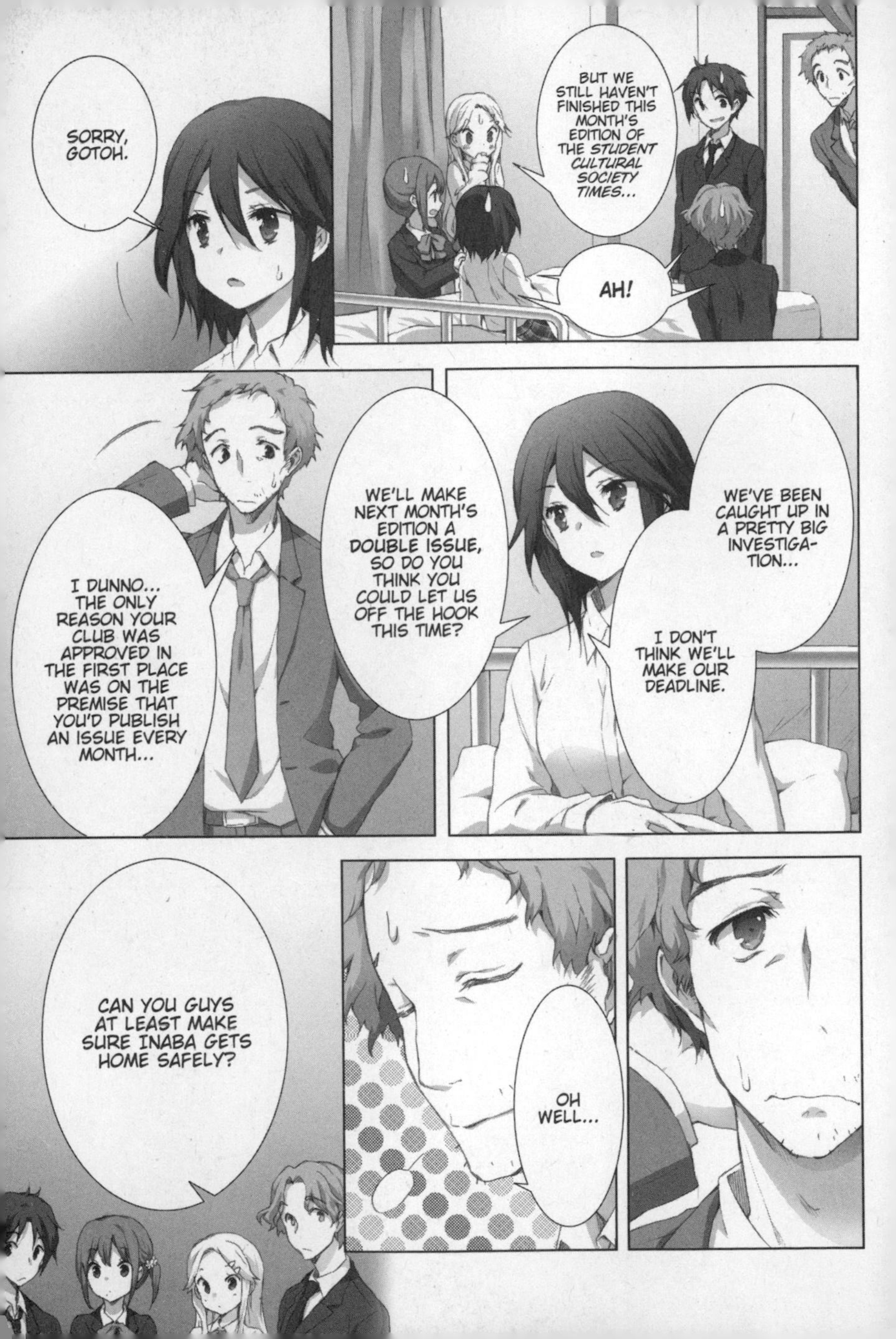
BUT WE STILL HAVEN'T FINISHED THIS MONTH'S EDITION OF THE *STUDENT CULTURAL SOCIETY TIMES*...
AH!
SORRY, GOTOH.
WE'VE BEEN CAUGHT UP IN A PRETTY BIG INVESTIGA-TION...
I DON'T THINK WE'LL MAKE OUR DEADLINE.
WE'LL MAKE NEXT MONTH'S EDITION A DOUBLE ISSUE, SO DO YOU THINK YOU COULD LET US OFF THE HOOK THIS TIME?
I DUNNO... THE ONLY REASON YOUR CLUB WAS APPROVED IN THE FIRST PLACE WAS ON THE PREMISE THAT YOU'D PUBLISH AN ISSUE EVERY MONTH...
OH WELL...
CAN YOU GUYS AT LEAST MAKE SURE INABA GETS HOME SAFELY?

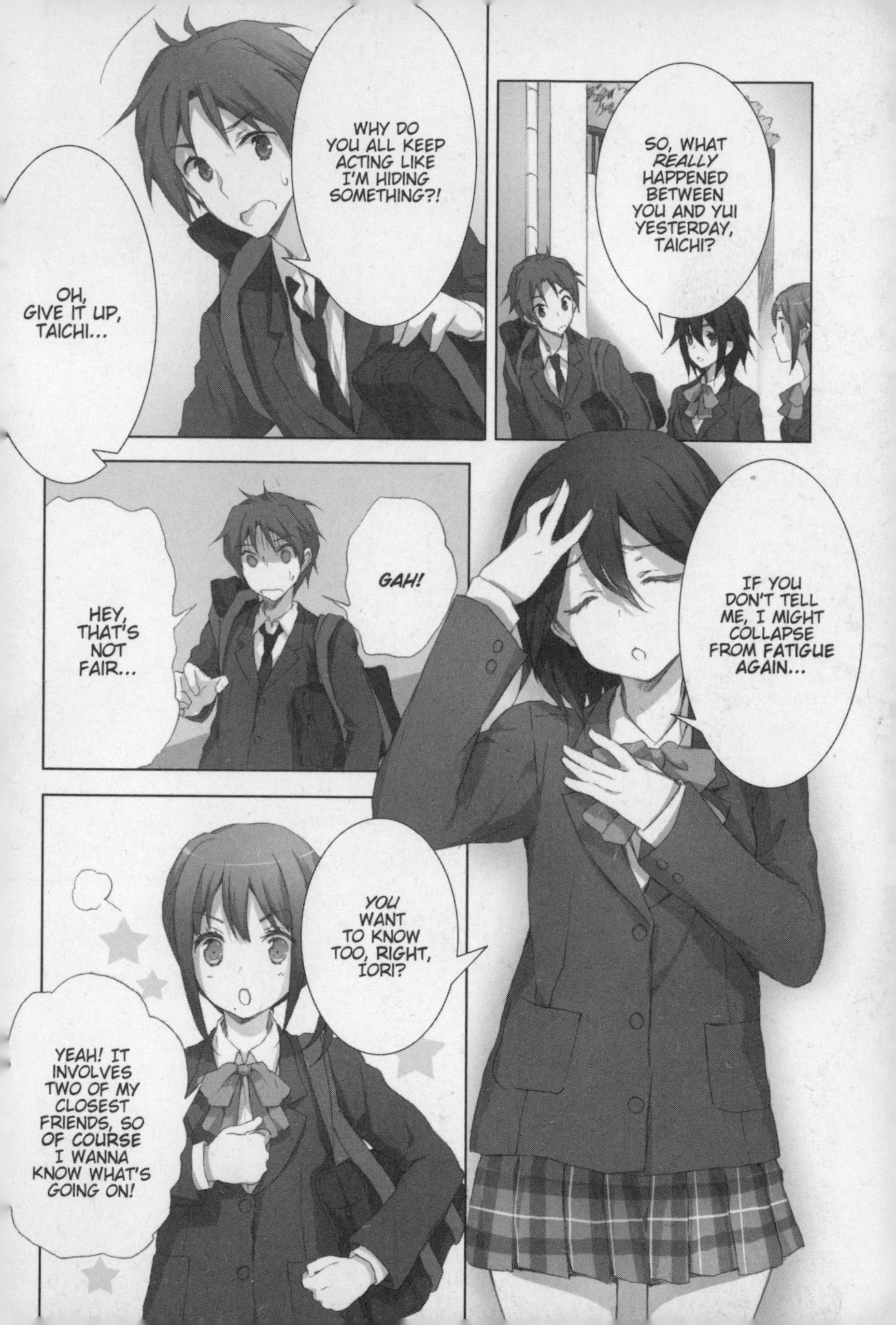
SO, WHAT *REALLY* HAPPENED BETWEEN YOU AND YUI YESTERDAY, TAICHI?
WHY DO YOU ALL KEEP ACTING LIKE I'M HIDING SOMETHING?!
OH, GIVE IT UP, TAICHI...
IF YOU DON'T TELL ME, I MIGHT COLLAPSE FROM FATIGUE AGAIN...
GAH!
HEY, THAT'S NOT FAIR...
YOU WANT TO KNOW TOO, RIGHT, IORI?
YEAH! IT INVOLVES TWO OF MY CLOSEST FRIENDS, SO OF COURSE I WANNA KNOW WHAT'S GOING ON!

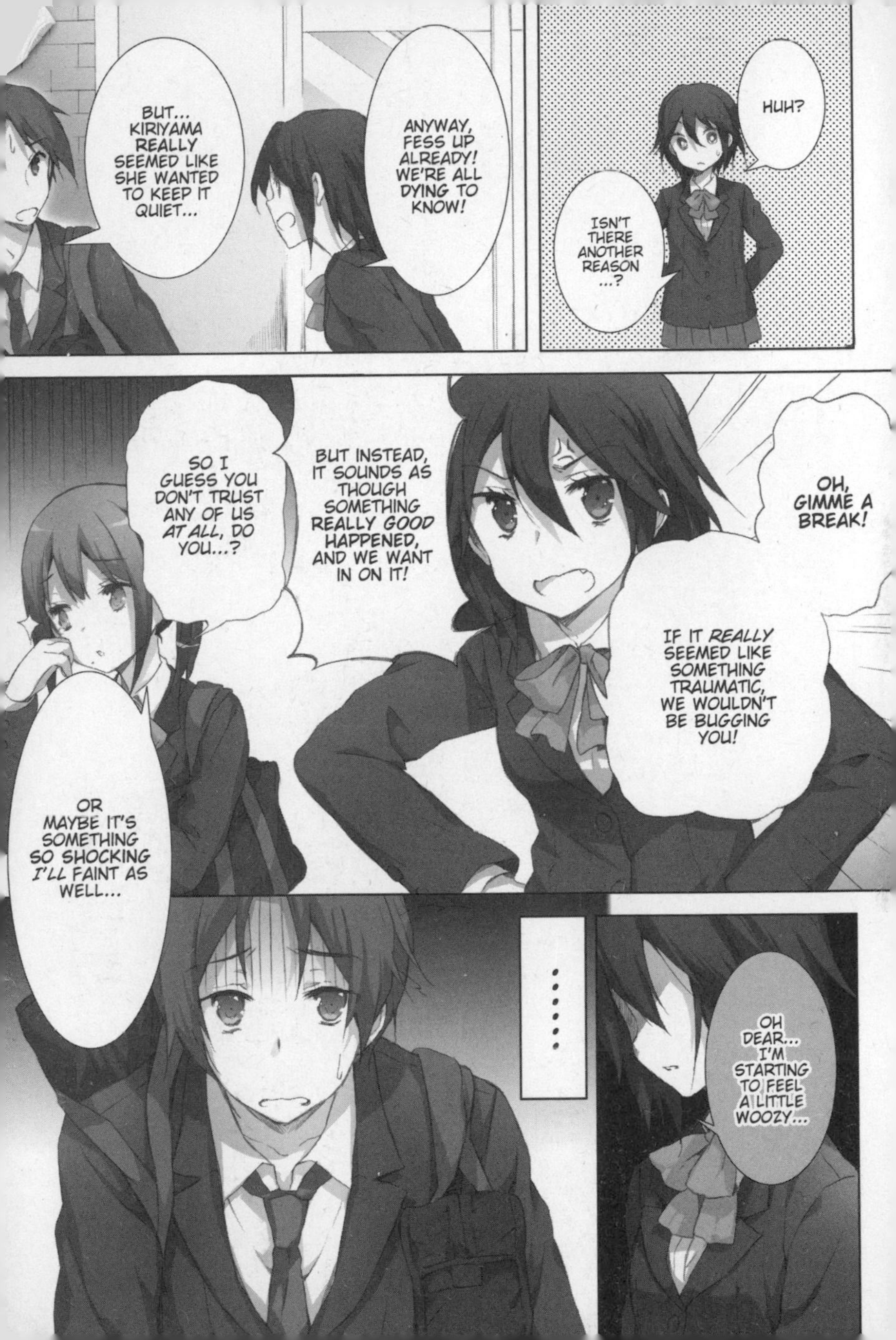
HUH?
ISN'T THERE ANOTHER REASON ...?
ANYWAY, FESS UP ALREADY! WE'RE ALL DYING TO KNOW!
BUT... KIRIYAMA REALLY SEEMED LIKE SHE WANTED TO KEEP IT QUIET...
OH, GIMME A BREAK!
IF IT *REALLY* SEEMED LIKE SOMETHING TRAUMATIC, WE WOULDN'T BE BUGGING YOU!
BUT INSTEAD, IT SOUNDS AS THOUGH SOMETHING REALLY *GOOD* HAPPENED, AND WE WANT IN ON IT!
SO I GUESS YOU DON'T TRUST ANY OF US *AT ALL*, DO YOU...?
OR MAYBE IT'S SOMETHING SO SHOCKING *I'LL* FAINT AS WELL...
OH DEAR... I'M STARTING TO FEEL A LITTLE WOOZY...
......

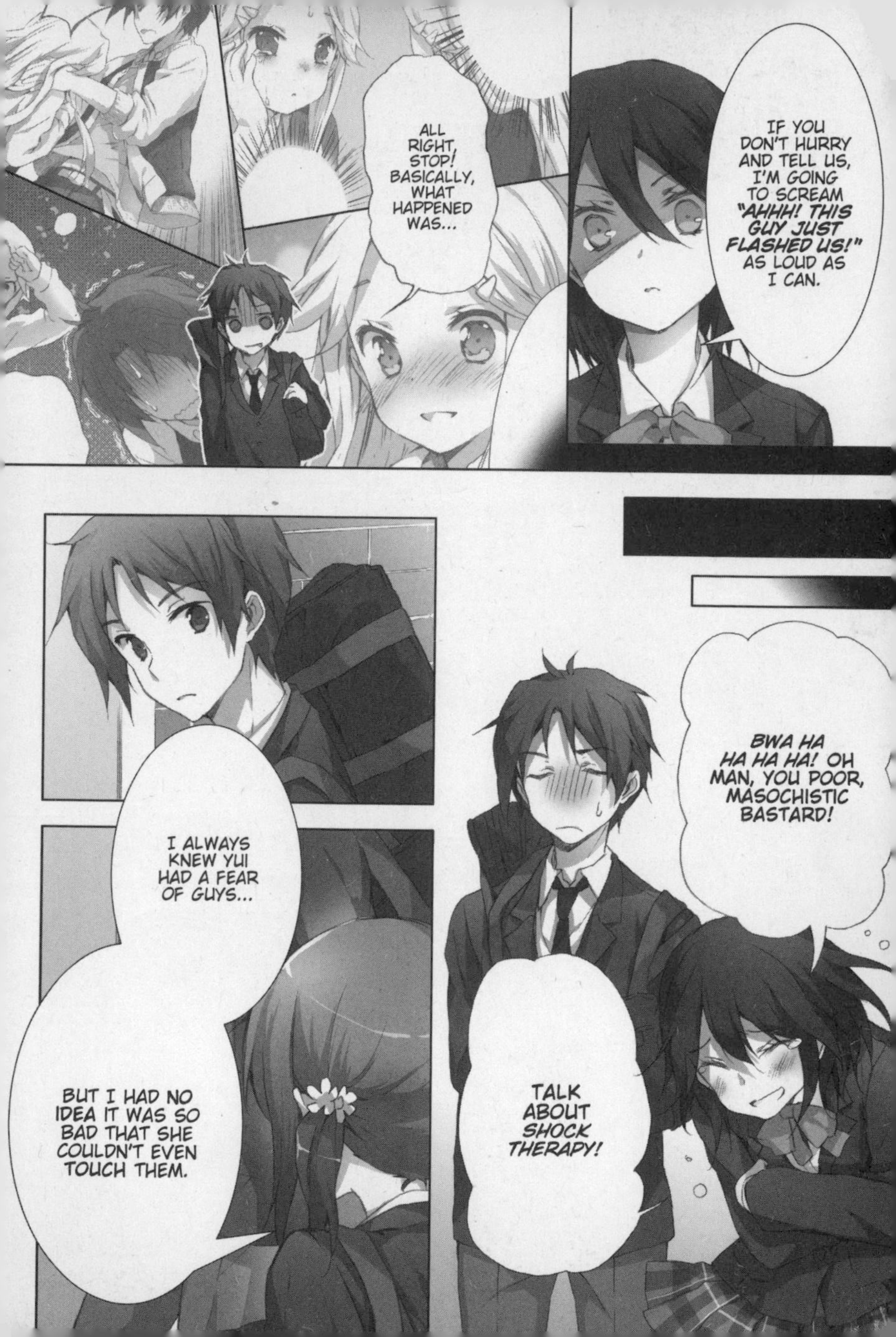
IF YOU DON'T HURRY AND TELL US, I'M GOING TO SCREAM *"AHHH! THIS GUY JUST FLASHED US!"* AS LOUD AS I CAN.
ALL RIGHT, STOP! BASICALLY, WHAT HAPPENED WAS...
BWA HA HA HA HA! OH MAN, YOU POOR, MASOCHISTIC BASTARD!
TALK ABOUT *SHOCK THERAPY!*
I ALWAYS KNEW YUI HAD A FEAR OF GUYS...
BUT I HAD NO IDEA IT WAS SO BAD THAT SHE COULDN'T EVEN TOUCH THEM.

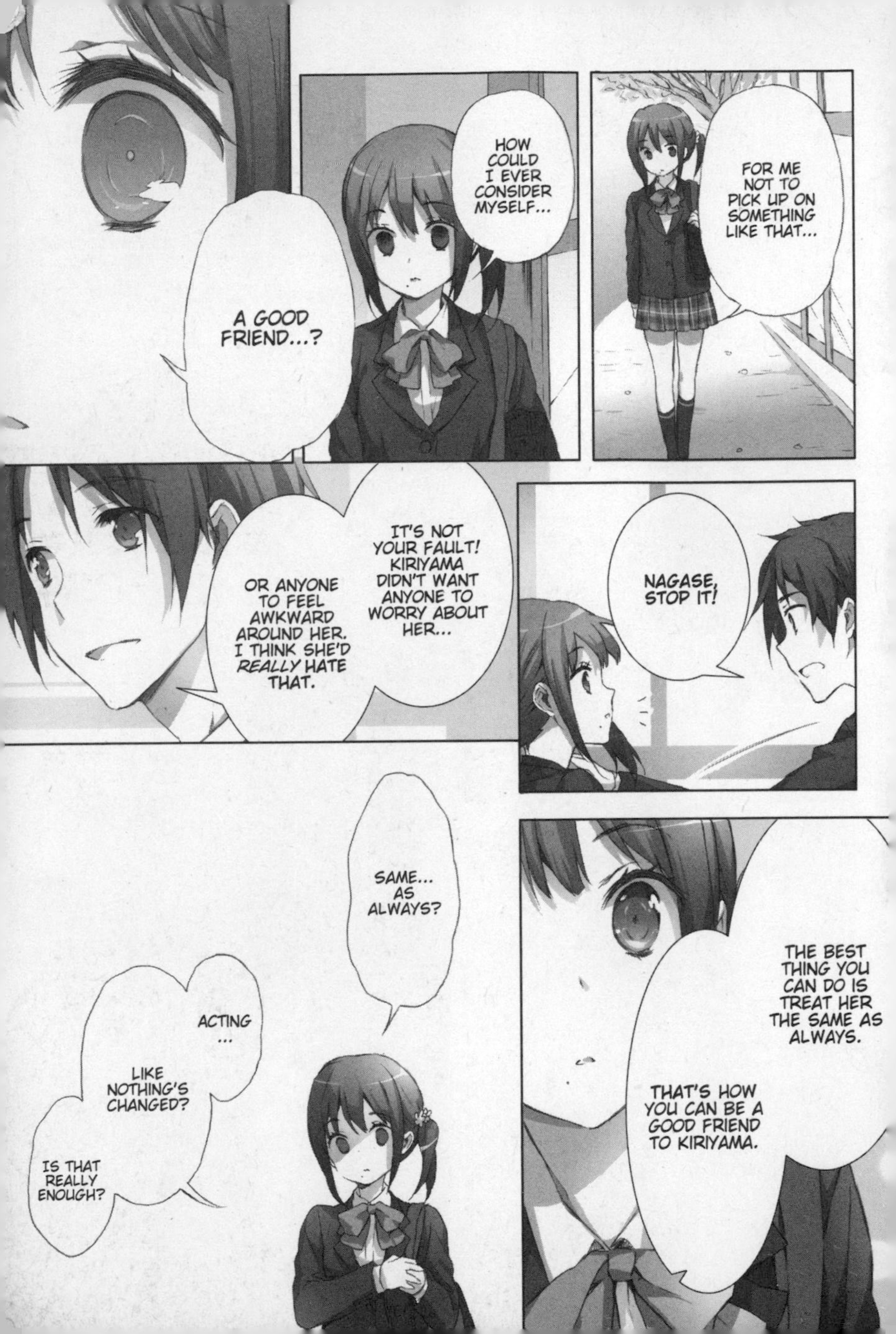
FOR ME NOT TO PICK UP ON SOMETHING LIKE THAT...
HOW COULD I EVER CONSIDER MYSELF...
A GOOD FRIEND...?
NAGASE, STOP IT!
IT'S NOT YOUR FAULT! KIRIYAMA DIDN'T WANT ANYONE TO WORRY ABOUT HER...
OR ANYONE TO FEEL AWKWARD AROUND HER. I THINK SHE'D *REALLY* HATE THAT.
THE BEST THING YOU CAN DO IS TREAT HER THE SAME AS ALWAYS.
THAT'S HOW YOU CAN BE A GOOD FRIEND TO KIRIYAMA.
SAME... AS ALWAYS?
ACTING...
LIKE NOTHING'S CHANGED?
IS THAT REALLY ENOUGH?

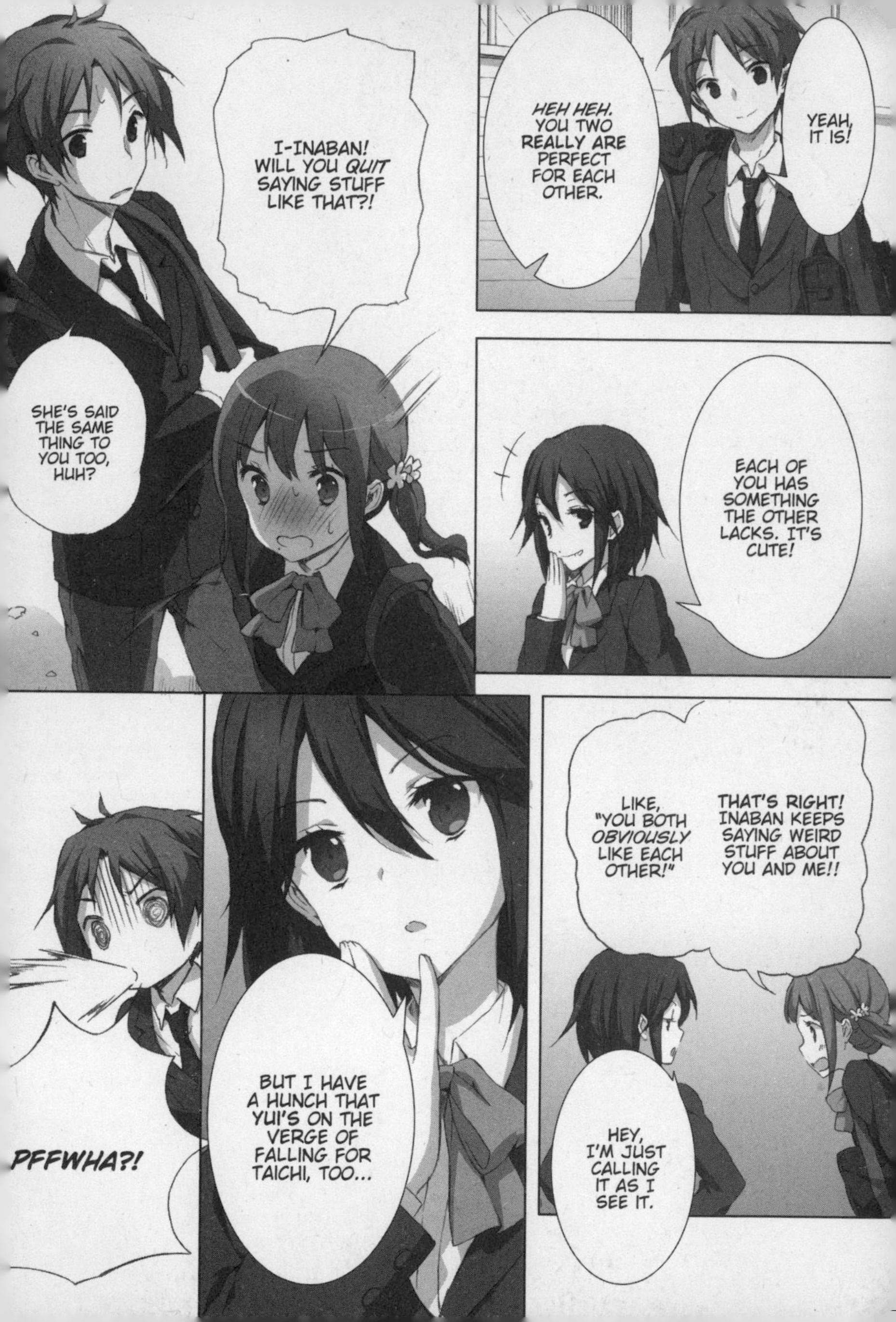
YEAH, IT IS!
HEH HEH. YOU TWO REALLY ARE PERFECT FOR EACH OTHER.
EACH OF YOU HAS SOMETHING THE OTHER LACKS. IT'S CUTE!
I-INABAN! WILL YOU *QUIT* SAYING STUFF LIKE THAT?!
SHE'S SAID THE SAME THING TO YOU TOO, HUH?
THAT'S RIGHT! INABAN KEEPS SAYING WEIRD STUFF ABOUT YOU AND ME!!
LIKE, "YOU BOTH *OBVIOUSLY* LIKE EACH OTHER!"
HEY, I'M JUST CALLING IT AS I SEE IT.
BUT I HAVE A HUNCH THAT YUI'S ON THE VERGE OF FALLING FOR TAICHI, TOO...
PFFWHA?!

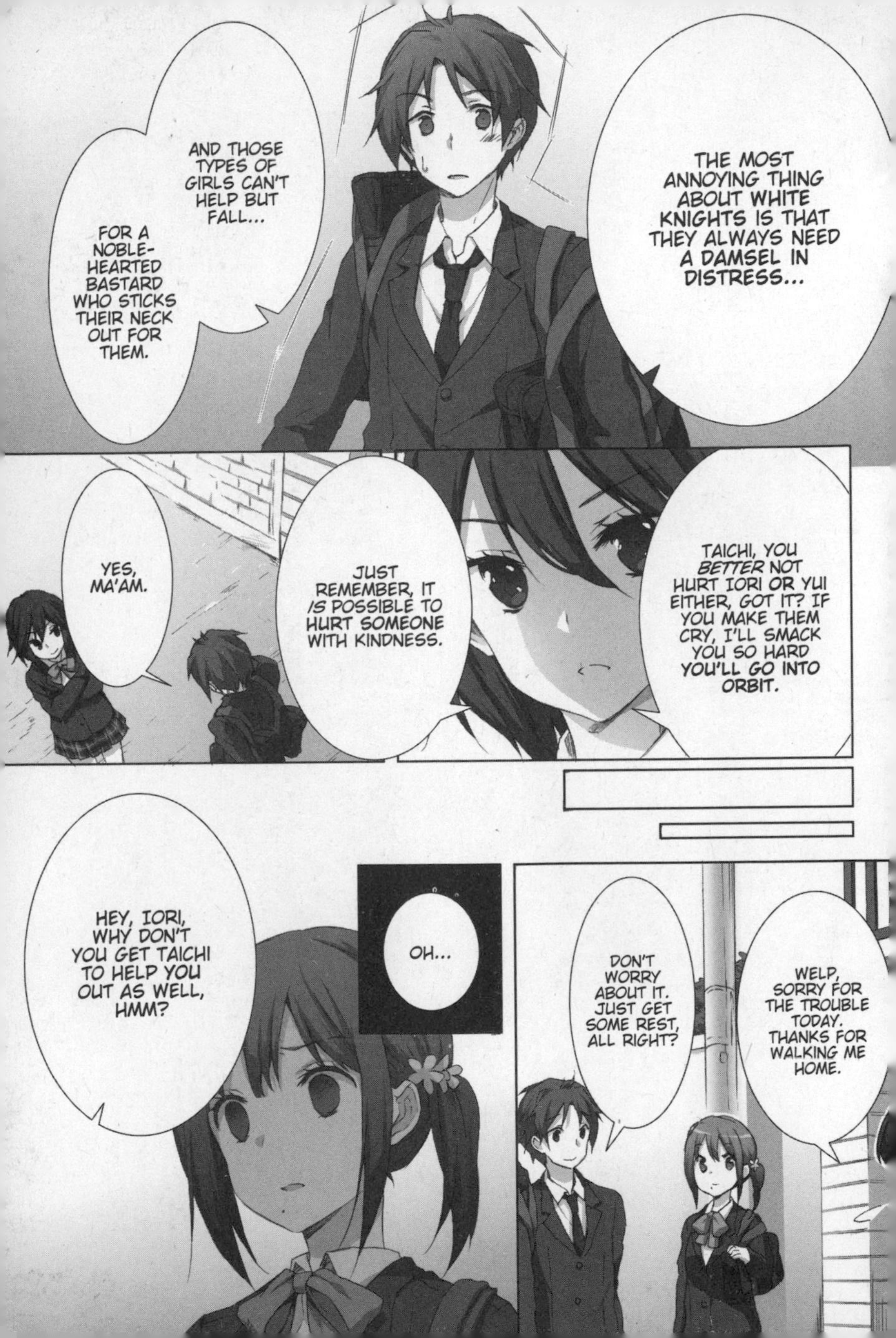
THE MOST ANNOYING THING ABOUT WHITE KNIGHTS IS THAT THEY ALWAYS NEED A DAMSEL IN DISTRESS...
AND THOSE TYPES OF GIRLS CAN'T HELP BUT FALL...
FOR A NOBLE-HEARTED BASTARD WHO STICKS THEIR NECK OUT FOR THEM.
TAICHI, YOU *BETTER* NOT HURT IORI OR YUI EITHER, GOT IT? IF YOU MAKE THEM CRY, I'LL SMACK YOU SO HARD YOU'LL GO INTO ORBIT.
JUST REMEMBER, IT *IS* POSSIBLE TO HURT SOMEONE WITH KINDNESS.
YES, MA'AM.
WELP, SORRY FOR THE TROUBLE TODAY. THANKS FOR WALKING ME HOME.
DON'T WORRY ABOUT IT. JUST GET SOME REST, ALL RIGHT?
OH...
HEY, IORI, WHY DON'T YOU GET TAICHI TO HELP YOU OUT AS WELL, HMM?

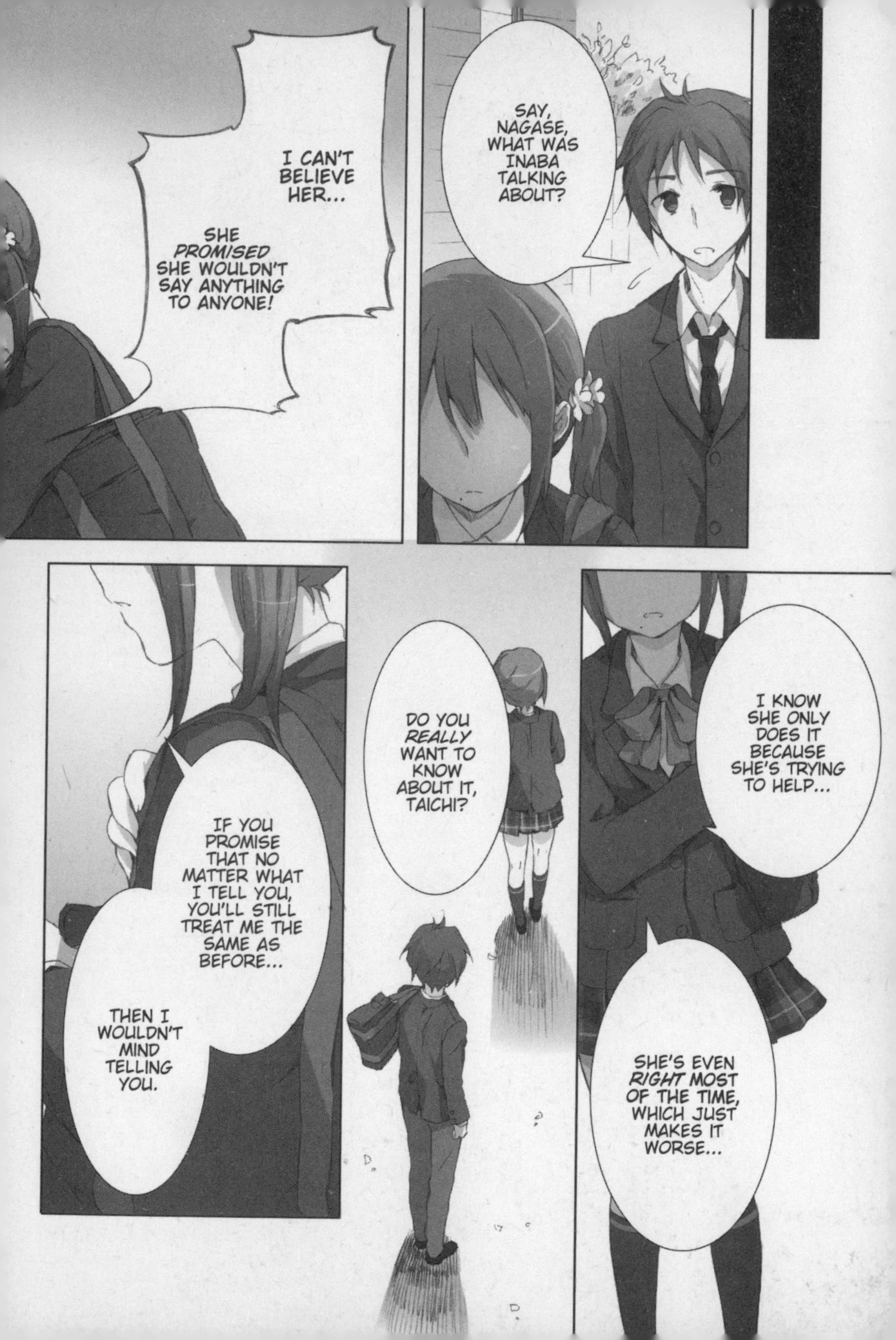
SAY, NAGASE, WHAT WAS INABA TALKING ABOUT?
I CAN'T BELIEVE HER...
SHE *PROMISED* SHE WOULDN'T SAY ANYTHING TO ANYONE!
I KNOW SHE ONLY DOES IT BECAUSE SHE'S TRYING TO HELP...
SHE'S EVEN *RIGHT* MOST OF THE TIME, WHICH JUST MAKES IT WORSE...
DO YOU *REALLY* WANT TO KNOW ABOUT IT, TAICHI?
IF YOU PROMISE THAT NO MATTER WHAT I TELL YOU, YOU'LL STILL TREAT ME THE SAME AS BEFORE...
THEN I WOULDN'T MIND TELLING YOU.

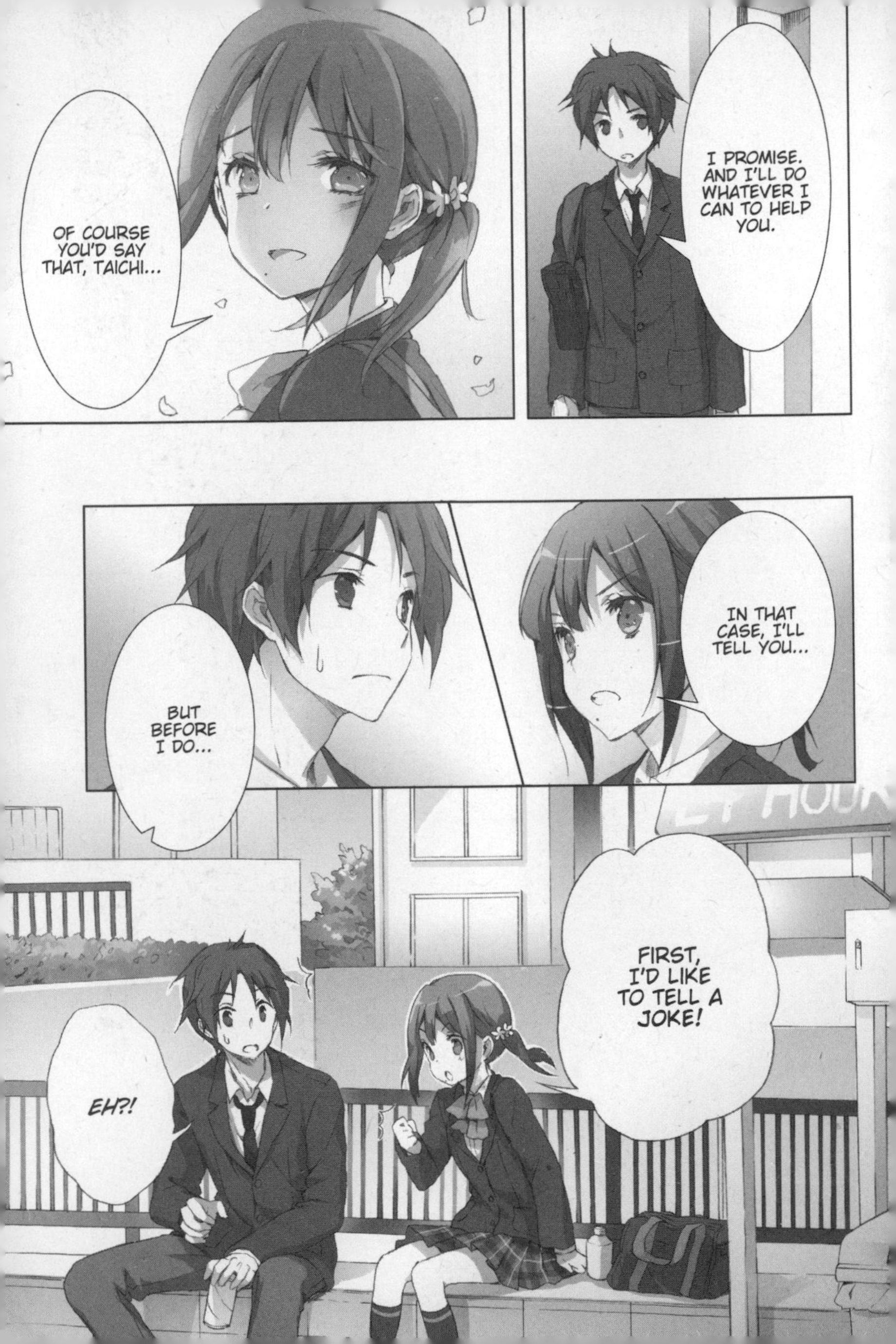
I PROMISE. AND I'LL DO WHATEVER I CAN TO HELP YOU.
OF COURSE YOU'D SAY THAT, TAICHI...
IN THAT CASE, I'LL TELL YOU...
BUT BEFORE I DO...
FIRST, I'D LIKE TO TELL A JOKE!
EH?!

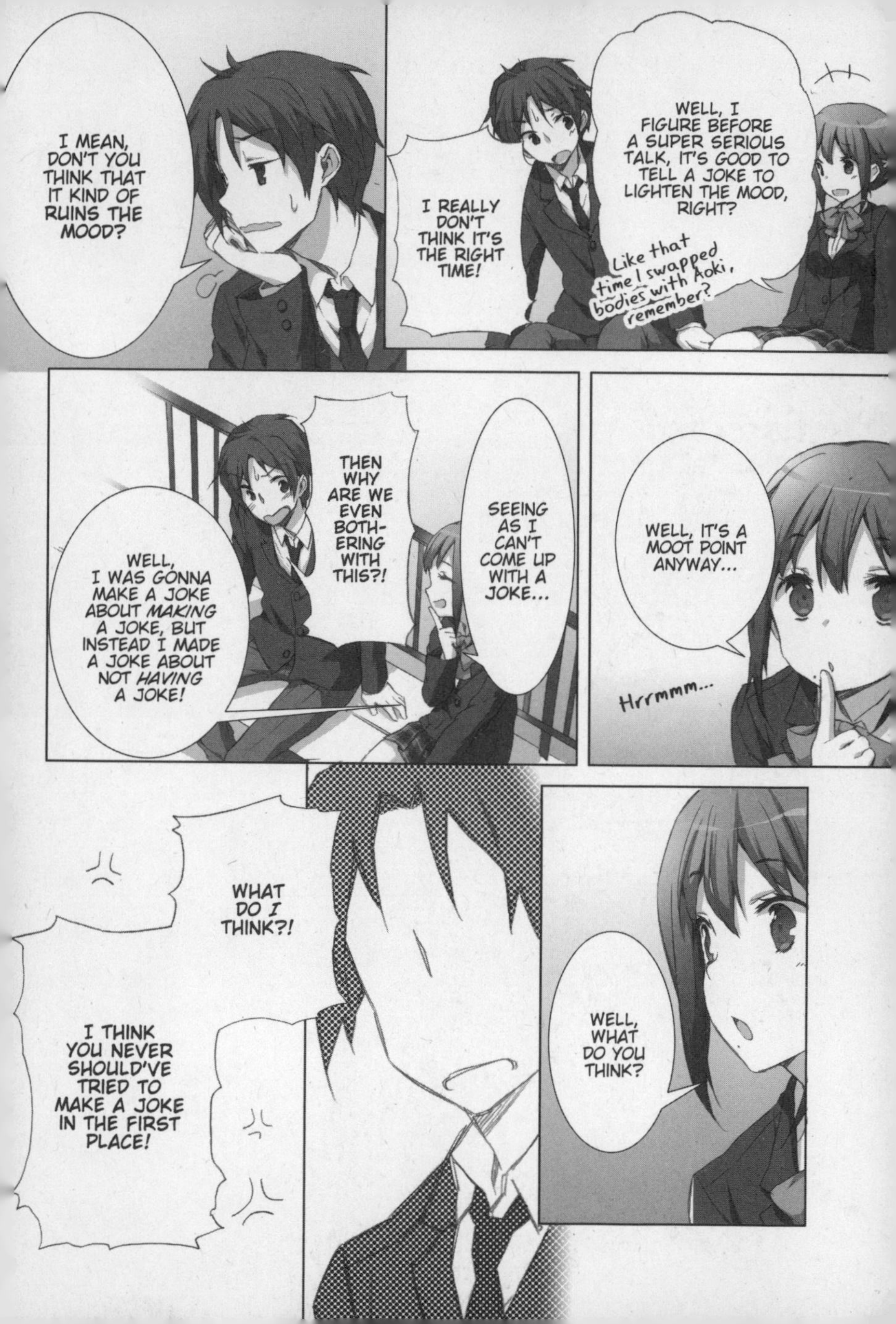
WELL, I FIGURE BEFORE A SUPER SERIOUS TALK, IT'S GOOD TO TELL A JOKE TO LIGHTEN THE MOOD, RIGHT?
Like that time I swapped bodies with Aoki, remember?
I REALLY DON'T THINK IT'S THE RIGHT TIME!
I MEAN, DON'T YOU THINK THAT IT KIND OF RUINS THE MOOD?
WELL, IT'S A MOOT POINT ANYWAY...
Hrrmmm...
SEEING AS I CAN'T COME UP WITH A JOKE...
THEN WHY ARE WE EVEN BOTHERING WITH THIS?!
WELL, I WAS GONNA MAKE A JOKE ABOUT *MAKING* A JOKE, BUT INSTEAD I MADE A JOKE ABOUT NOT *HAVING* A JOKE!
WELL, WHAT DO YOU THINK?
WHAT DO *I* THINK?!
I THINK YOU NEVER SHOULD'VE TRIED TO MAKE A JOKE IN THE FIRST PLACE!

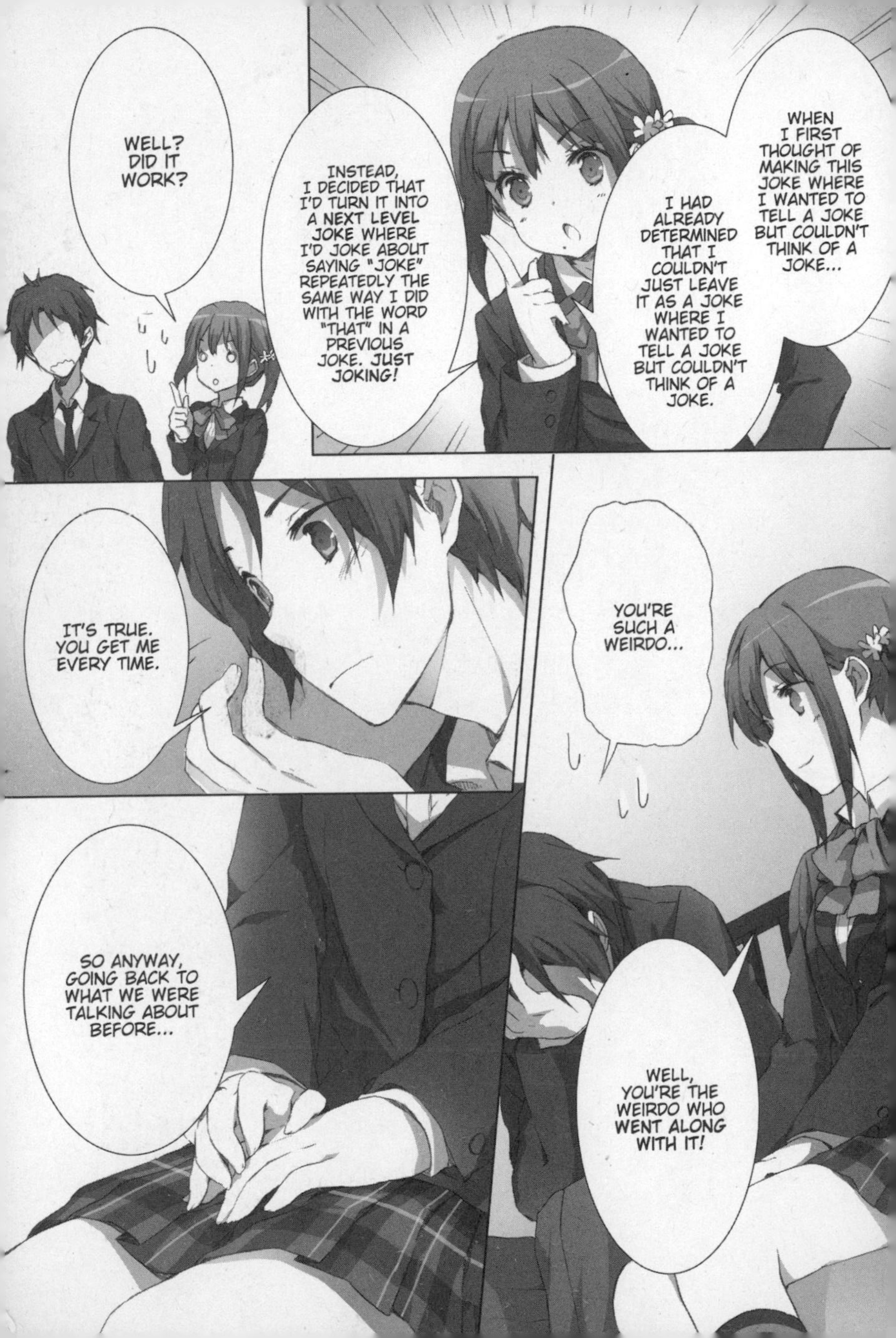
WHEN I FIRST THOUGHT OF MAKING THIS JOKE WHERE I WANTED TO TELL A JOKE BUT COULDN'T THINK OF A JOKE...
I HAD ALREADY DETERMINED THAT I COULDN'T JUST LEAVE IT AS A JOKE WHERE I WANTED TO TELL A JOKE BUT COULDN'T THINK OF A JOKE.
INSTEAD, I DECIDED THAT I'D TURN IT INTO A NEXT LEVEL JOKE WHERE I'D JOKE ABOUT SAYING "JOKE" REPEATEDLY THE SAME WAY I DID WITH THE WORD "THAT" IN A PREVIOUS JOKE. JUST JOKING!
WELL? DID IT WORK?
YOU'RE SUCH A WEIRDO...
WELL, YOU'RE THE WEIRDO WHO WENT ALONG WITH IT!
IT'S TRUE. YOU GET ME EVERY TIME.
SO ANYWAY, GOING BACK TO WHAT WE WERE TALKING ABOUT BEFORE...

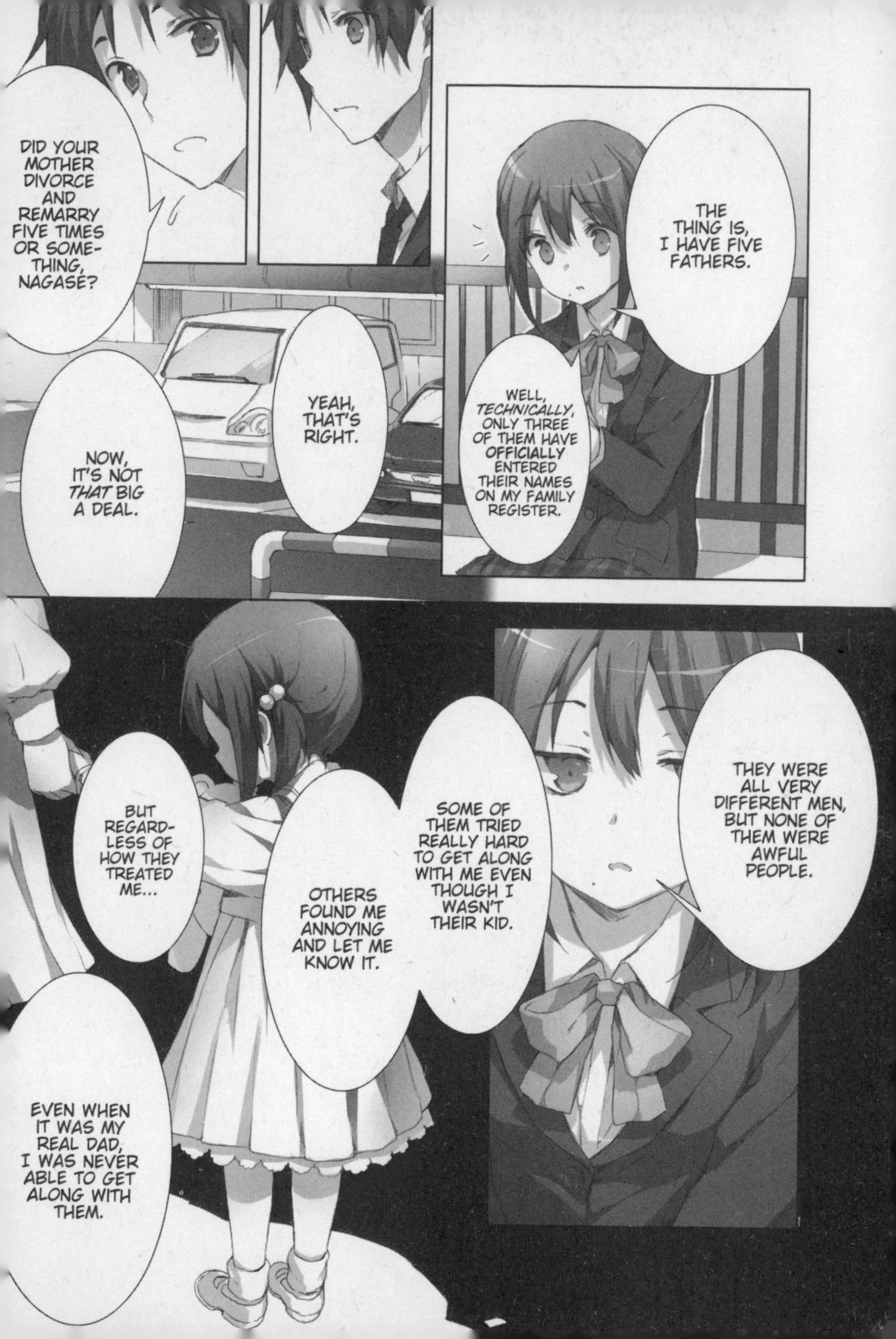
THE THING IS, I HAVE FIVE FATHERS.
WELL, *TECHNICALLY*, ONLY THREE OF THEM HAVE OFFICIALLY ENTERED THEIR NAMES ON MY FAMILY REGISTER.
DID YOUR MOTHER DIVORCE AND REMARRY FIVE TIMES OR SOME-THING, NAGASE?
YEAH, THAT'S RIGHT.
NOW, IT'S NOT *THAT* BIG A DEAL.
THEY WERE ALL VERY DIFFERENT MEN, BUT NONE OF THEM WERE AWFUL PEOPLE.
SOME OF THEM TRIED REALLY HARD TO GET ALONG WITH ME EVEN THOUGH I WASN'T THEIR KID.
OTHERS FOUND ME ANNOYING AND LET ME KNOW IT.
BUT REGARD-LESS OF HOW THEY TREATED ME...
EVEN WHEN IT WAS MY REAL DAD, I WAS NEVER ABLE TO GET ALONG WITH THEM.

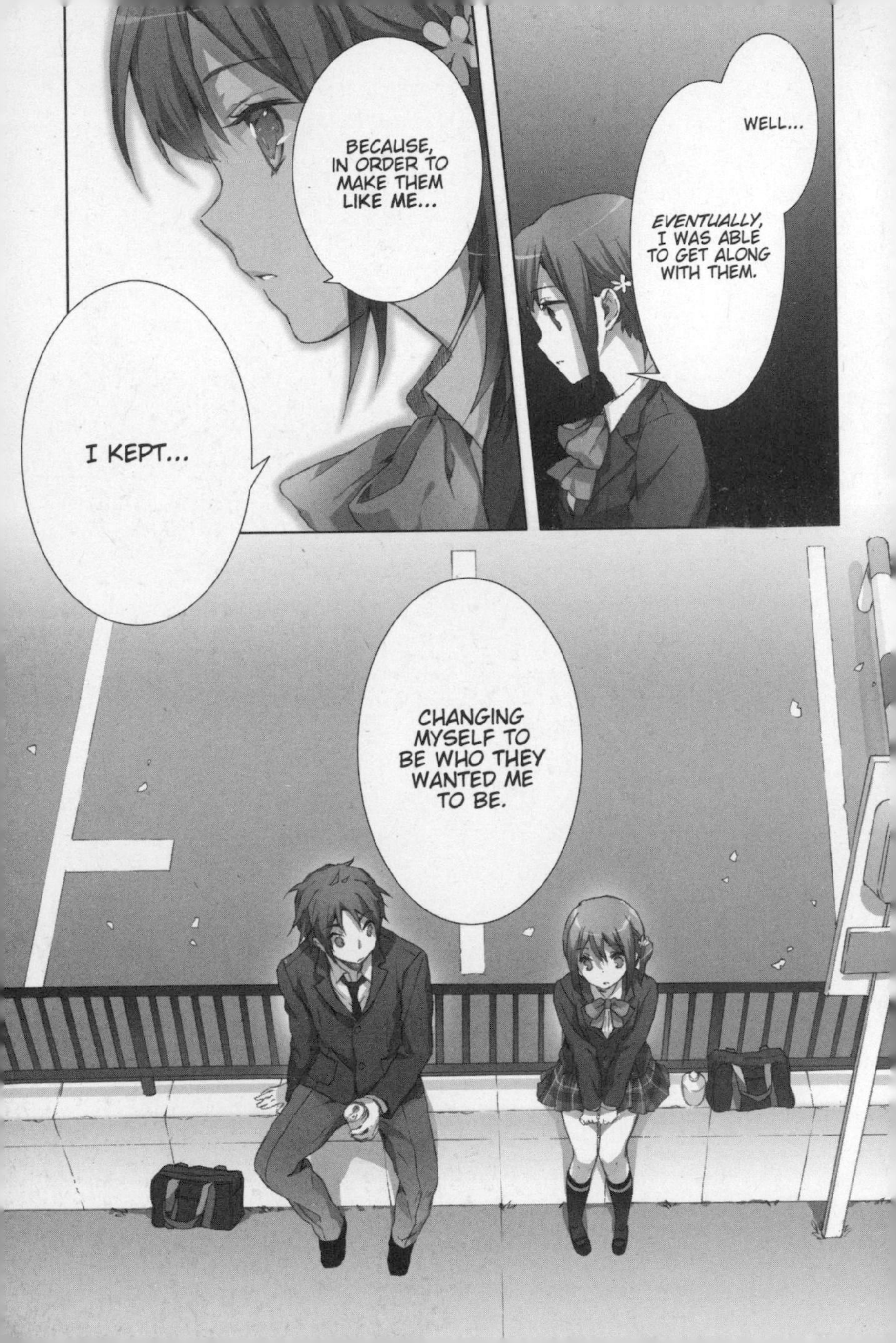
WELL...
EVENTUALLY, I WAS ABLE TO GET ALONG WITH THEM.
BECAUSE, IN ORDER TO MAKE THEM LIKE ME...
I KEPT...
CHANGING MYSELF TO BE WHO THEY WANTED ME TO BE.

KOKORO CONNECT

KOKORO CONNECT

Chapter 8

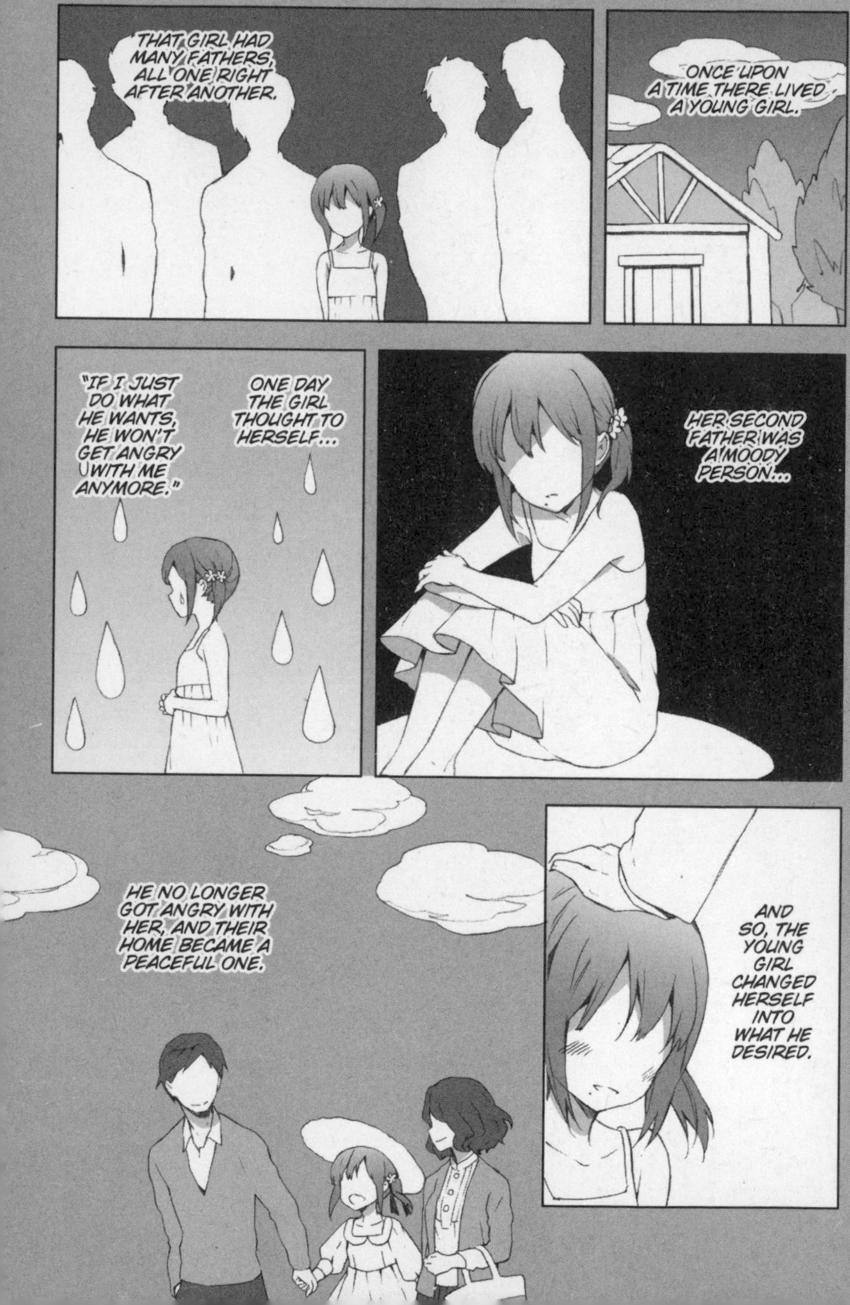
ONCE UPON A TIME THERE LIVED A YOUNG GIRL.
THAT GIRL HAD MANY FATHERS, ALL ONE RIGHT AFTER ANOTHER.
HER SECOND FATHER WAS A MOODY PERSON...
ONE DAY THE GIRL THOUGHT TO HERSELF...
"IF I JUST DO WHAT HE WANTS, HE WON'T GET ANGRY WITH ME ANYMORE."
AND SO, THE YOUNG GIRL CHANGED HERSELF INTO WHAT HE DESIRED.
HE NO LONGER GOT ANGRY WITH HER, AND THEIR HOME BECAME A PEACEFUL ONE.

AND THUS, THE YOUNG GIRL FOUND SHE WAS ABLE TO GET ALONG WELL WITH HER THIRD AND FOURTH FATHERS, AND THEIR CHILDREN AS WELL.

"IF I DO THIS, MAYBE THEY'LL LIKE ME."

"IF I DO THIS, MAYBE THEY'LL STAY."

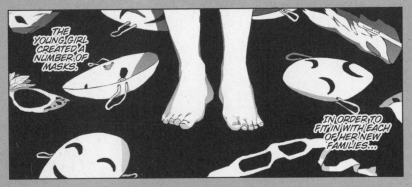

THE YOUNG GIRL CREATED A NUMBER OF MASKS.

IN ORDER TO FIT IN WITH EACH OF HER NEW FAMILIES...

THIS...

SHE SUPPRESSED HER OWN LIKES AND DISLIKES TO SUIT THE PEOPLE AROUND HER. OVER THE YEARS, THE YOUNG GIRL REINVENTED HERSELF OVER AND OVER AGAIN.

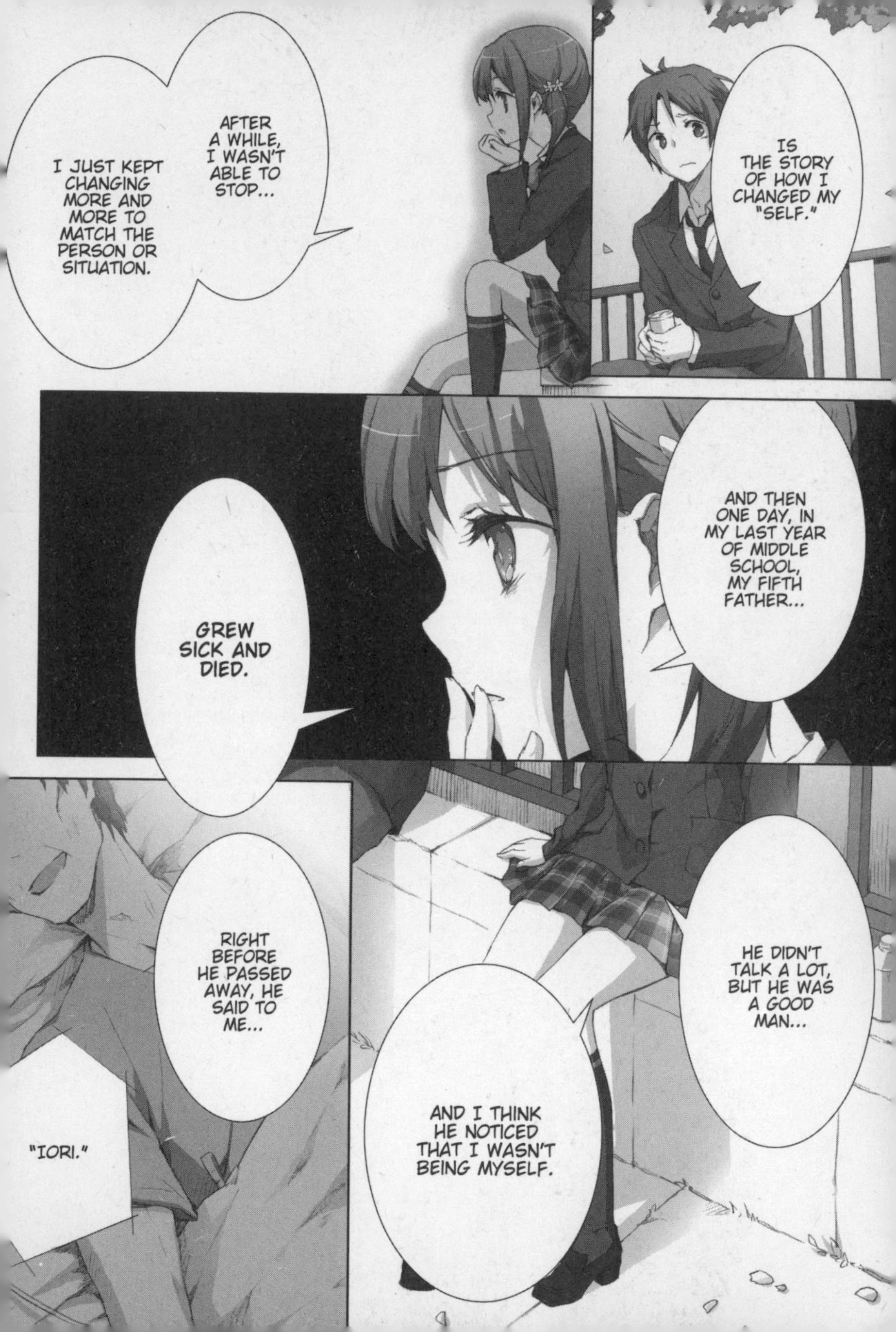
IS THE STORY OF HOW I CHANGED MY "SELF."
AFTER A WHILE, I WASN'T ABLE TO STOP...
I JUST KEPT CHANGING MORE AND MORE TO MATCH THE PERSON OR SITUATION.
AND THEN ONE DAY, IN MY LAST YEAR OF MIDDLE SCHOOL, MY FIFTH FATHER...
GREW SICK AND DIED.
HE DIDN'T TALK A LOT, BUT HE WAS A GOOD MAN...
AND I THINK HE NOTICED THAT I WASN'T BEING MYSELF.
RIGHT BEFORE HE PASSED AWAY, HE SAID TO ME...
"IORI."

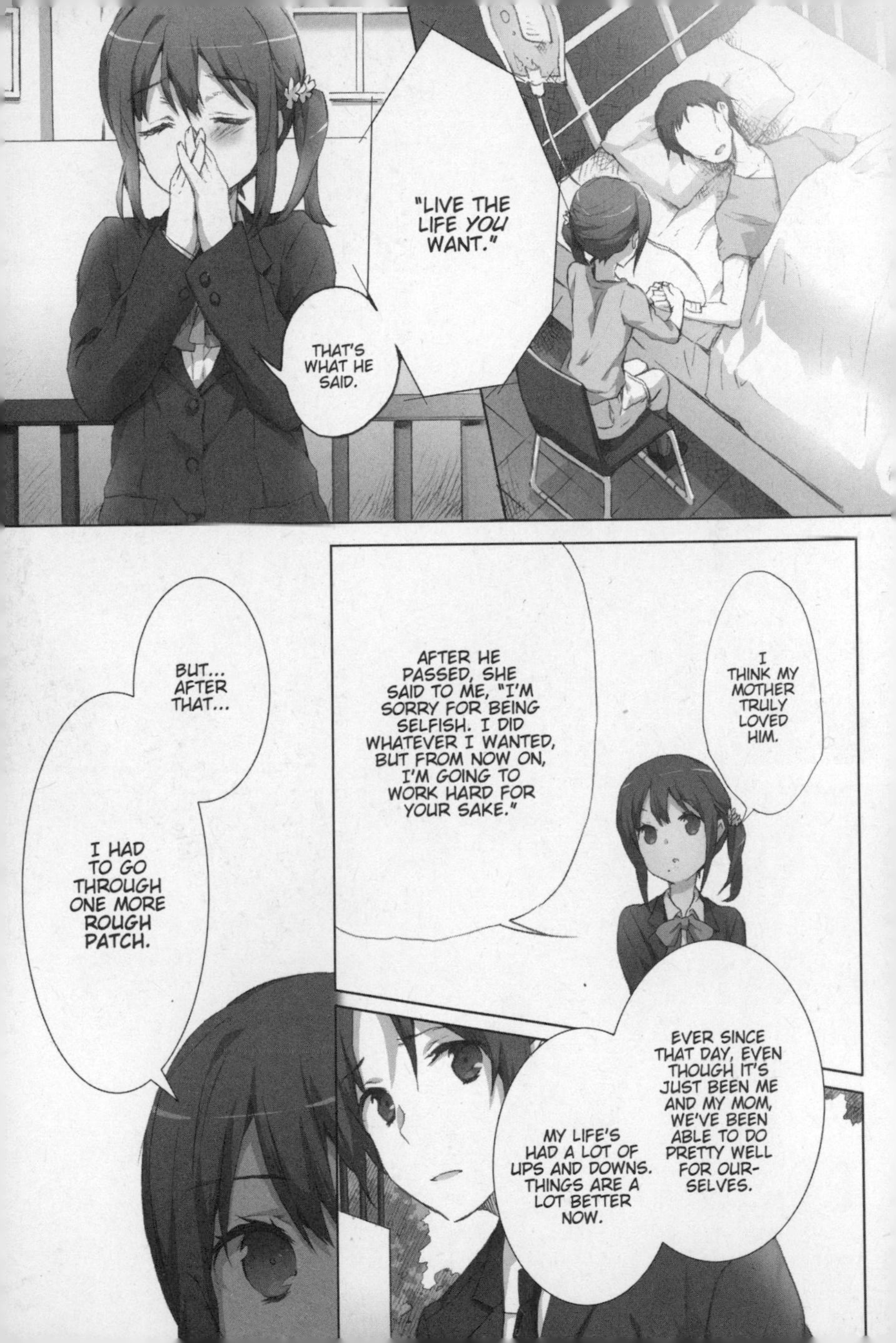
"LIVE THE LIFE YOU WANT."
THAT'S WHAT HE SAID.
I THINK MY MOTHER TRULY LOVED HIM.
AFTER HE PASSED, SHE SAID TO ME, "I'M SORRY FOR BEING SELFISH. I DID WHATEVER I WANTED, BUT FROM NOW ON, I'M GOING TO WORK HARD FOR YOUR SAKE."
EVER SINCE THAT DAY, EVEN THOUGH IT'S JUST BEEN ME AND MY MOM, WE'VE BEEN ABLE TO DO PRETTY WELL FOR OUR-SELVES.
MY LIFE'S HAD A LOT OF UPS AND DOWNS. THINGS ARE A LOT BETTER NOW.
BUT... AFTER THAT...
I HAD TO GO THROUGH ONE MORE ROUGH PATCH.

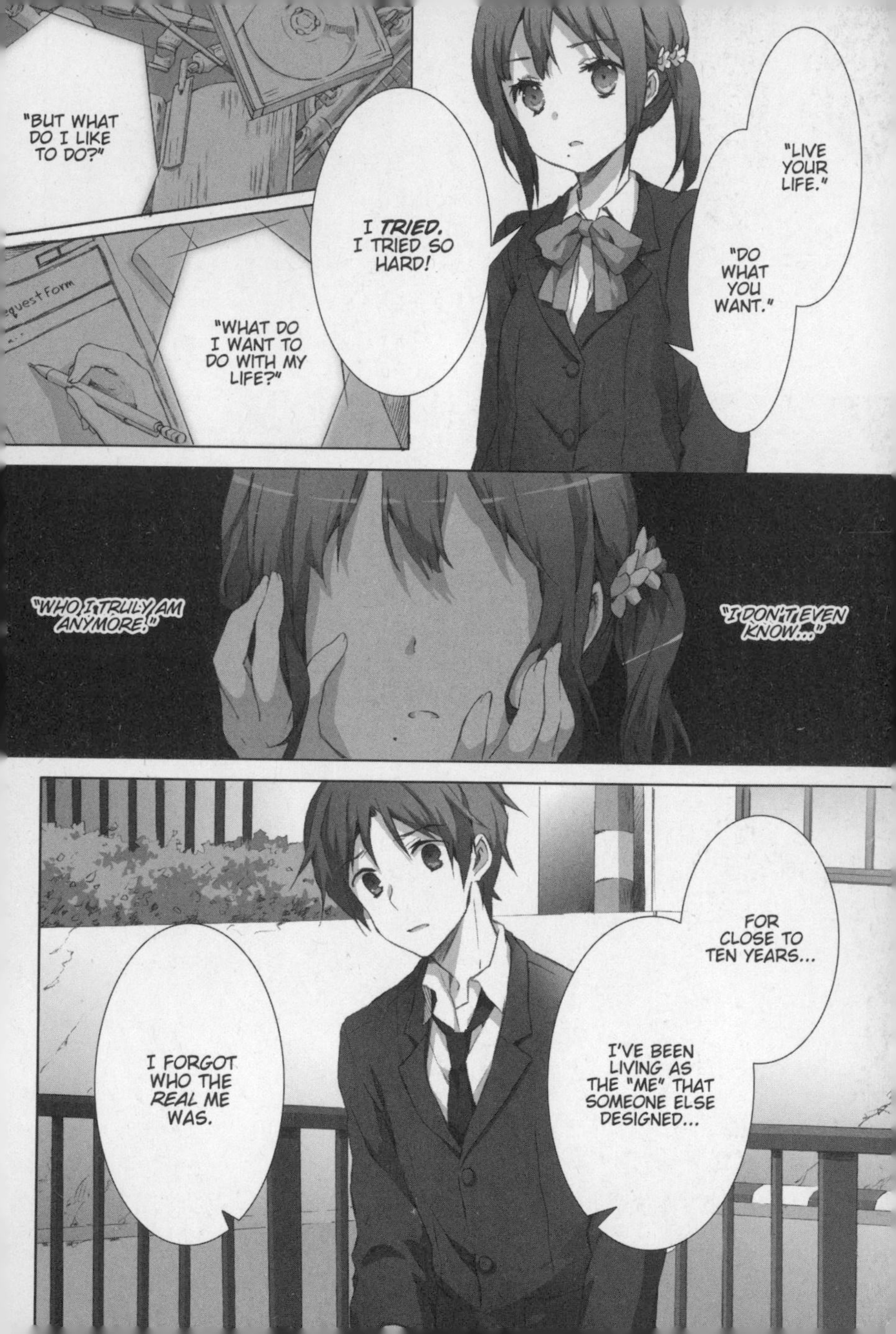
"LIVE YOUR LIFE."
"DO WHAT YOU WANT."
I *TRIED.* I TRIED SO HARD!
"BUT WHAT DO I LIKE TO DO?"
"WHAT DO I WANT TO DO WITH MY LIFE?"
"I DON'T EVEN KNOW..."
"WHO I TRULY AM ANYMORE."
FOR CLOSE TO TEN YEARS...
I'VE BEEN LIVING AS THE "ME" THAT SOMEONE ELSE DESIGNED...
I FORGOT WHO THE *REAL* ME WAS.

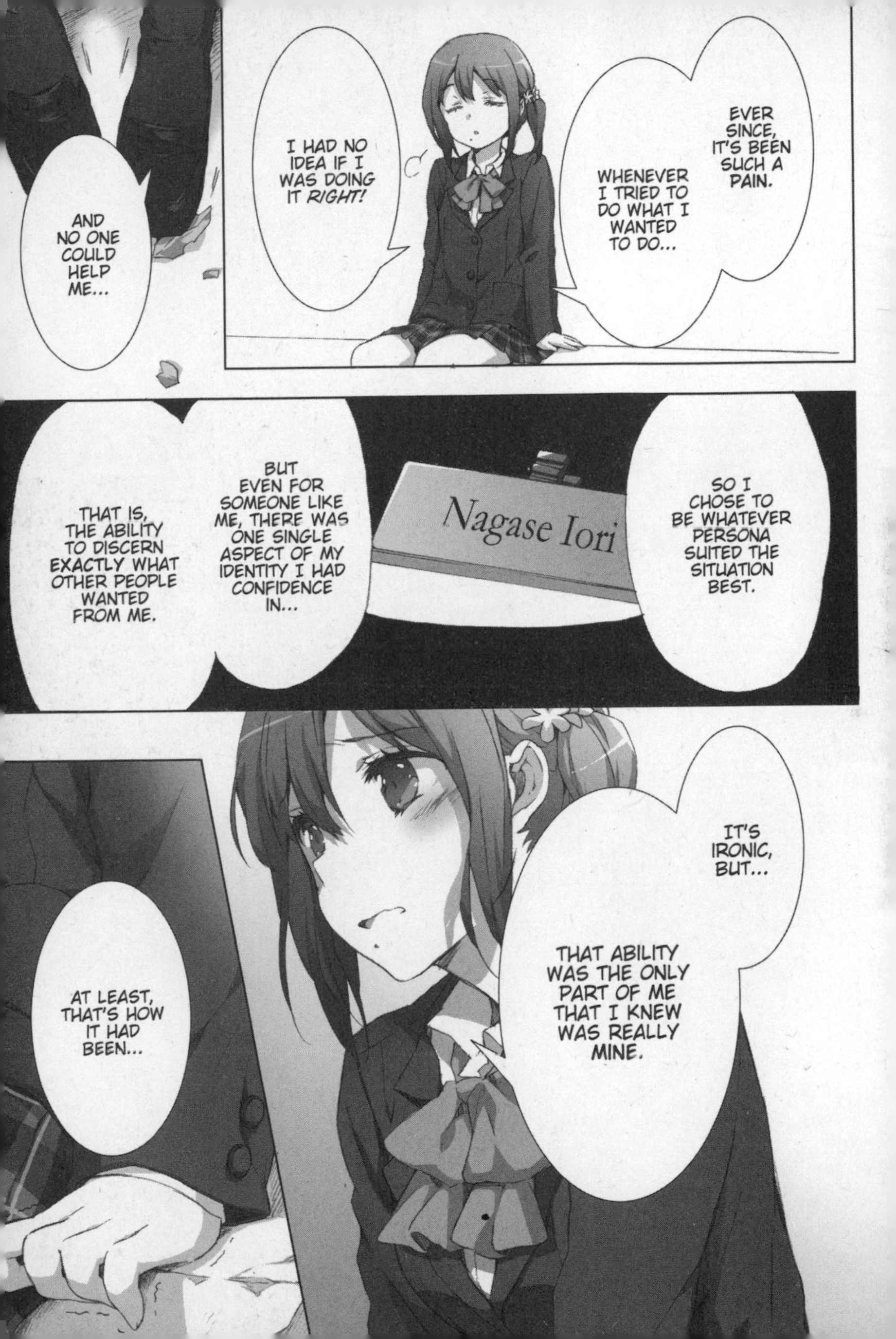
EVER SINCE, IT'S BEEN SUCH A PAIN.
WHENEVER I TRIED TO DO WHAT I WANTED TO DO...
I HAD NO IDEA IF I WAS DOING IT *RIGHT!*
AND NO ONE COULD HELP ME...
SO I CHOSE TO BE WHATEVER PERSONA SUITED THE SITUATION BEST.
Nagase Iori
BUT EVEN FOR SOMEONE LIKE ME, THERE WAS ONE SINGLE ASPECT OF MY IDENTITY I HAD CONFIDENCE IN...
THAT IS, THE ABILITY TO DISCERN EXACTLY WHAT OTHER PEOPLE WANTED FROM ME.
IT'S IRONIC, BUT...
THAT ABILITY WAS THE ONLY PART OF ME THAT I KNEW WAS REALLY MINE.
AT LEAST, THAT'S HOW IT HAD BEEN...

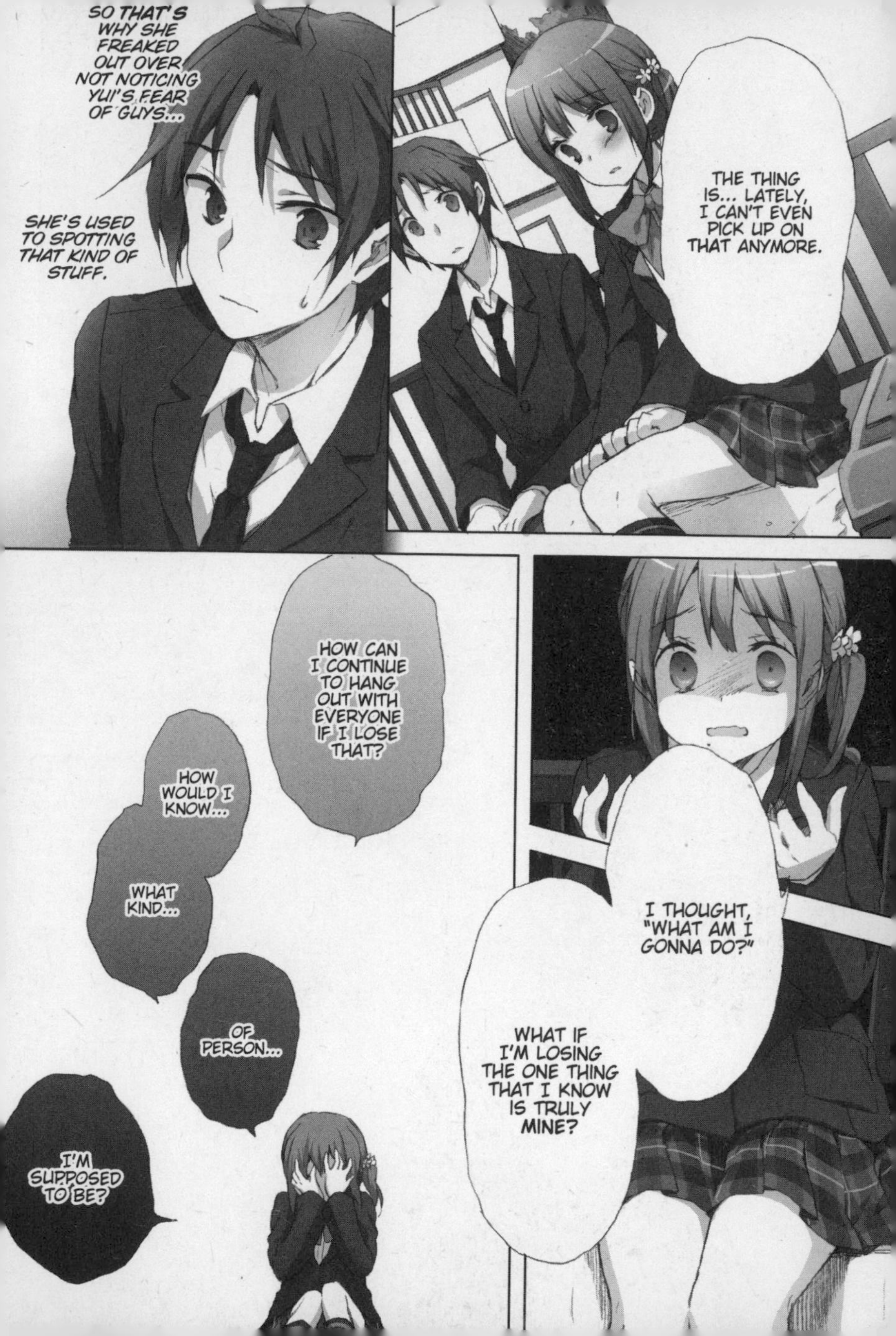
THE THING IS... LATELY, I CAN'T EVEN PICK UP ON THAT ANYMORE.
SO THAT'S WHY SHE FREAKED OUT OVER NOT NOTICING YUI'S FEAR OF GUYS...
SHE'S USED TO SPOTTING THAT KIND OF STUFF.
I THOUGHT, "WHAT AM I GONNA DO?"
WHAT IF I'M LOSING THE ONE THING THAT I KNOW IS TRULY MINE?
HOW CAN I CONTINUE TO HANG OUT WITH EVERYONE IF I LOSE THAT?
HOW WOULD I KNOW...
WHAT KIND...
OF PERSON...
I'M SUPPOSED TO BE?

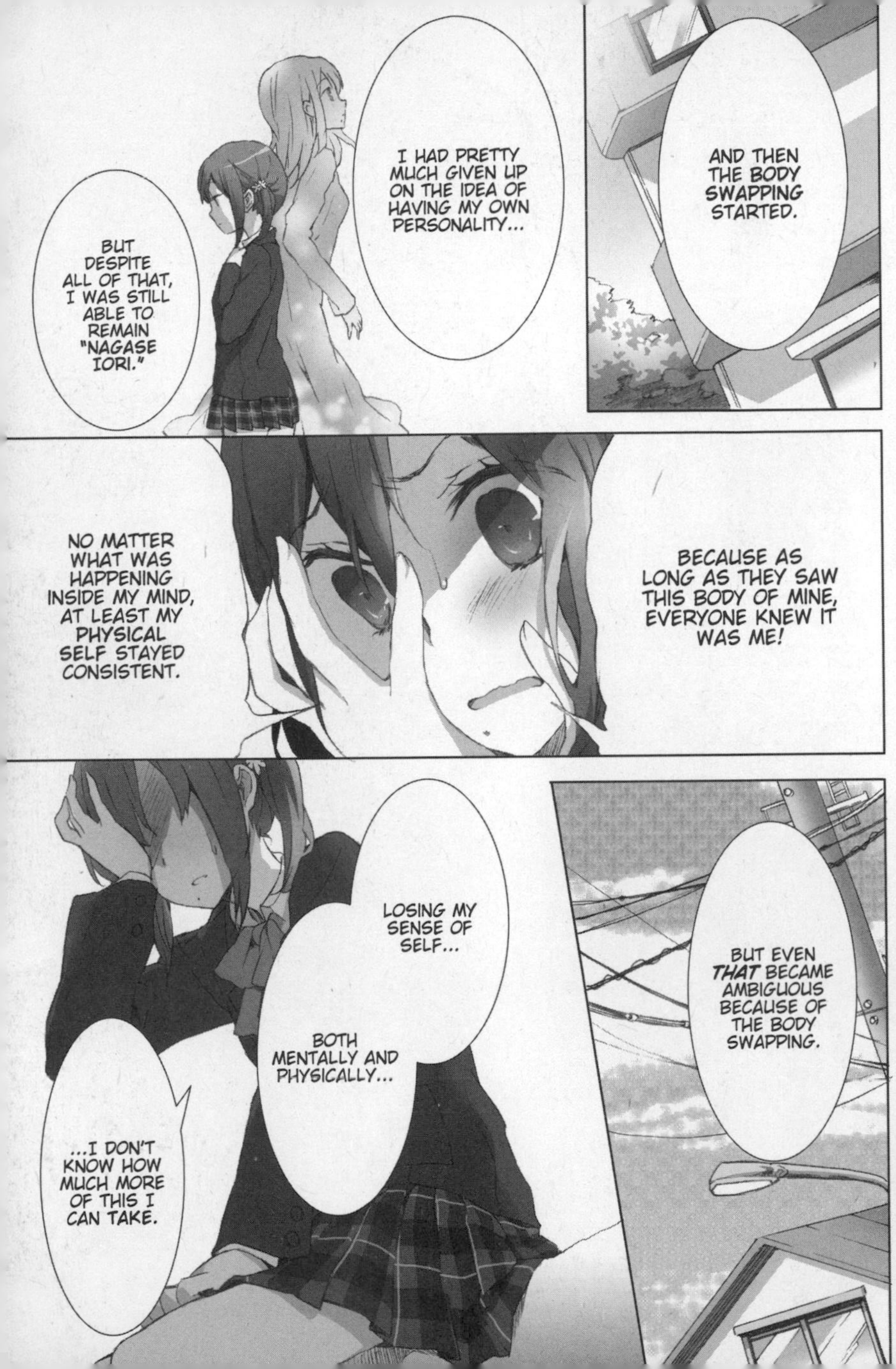
AND THEN THE BODY SWAPPING STARTED.
I HAD PRETTY MUCH GIVEN UP ON THE IDEA OF HAVING MY OWN PERSONALITY...
BUT DESPITE ALL OF THAT, I WAS STILL ABLE TO REMAIN "NAGASE IORI."
BECAUSE AS LONG AS THEY SAW THIS BODY OF MINE, EVERYONE KNEW IT WAS ME!
NO MATTER WHAT WAS HAPPENING INSIDE MY MIND, AT LEAST MY PHYSICAL SELF STAYED CONSISTENT.
BUT EVEN *THAT* BECAME AMBIGUOUS BECAUSE OF THE BODY SWAPPING.
LOSING MY SENSE OF SELF...
BOTH MENTALLY AND PHYSICALLY...
...I DON'T KNOW HOW MUCH MORE OF THIS I CAN TAKE.

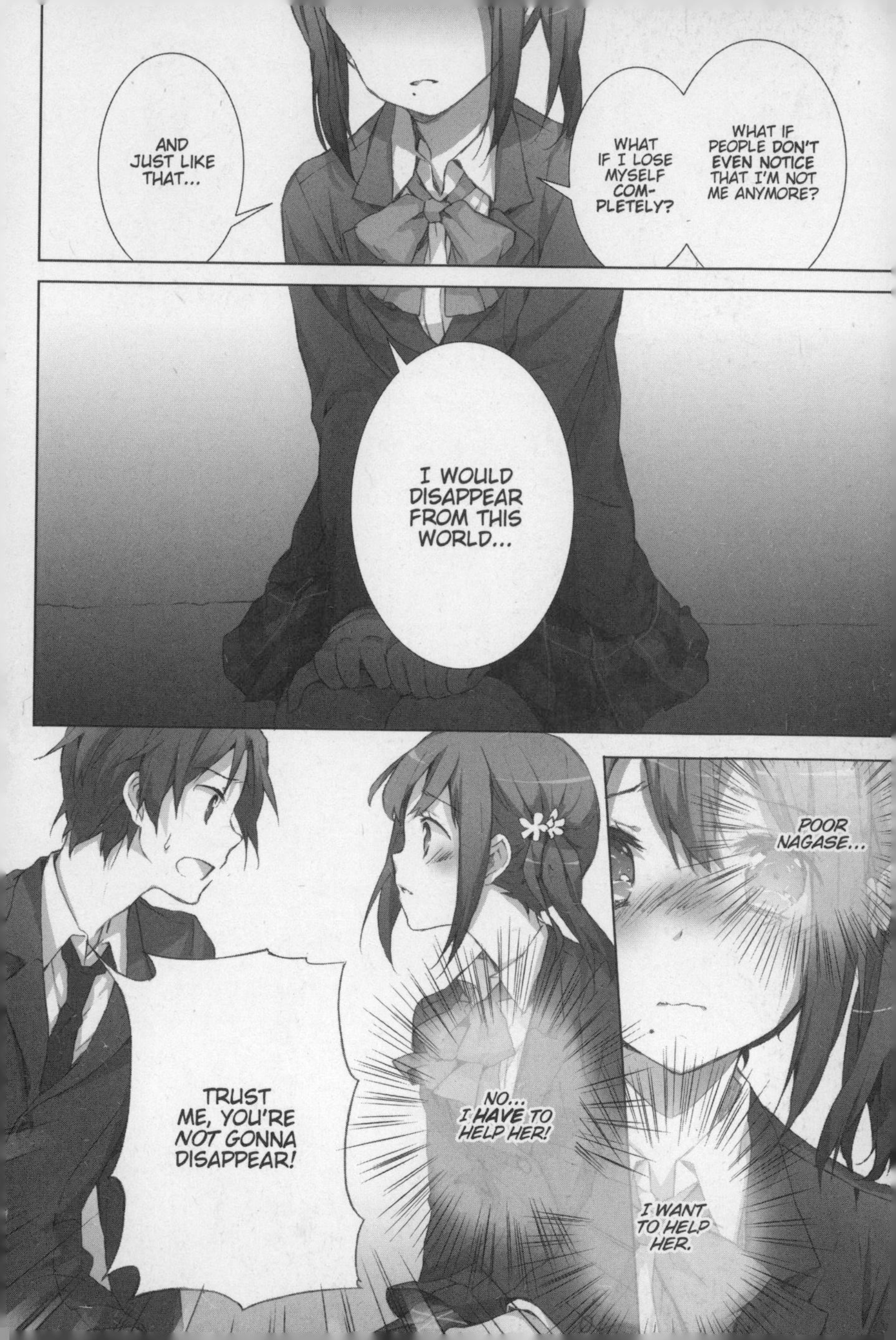

WHAT IF PEOPLE DON'T EVEN NOTICE THAT I'M NOT ME ANYMORE?
WHAT IF I LOSE MYSELF COM-PLETELY?
AND JUST LIKE THAT...
I WOULD DISAPPEAR FROM THIS WORLD...
POOR NAGASE...
NO... I HAVE TO HELP HER!
I WANT TO HELP HER.
TRUST ME, YOU'RE NOT GONNA DISAPPEAR!

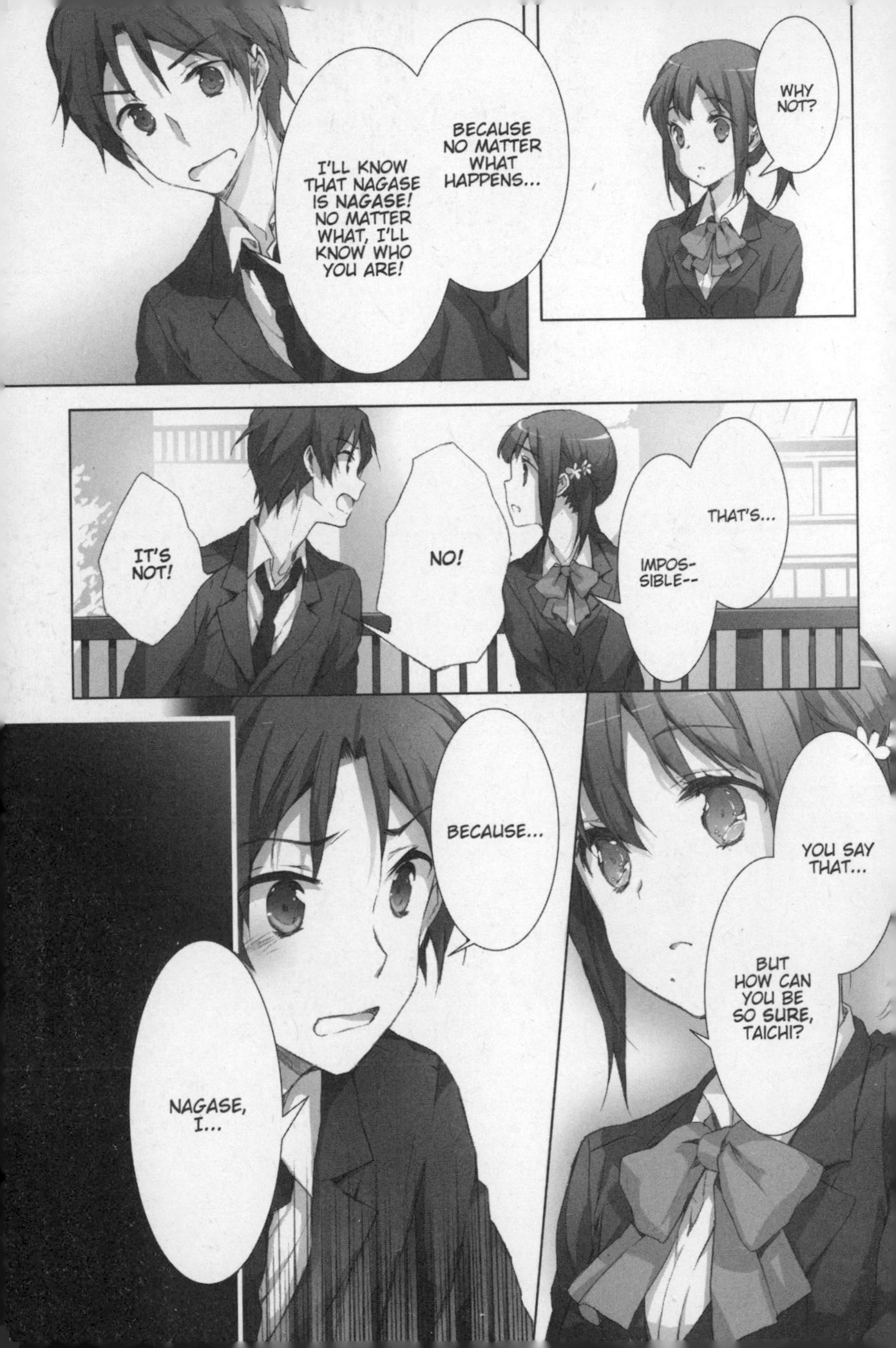
WHY NOT?
BECAUSE NO MATTER WHAT HAPPENS...
I'LL KNOW THAT NAGASE IS NAGASE! NO MATTER WHAT, I'LL KNOW WHO YOU ARE!
THAT'S...
IMPOS-SIBLE--
NO!
IT'S NOT!
YOU SAY THAT...
BUT HOW CAN YOU BE SO SURE, TAICHI?
BECAUSE...
NAGASE, I...

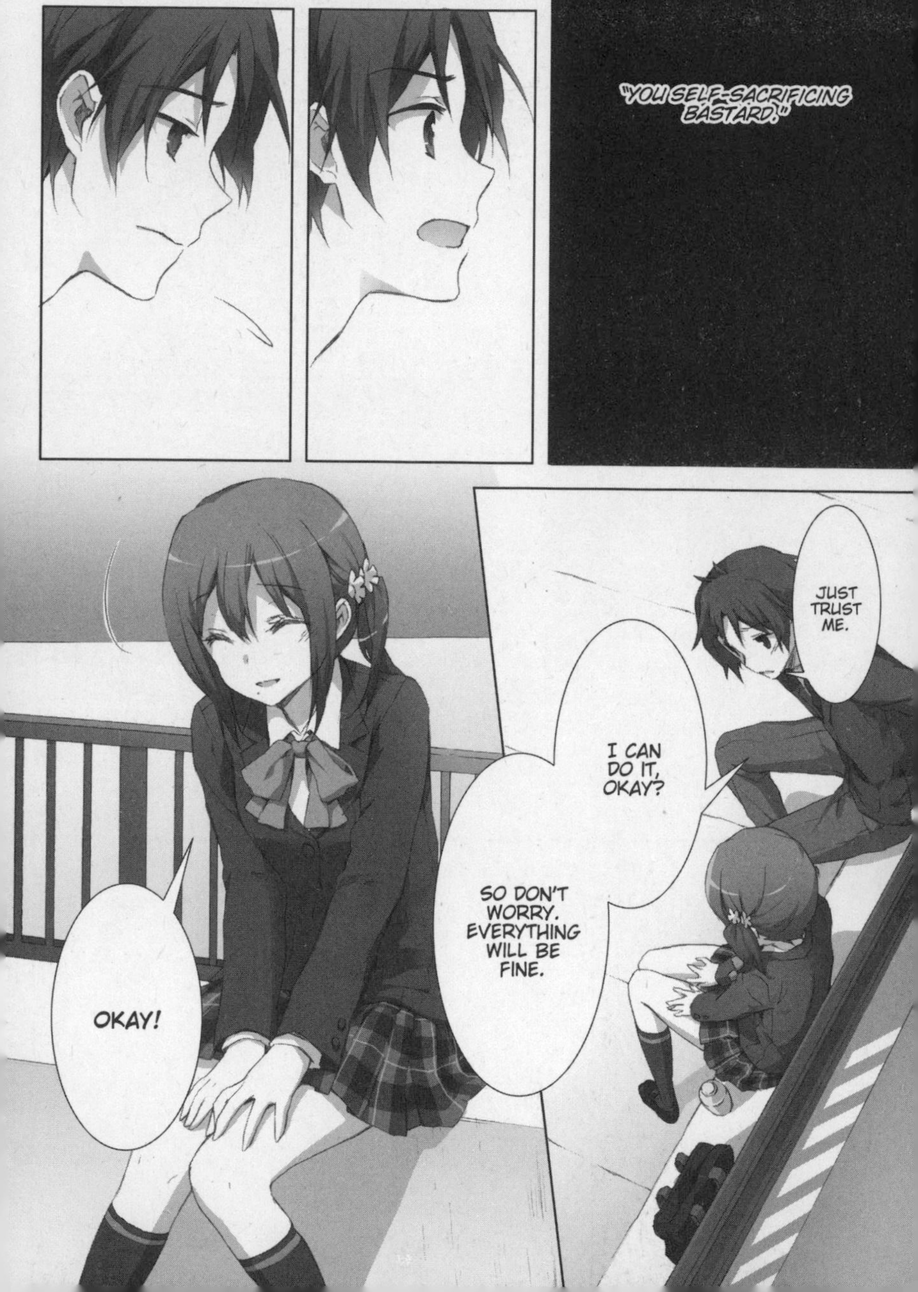
"YOU SELF-SACRIFICING BASTARD."
JUST TRUST ME.
I CAN DO IT, OKAY?
SO DON'T WORRY. EVERYTHING WILL BE FINE.
OKAY!

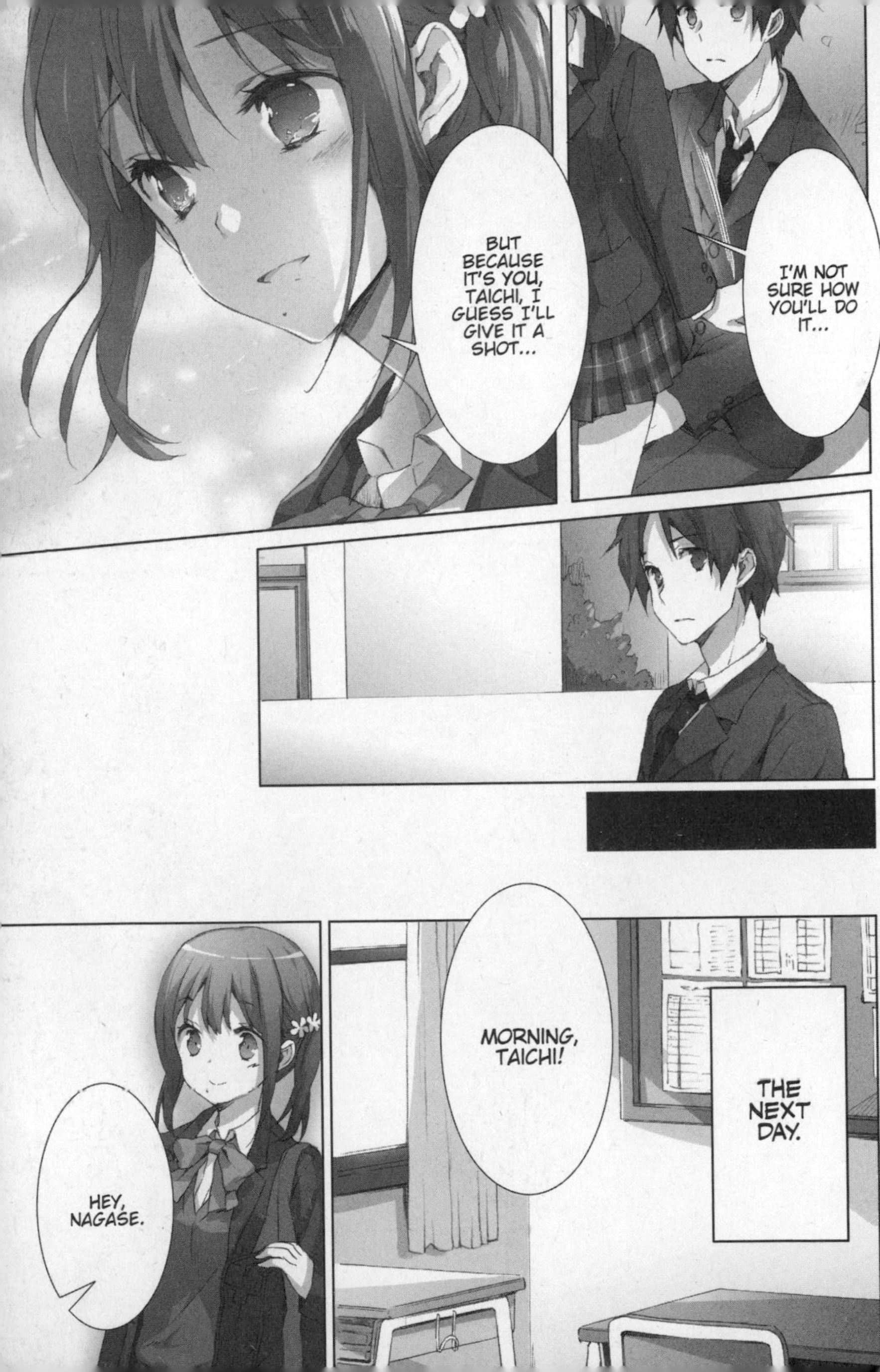
I'M NOT SURE HOW YOU'LL DO IT...
BUT BECAUSE IT'S YOU, TAICHI, I GUESS I'LL GIVE IT A SHOT...
THE NEXT DAY.
MORNING, TAICHI!
HEY, NAGASE.

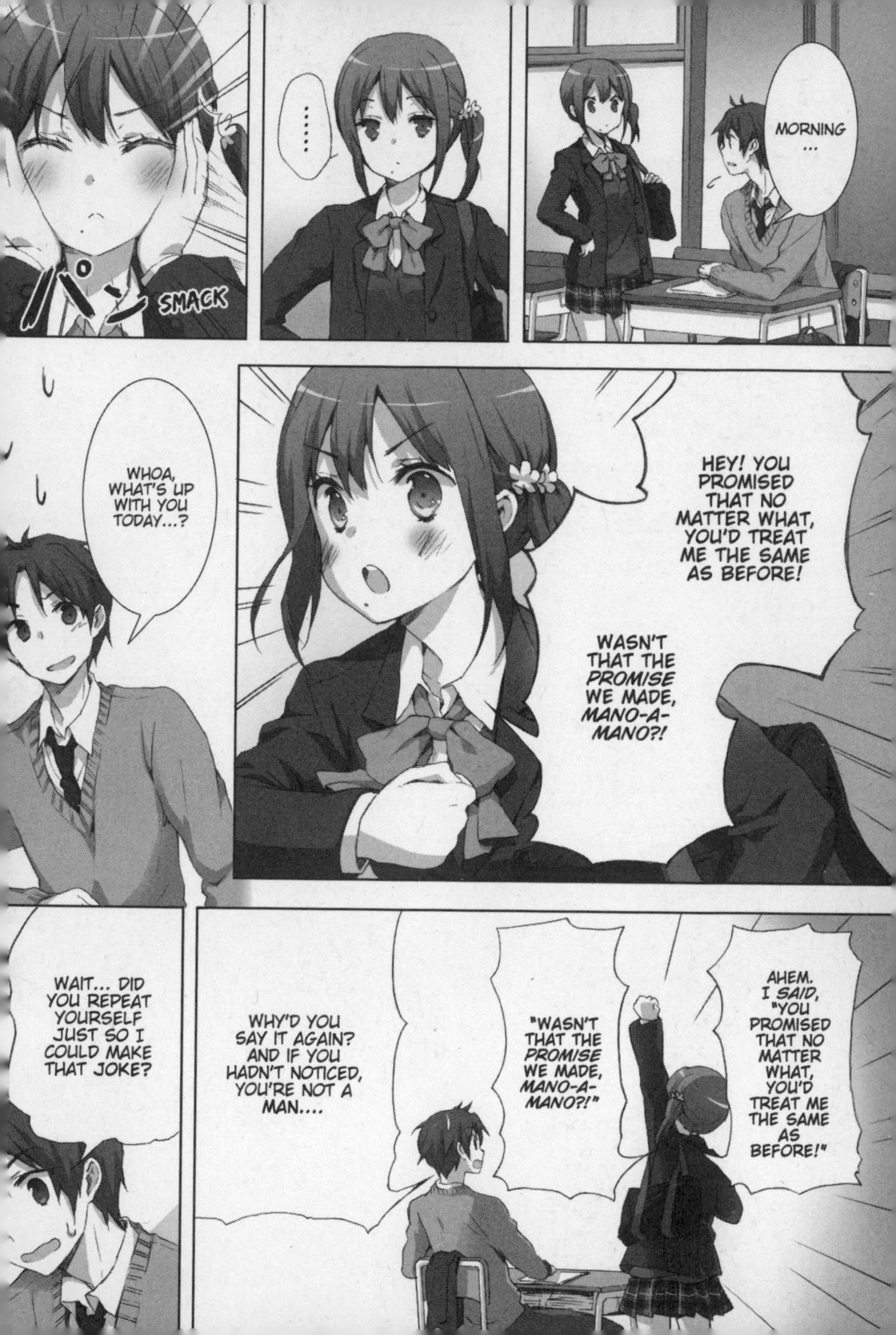
MORNING ...
......
SMACK
HEY! YOU PROMISED THAT NO MATTER WHAT, YOU'D TREAT ME THE SAME AS BEFORE!
WASN'T THAT THE *PROMISE* WE MADE, *MANO-A-MANO?!*
WHOA, WHAT'S UP WITH YOU TODAY...?
AHEM. I *SAID*, "YOU PROMISED THAT NO MATTER WHAT, YOU'D TREAT ME THE SAME AS BEFORE!"
"WASN'T THAT THE *PROMISE* WE MADE, *MANO-A-MANO?!*"
WHY'D YOU SAY IT AGAIN? AND IF YOU HADN'T NOTICED, YOU'RE NOT A MAN....
WAIT... DID YOU REPEAT YOURSELF JUST SO I COULD MAKE THAT JOKE?

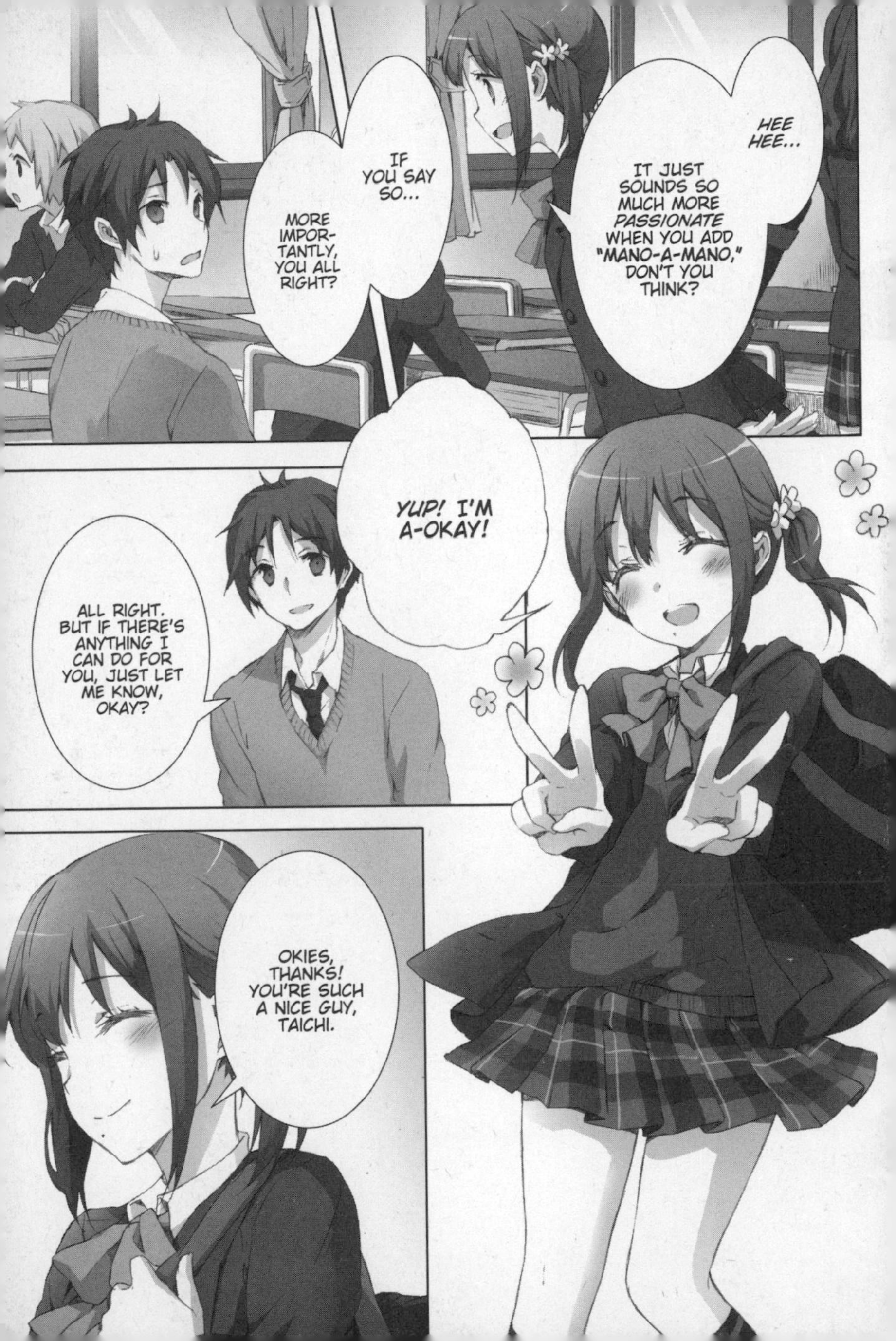
HEE HEE...
IT JUST SOUNDS SO MUCH MORE PASSIONATE WHEN YOU ADD "MANO-A-MANO," DON'T YOU THINK?
IF YOU SAY SO...
MORE IMPORTANTLY, YOU ALL RIGHT?
YUP! I'M A-OKAY!
ALL RIGHT. BUT IF THERE'S ANYTHING I CAN DO FOR YOU, JUST LET ME KNOW, OKAY?
OKIES, THANKS! YOU'RE SUCH A NICE GUY, TAICHI.

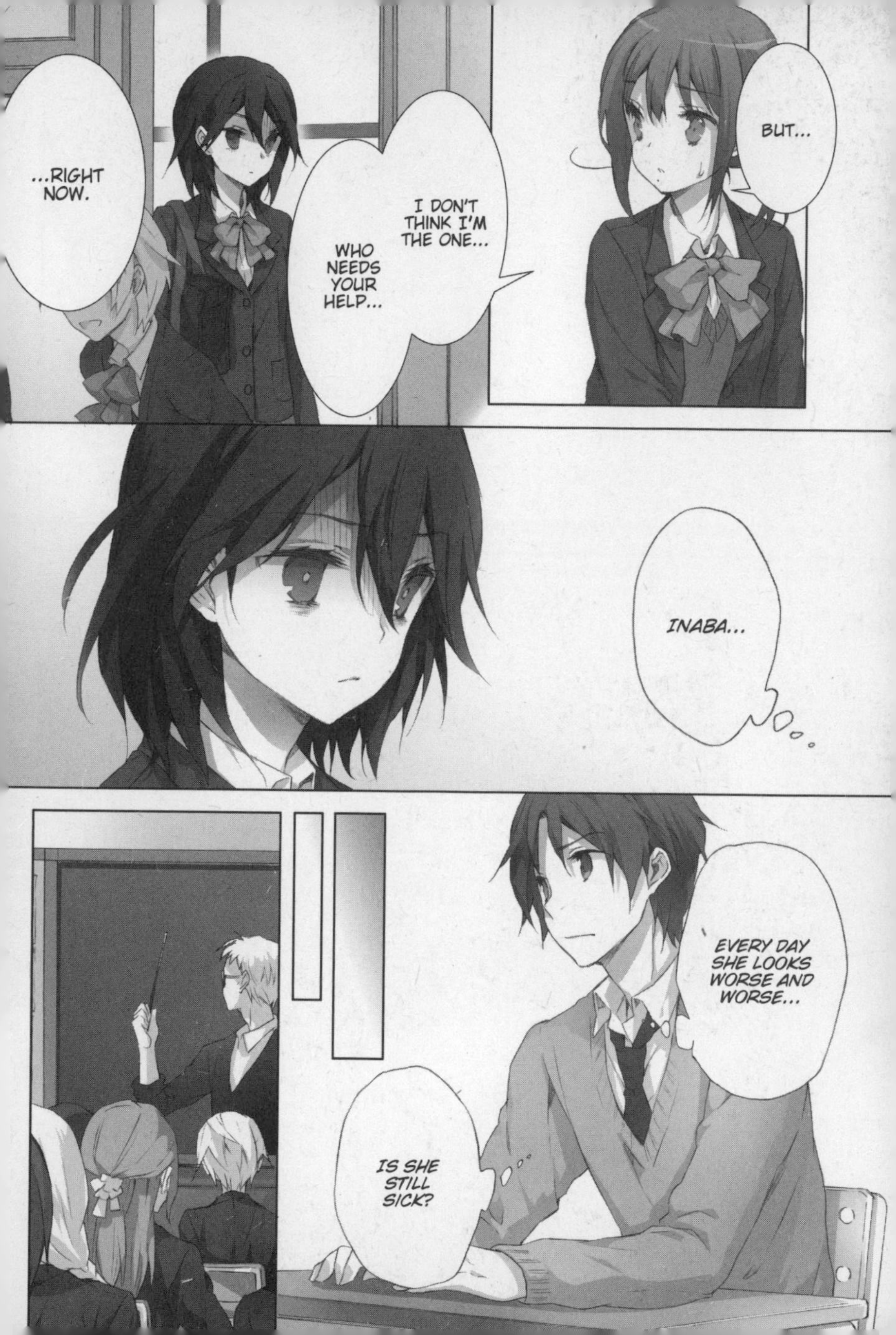
BUT...
I DON'T THINK I'M THE ONE...
WHO NEEDS YOUR HELP...
...RIGHT NOW.
INABA...
EVERY DAY SHE LOOKS WORSE AND WORSE...
IS SHE STILL SICK?

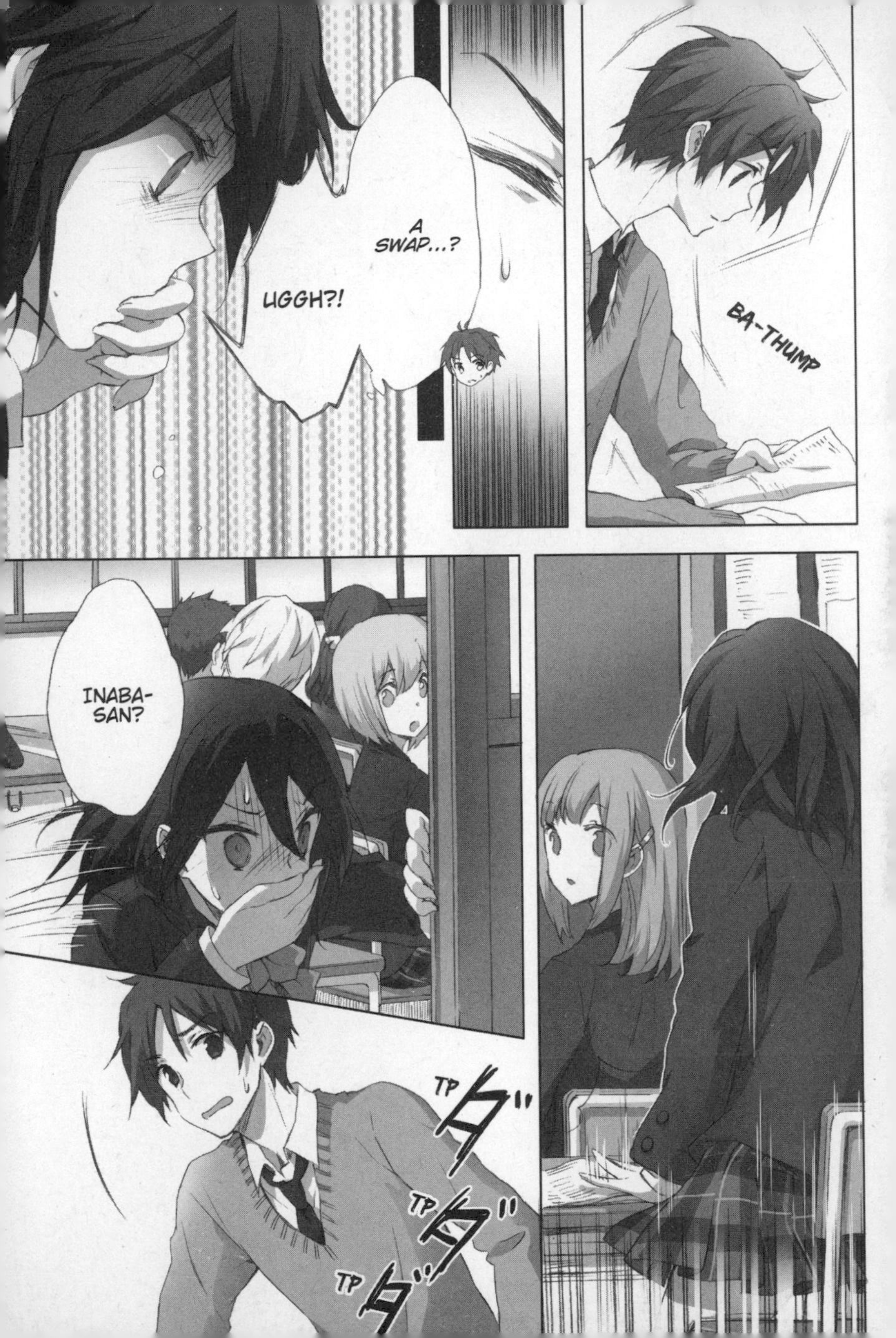

BA-THUMP
A SWAP...?
UGGH?!
INABA-SAN?
TP ダ
TP ダ
TP ダ

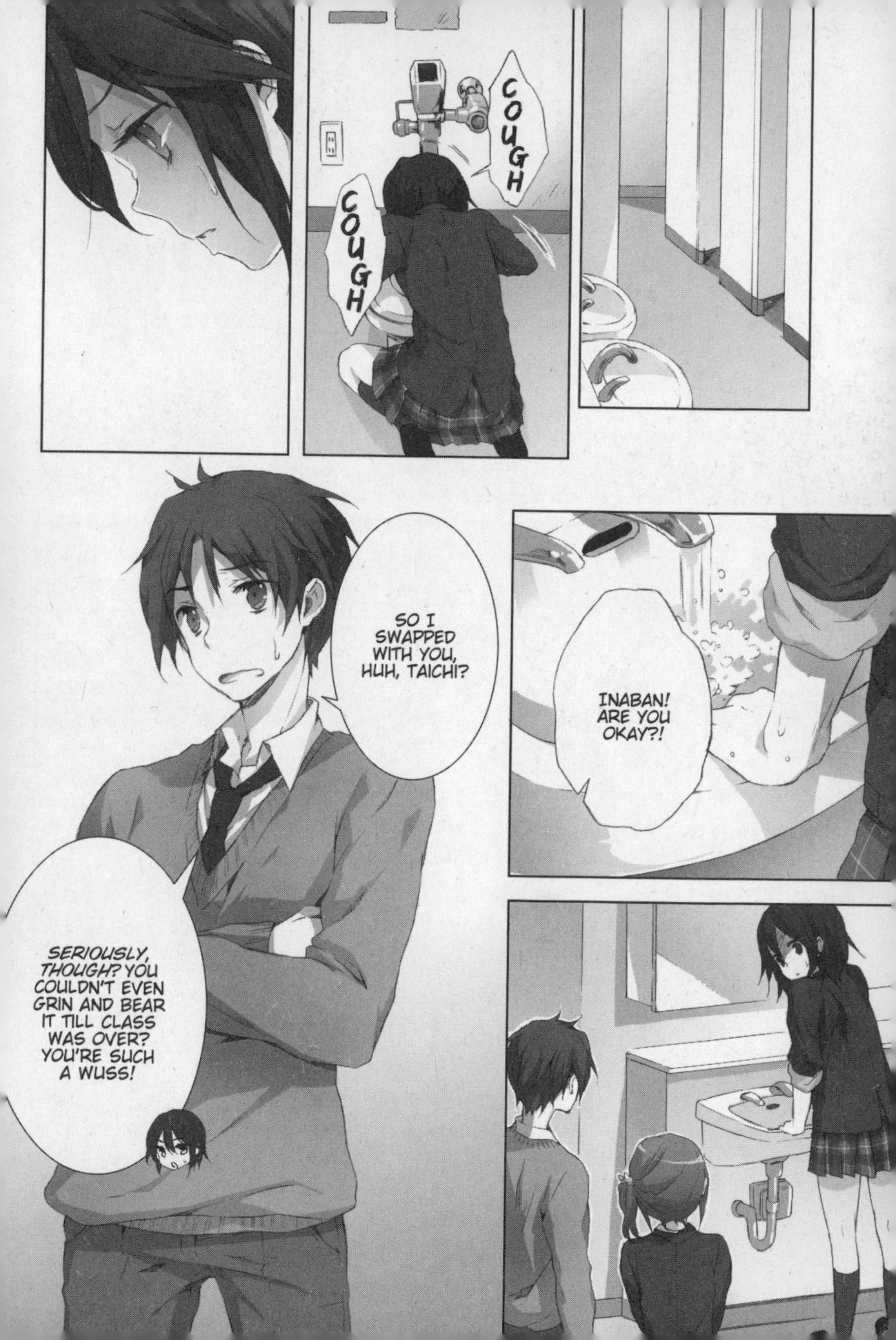
COUGH
COUGH
INABAN! ARE YOU OKAY?!
SO I SWAPPED WITH YOU, HUH, TAICHI?
SERIOUSLY, THOUGH? YOU COULDN'T EVEN GRIN AND BEAR IT TILL CLASS WAS OVER? YOU'RE SUCH A WUSS!

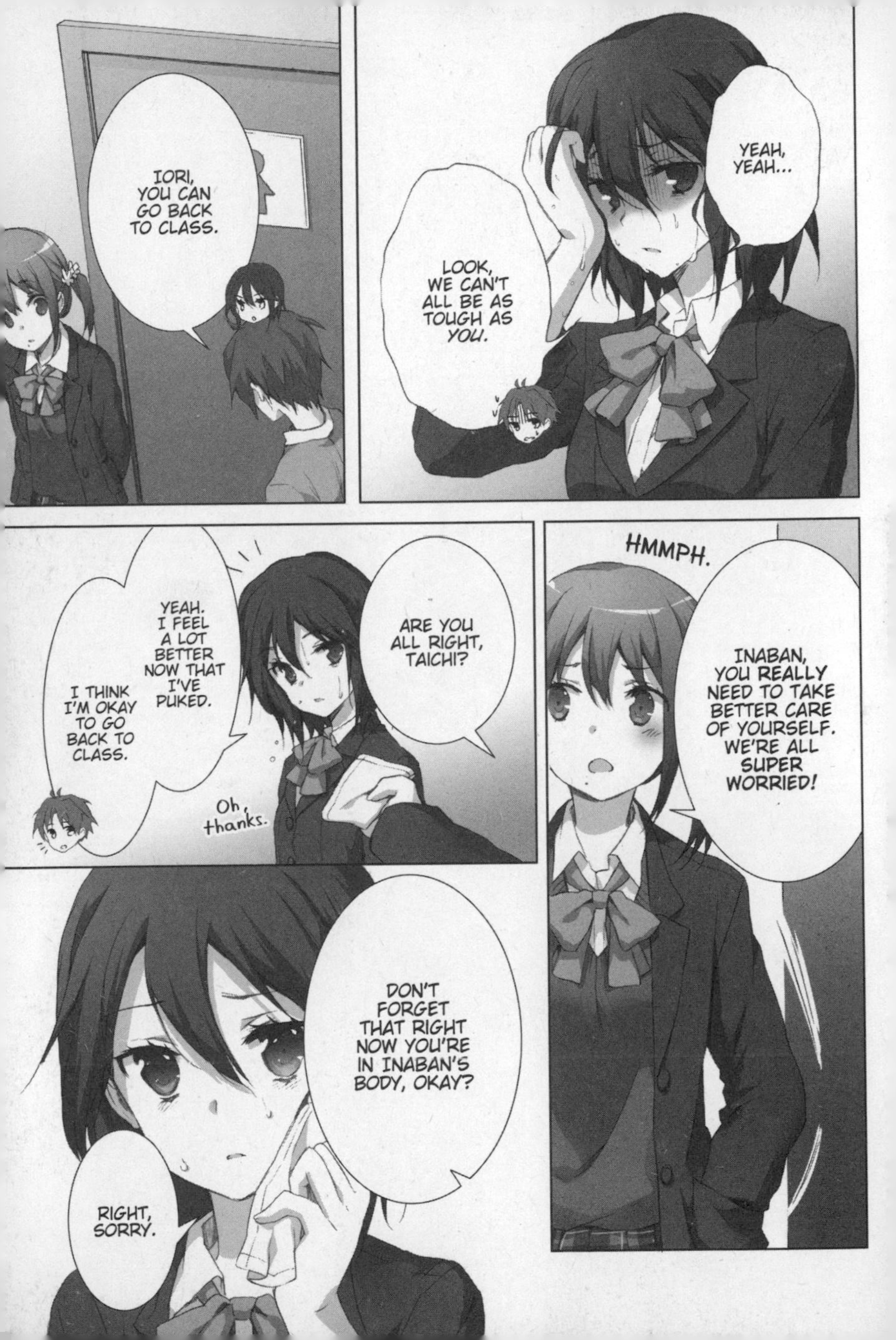
YEAH, YEAH...
LOOK, WE CAN'T ALL BE AS TOUGH AS YOU.
IORI, YOU CAN GO BACK TO CLASS.
HMMPH.
INABAN, YOU REALLY NEED TO TAKE BETTER CARE OF YOURSELF. WE'RE ALL SUPER WORRIED!
ARE YOU ALL RIGHT, TAICHI?
YEAH. I FEEL A LOT BETTER NOW THAT I'VE PUKED.
I THINK I'M OKAY TO GO BACK TO CLASS.
Oh, thanks.
DON'T FORGET THAT RIGHT NOW YOU'RE IN INABAN'S BODY, OKAY?
RIGHT, SORRY.

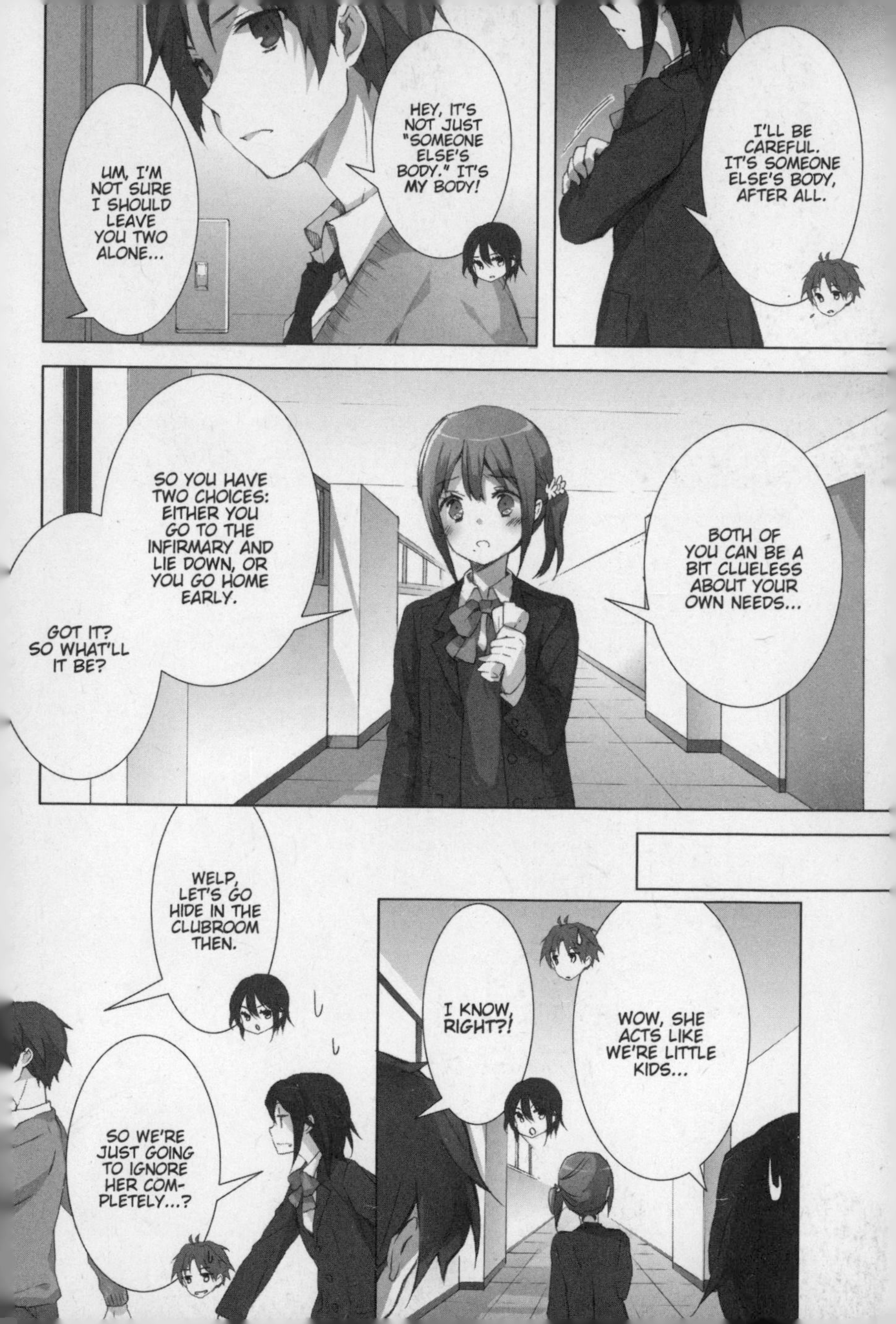
I'LL BE CAREFUL. IT'S SOMEONE ELSE'S BODY, AFTER ALL.
HEY, IT'S NOT JUST "SOMEONE ELSE'S BODY." IT'S MY BODY!
UM, I'M NOT SURE I SHOULD LEAVE YOU TWO ALONE...
BOTH OF YOU CAN BE A BIT CLUELESS ABOUT YOUR OWN NEEDS...
SO YOU HAVE TWO CHOICES: EITHER YOU GO TO THE INFIRMARY AND LIE DOWN, OR YOU GO HOME EARLY.
GOT IT? SO WHAT'LL IT BE?
WOW, SHE ACTS LIKE WE'RE LITTLE KIDS...
I KNOW, RIGHT?!
WELP, LET'S GO HIDE IN THE CLUBROOM THEN.
SO WE'RE JUST GOING TO IGNORE HER COM-PLETELY...?

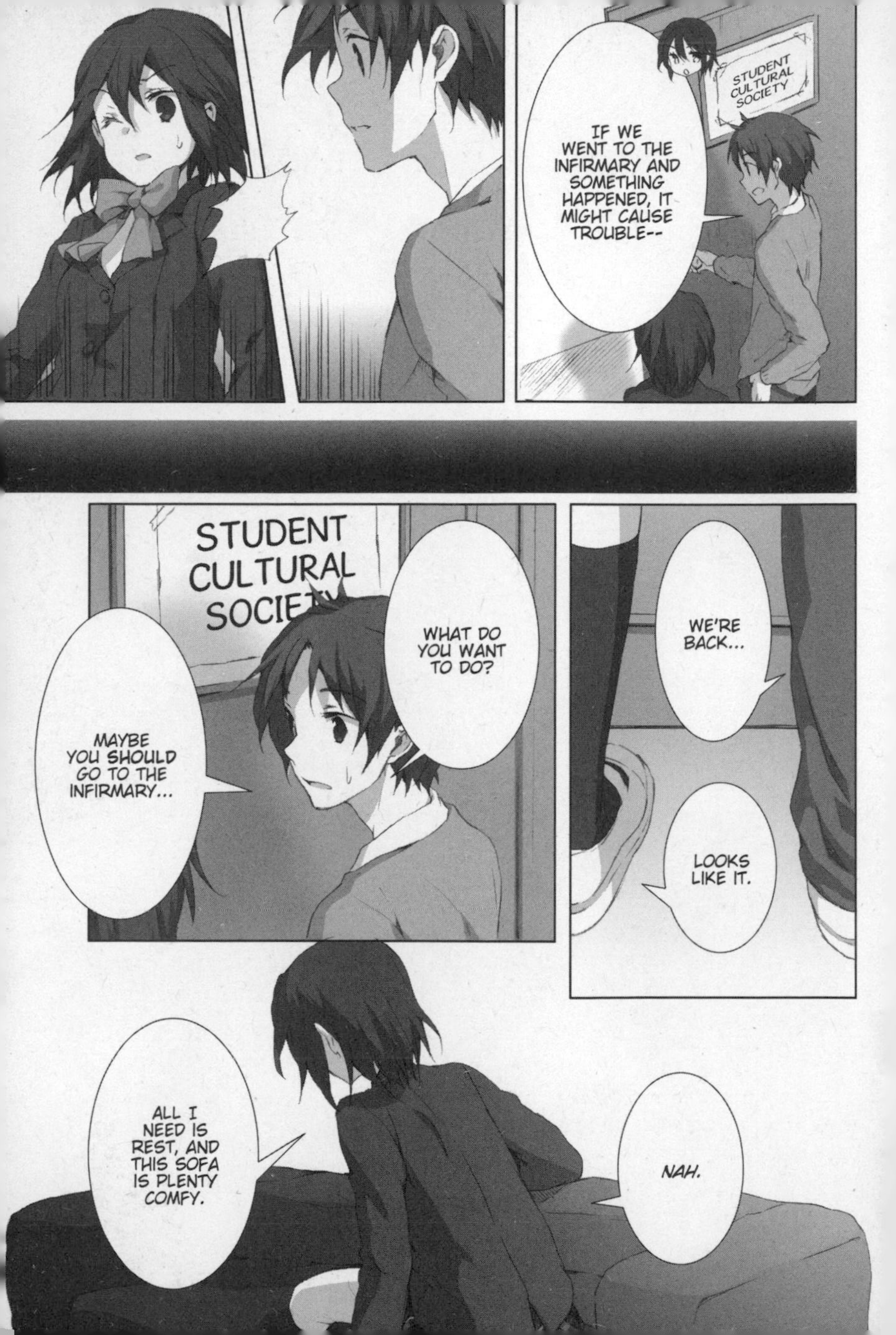
STUDENT CULTURAL SOCIETY
IF WE WENT TO THE INFIRMARY AND SOMETHING HAPPENED, IT MIGHT CAUSE TROUBLE--
WE'RE BACK...
LOOKS LIKE IT.
STUDENT CULTURAL SOCIET
WHAT DO YOU WANT TO DO?
MAYBE YOU SHOULD GO TO THE INFIRMARY...
NAH.
ALL I NEED IS REST, AND THIS SOFA IS PLENTY COMFY.

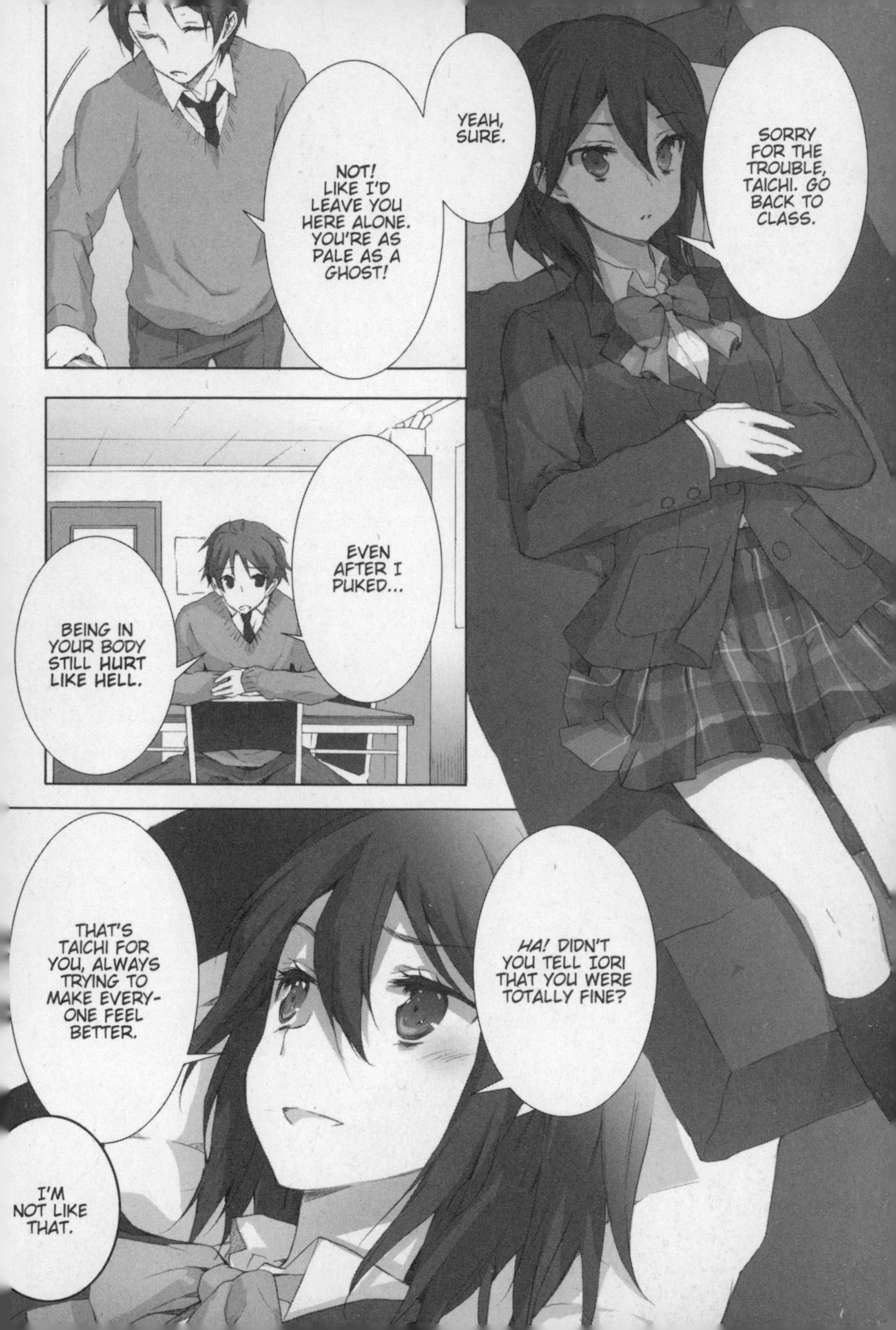
SORRY FOR THE TROUBLE, TAICHI. GO BACK TO CLASS.
YEAH, SURE.
NOT! LIKE I'D LEAVE YOU HERE ALONE. YOU'RE AS PALE AS A GHOST!
EVEN AFTER I PUKED...
BEING IN YOUR BODY STILL HURT LIKE HELL.
HA! DIDN'T YOU TELL IORI THAT YOU WERE TOTALLY FINE?
THAT'S TAICHI FOR YOU, ALWAYS TRYING TO MAKE EVERY-ONE FEEL BETTER.
I'M NOT LIKE THAT.

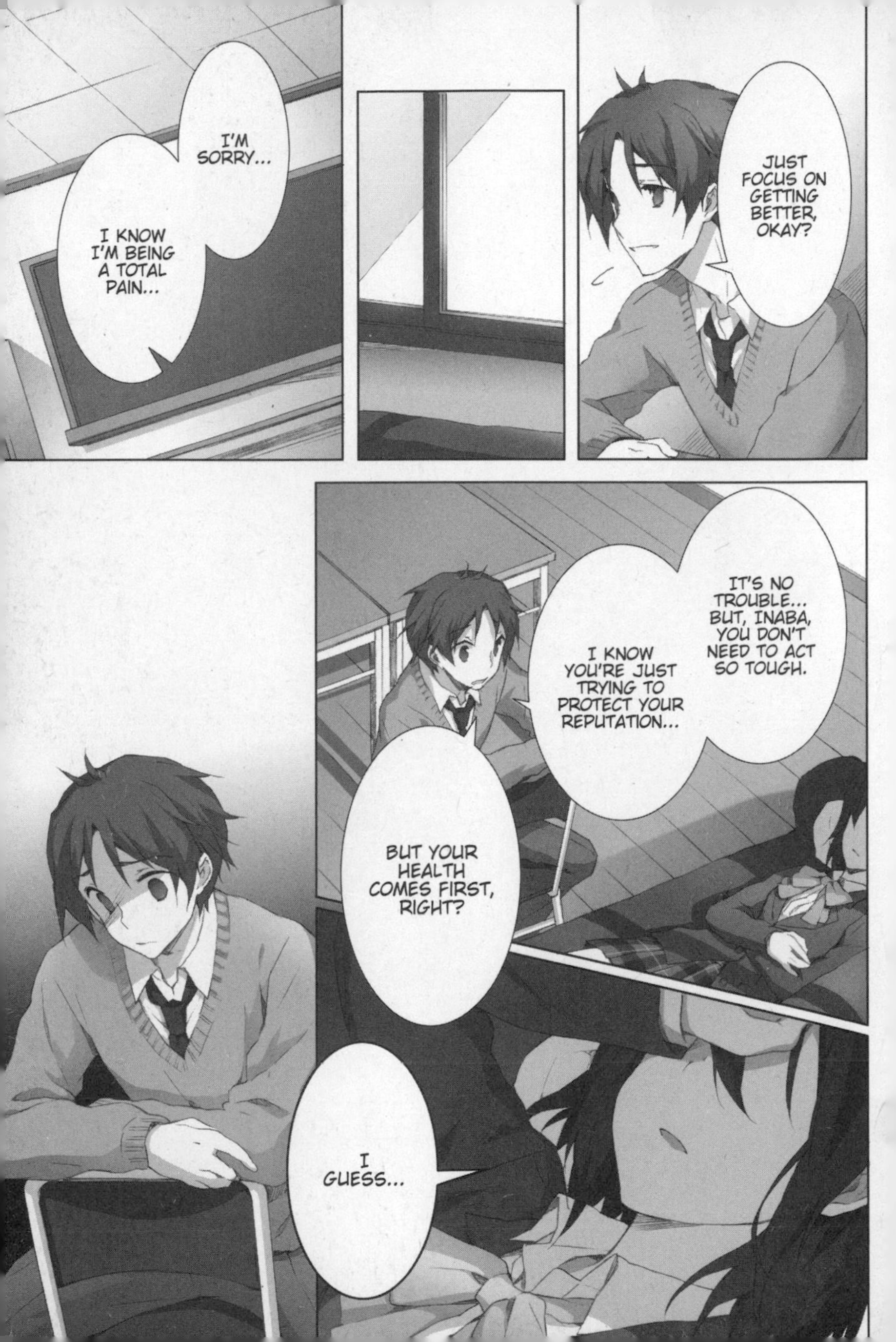
JUST FOCUS ON GETTING BETTER, OKAY?
I'M SORRY...
I KNOW I'M BEING A TOTAL PAIN...
IT'S NO TROUBLE... BUT, INABA, YOU DON'T NEED TO ACT SO TOUGH.
I KNOW YOU'RE JUST TRYING TO PROTECT YOUR REPUTATION...
BUT YOUR HEALTH COMES FIRST, RIGHT?
I GUESS...

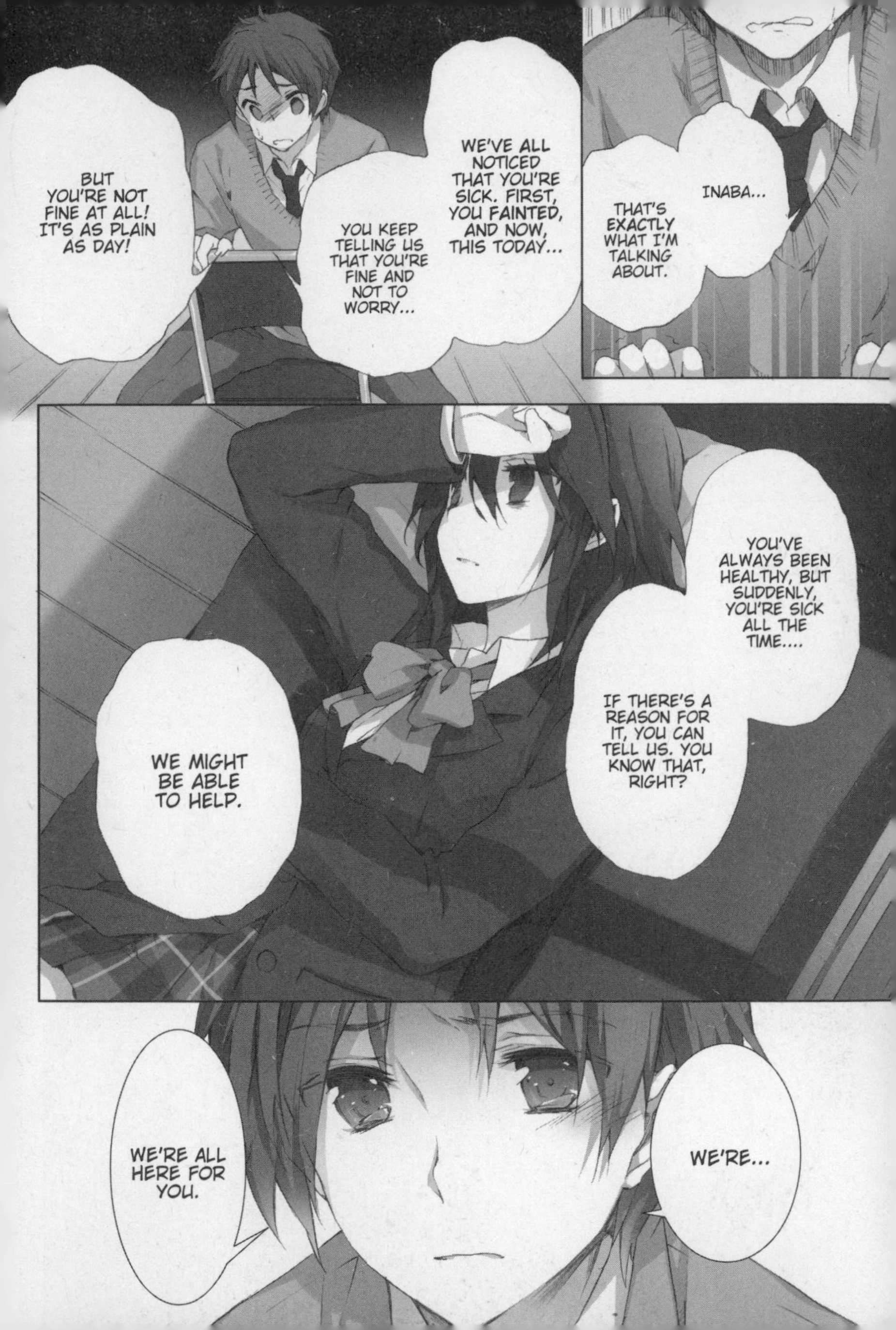
INABA...
THAT'S EXACTLY WHAT I'M TALKING ABOUT.
WE'VE ALL NOTICED THAT YOU'RE SICK. FIRST, YOU FAINTED, AND NOW, THIS TODAY...
YOU KEEP TELLING US THAT YOU'RE FINE AND NOT TO WORRY...
BUT YOU'RE NOT FINE AT ALL! IT'S AS PLAIN AS DAY!
YOU'VE ALWAYS BEEN HEALTHY, BUT SUDDENLY, YOU'RE SICK ALL THE TIME....
IF THERE'S A REASON FOR IT, YOU CAN TELL US. YOU KNOW THAT, RIGHT?
WE MIGHT BE ABLE TO HELP.
WE'RE...
WE'RE ALL HERE FOR YOU.

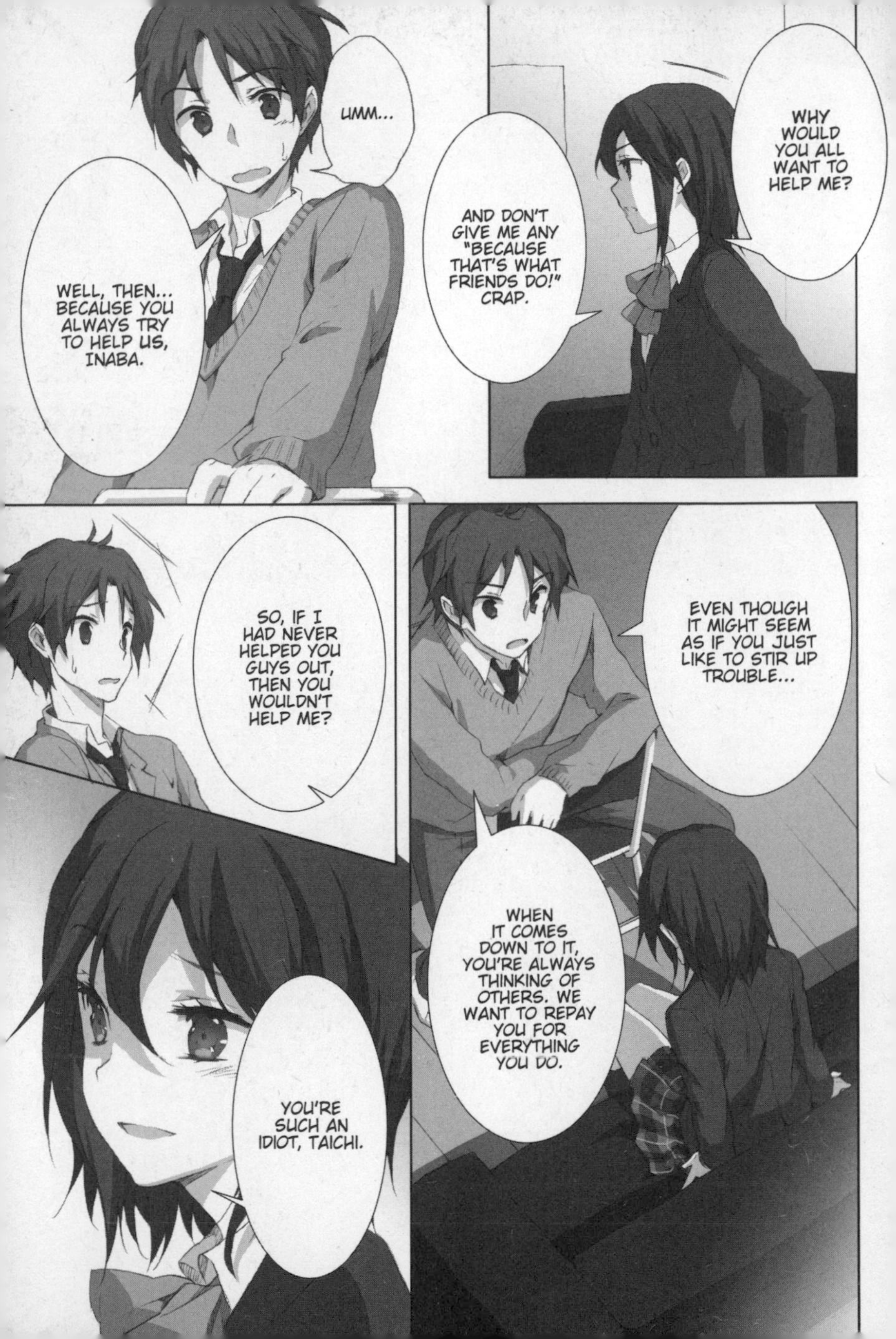
WHY WOULD YOU ALL WANT TO HELP ME?
AND DON'T GIVE ME ANY "BECAUSE THAT'S WHAT FRIENDS DO!" CRAP.
UMM...
WELL, THEN... BECAUSE YOU ALWAYS TRY TO HELP US, INABA.
EVEN THOUGH IT MIGHT SEEM AS IF YOU JUST LIKE TO STIR UP TROUBLE...
WHEN IT COMES DOWN TO IT, YOU'RE ALWAYS THINKING OF OTHERS. WE WANT TO REPAY YOU FOR EVERYTHING YOU DO.
SO, IF I HAD NEVER HELPED YOU GUYS OUT, THEN YOU WOULDN'T HELP ME?
YOU'RE SUCH AN IDIOT, TAICHI.

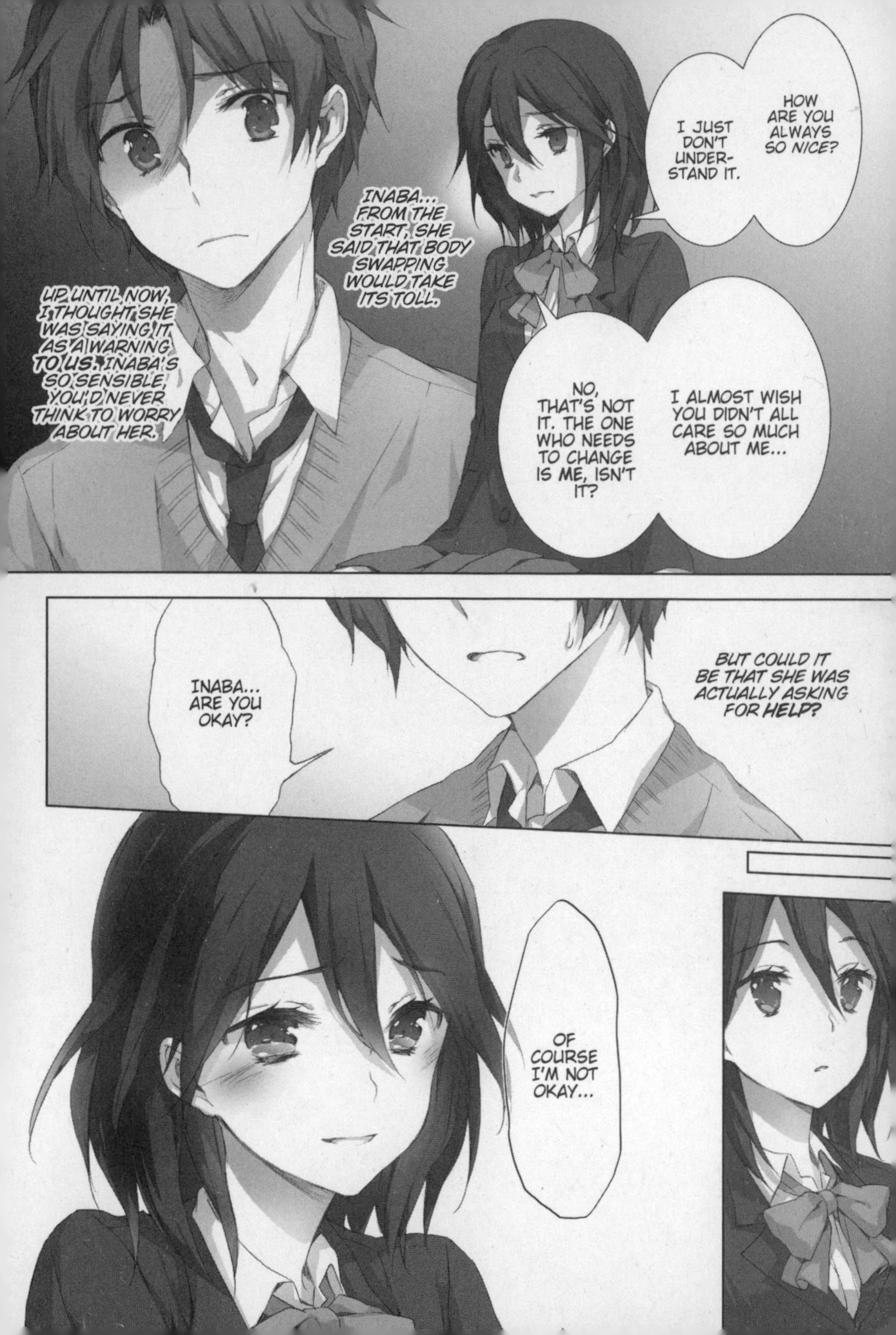
HOW ARE YOU ALWAYS SO *NICE?*
I JUST DON'T UNDER-STAND IT.
I ALMOST WISH YOU DIDN'T ALL CARE SO MUCH ABOUT ME...
NO, THAT'S NOT IT. THE ONE WHO NEEDS TO CHANGE IS ME, ISN'T IT?
INABA... FROM THE START, SHE SAID THAT BODY SWAPPING WOULD TAKE ITS TOLL.
UP UNTIL NOW, I THOUGHT SHE WAS SAYING IT AS A WARNING **TO US.** INABA'S SO SENSIBLE, YOU'D NEVER THINK TO WORRY ABOUT HER.
BUT COULD IT BE THAT SHE WAS ACTUALLY ASKING FOR **HELP?**
INABA... ARE YOU OKAY?
OF COURSE I'M NOT OKAY...

KOKORO CONNECT

I wanted to try dressing Yui in a Lolita outfit.

KOKORO CONNECT
Chapter 9

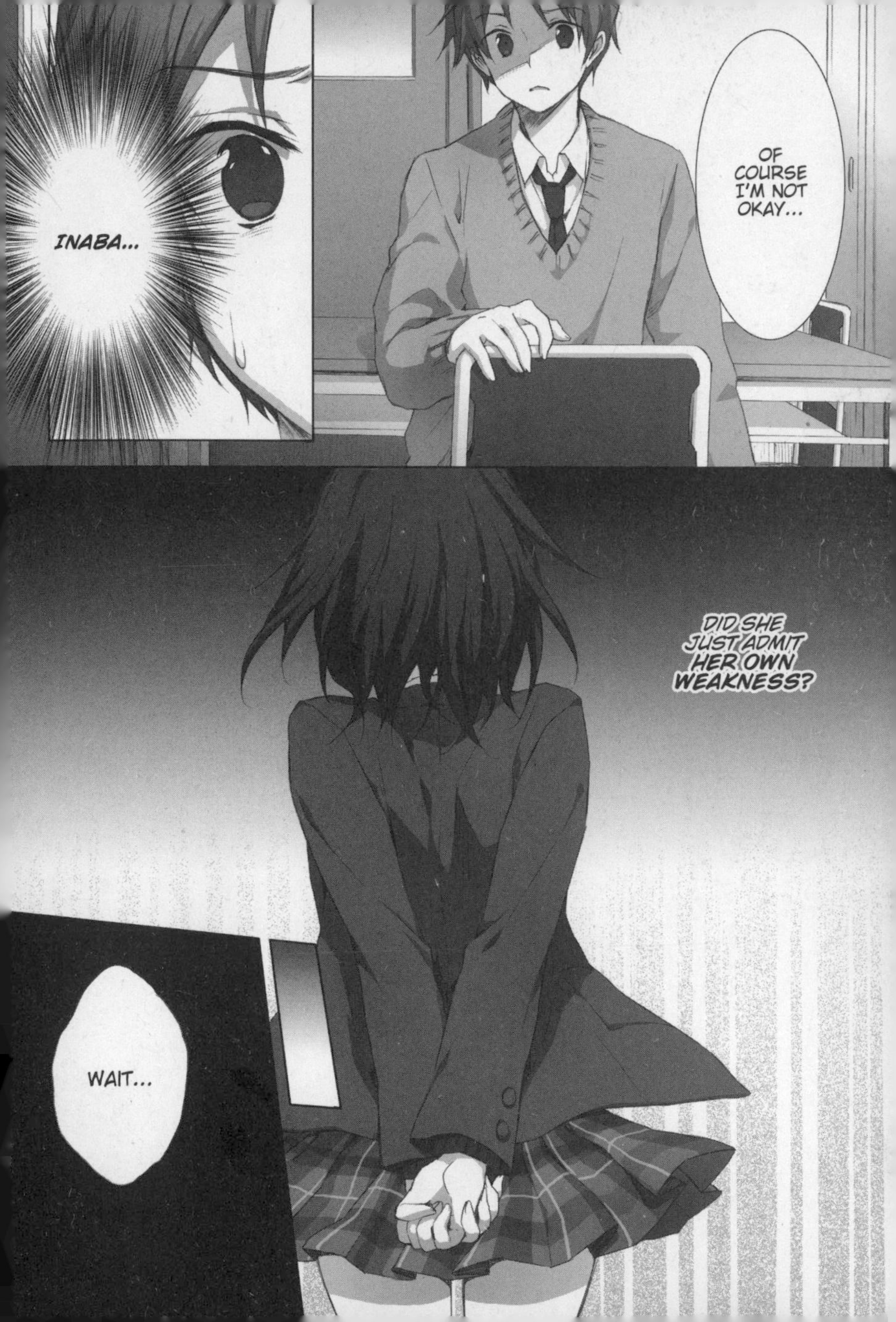
OF COURSE I'M NOT OKAY...
INABA...
DID SHE JUST ADMIT HER OWN WEAKNESS?
WAIT...

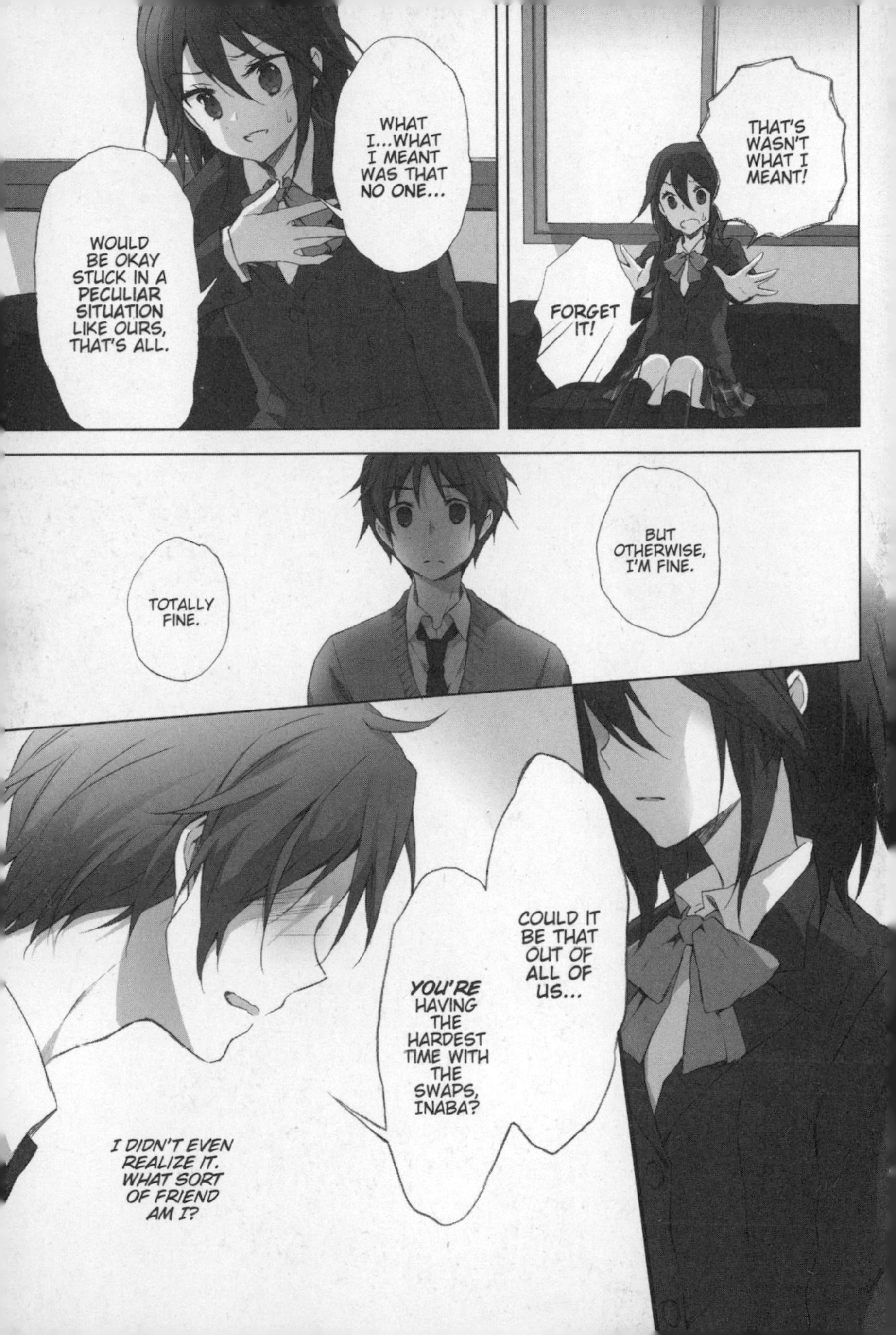
THAT'S WASN'T WHAT I MEANT!
FORGET IT!
WHAT I...WHAT I MEANT WAS THAT NO ONE...
WOULD BE OKAY STUCK IN A PECULIAR SITUATION LIKE OURS, THAT'S ALL.
BUT OTHERWISE, I'M FINE.
TOTALLY FINE.
COULD IT BE THAT OUT OF ALL OF US...
YOU'RE HAVING THE HARDEST TIME WITH THE SWAPS, INABA?
I DIDN'T EVEN REALIZE IT. WHAT SORT OF FRIEND AM I?

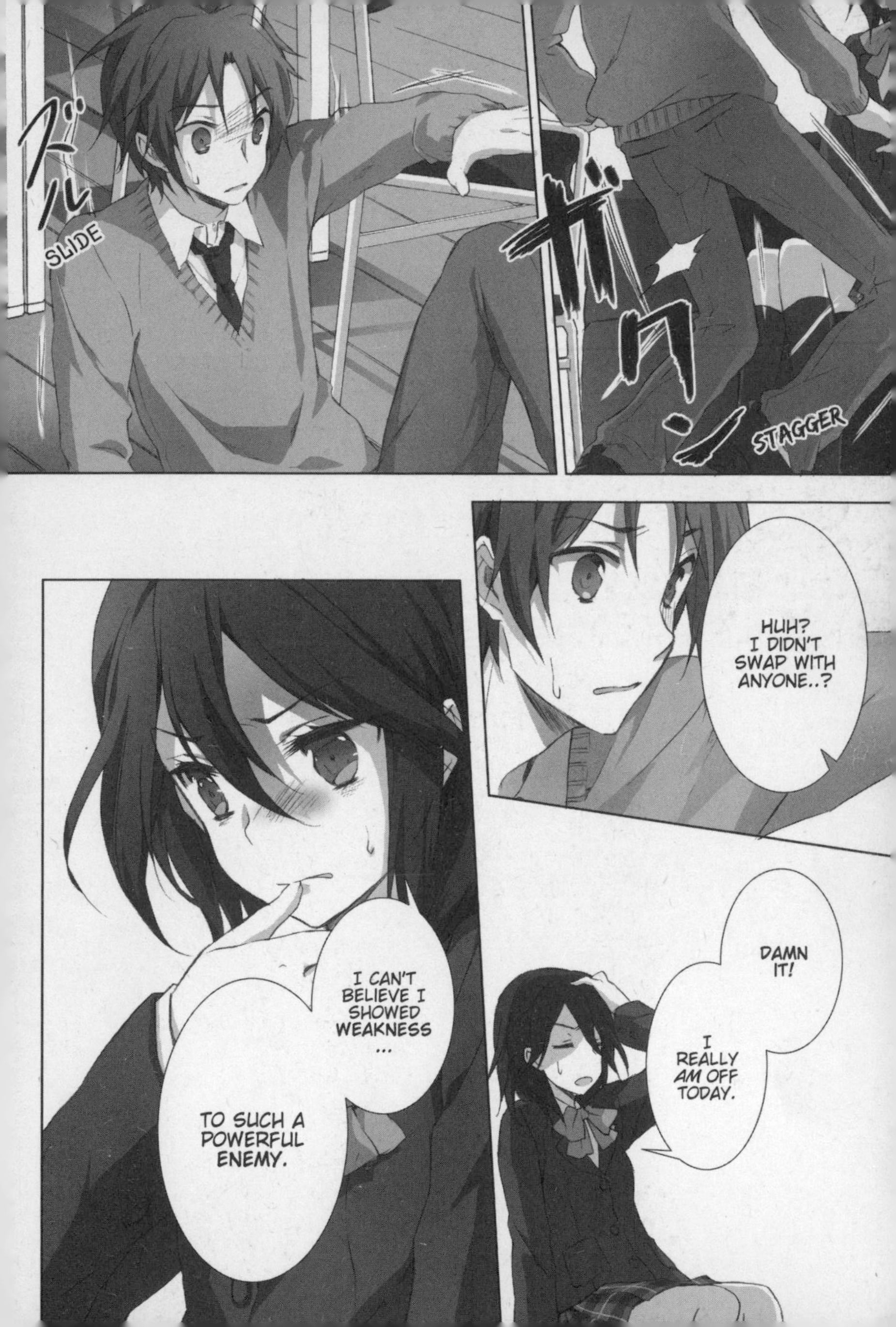

STAGGER
SLIDE
HUH? I DIDN'T SWAP WITH ANYONE..?
DAMN IT!
I REALLY AM OFF TODAY.
I CAN'T BELIEVE I SHOWED WEAKNESS ...
TO SUCH A POWERFUL ENEMY.

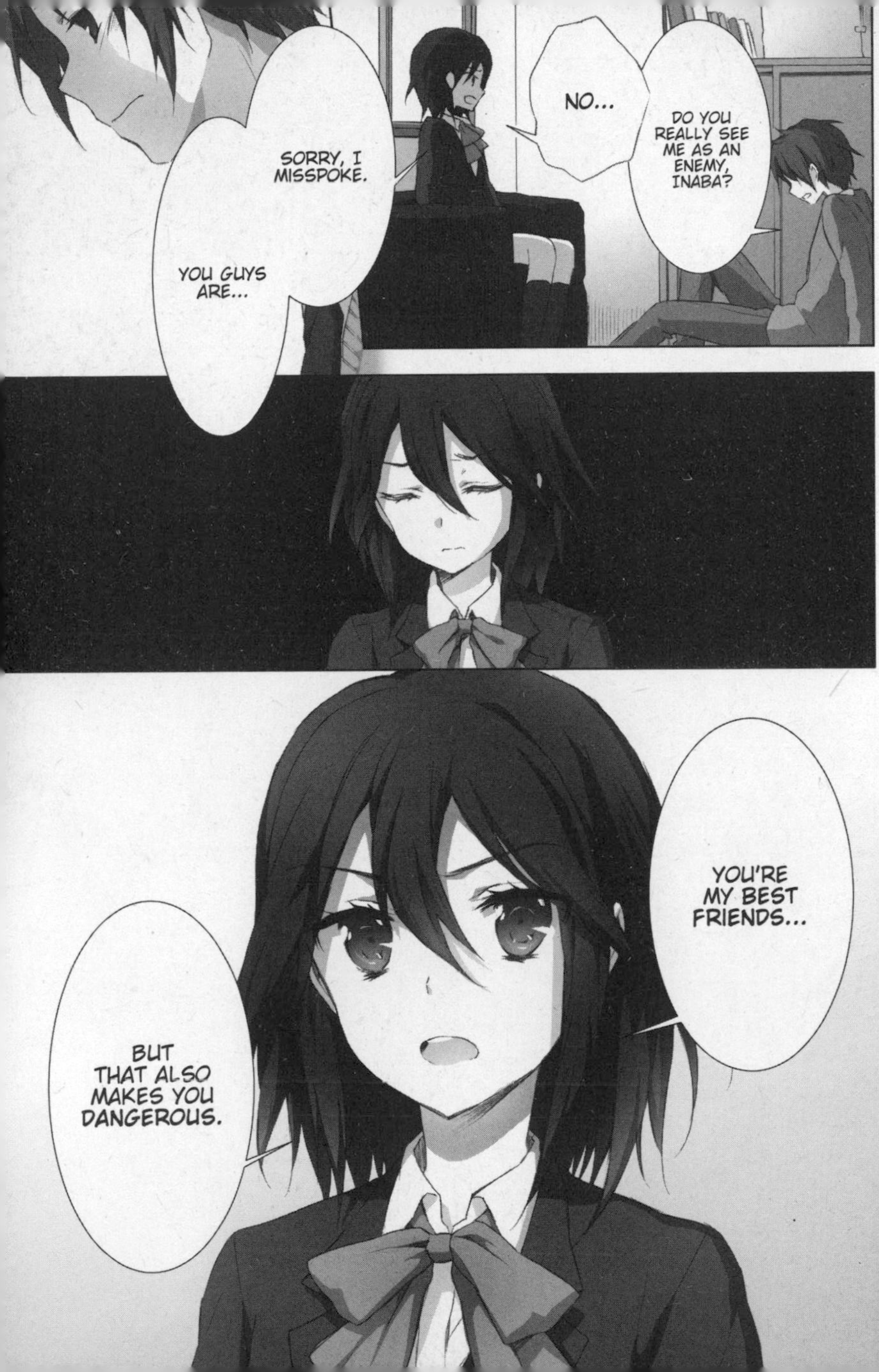
DO YOU REALLY SEE ME AS AN ENEMY, INABA?
NO...
SORRY, I MISSPOKE.
YOU GUYS ARE...
YOU'RE MY BEST FRIENDS...
BUT THAT ALSO MAKES YOU DANGEROUS.

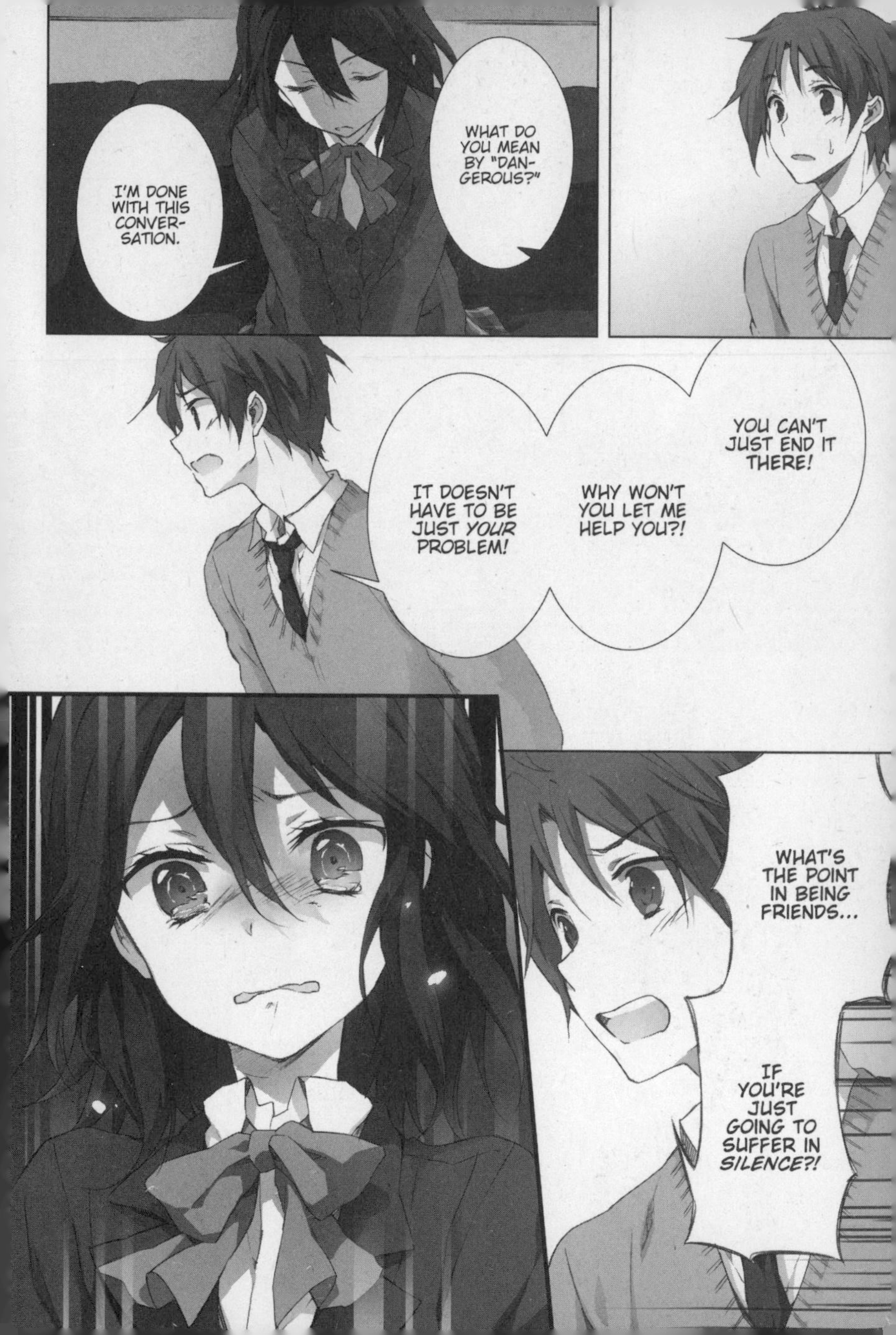
WHAT DO YOU MEAN BY "DANGEROUS?"
I'M DONE WITH THIS CONVERSATION.
YOU CAN'T JUST END IT THERE!
WHY WON'T YOU LET ME HELP YOU?!
IT DOESN'T HAVE TO BE JUST *YOUR* PROBLEM!
WHAT'S THE POINT IN BEING FRIENDS...
IF YOU'RE JUST GOING TO SUFFER IN *SILENCE*?!

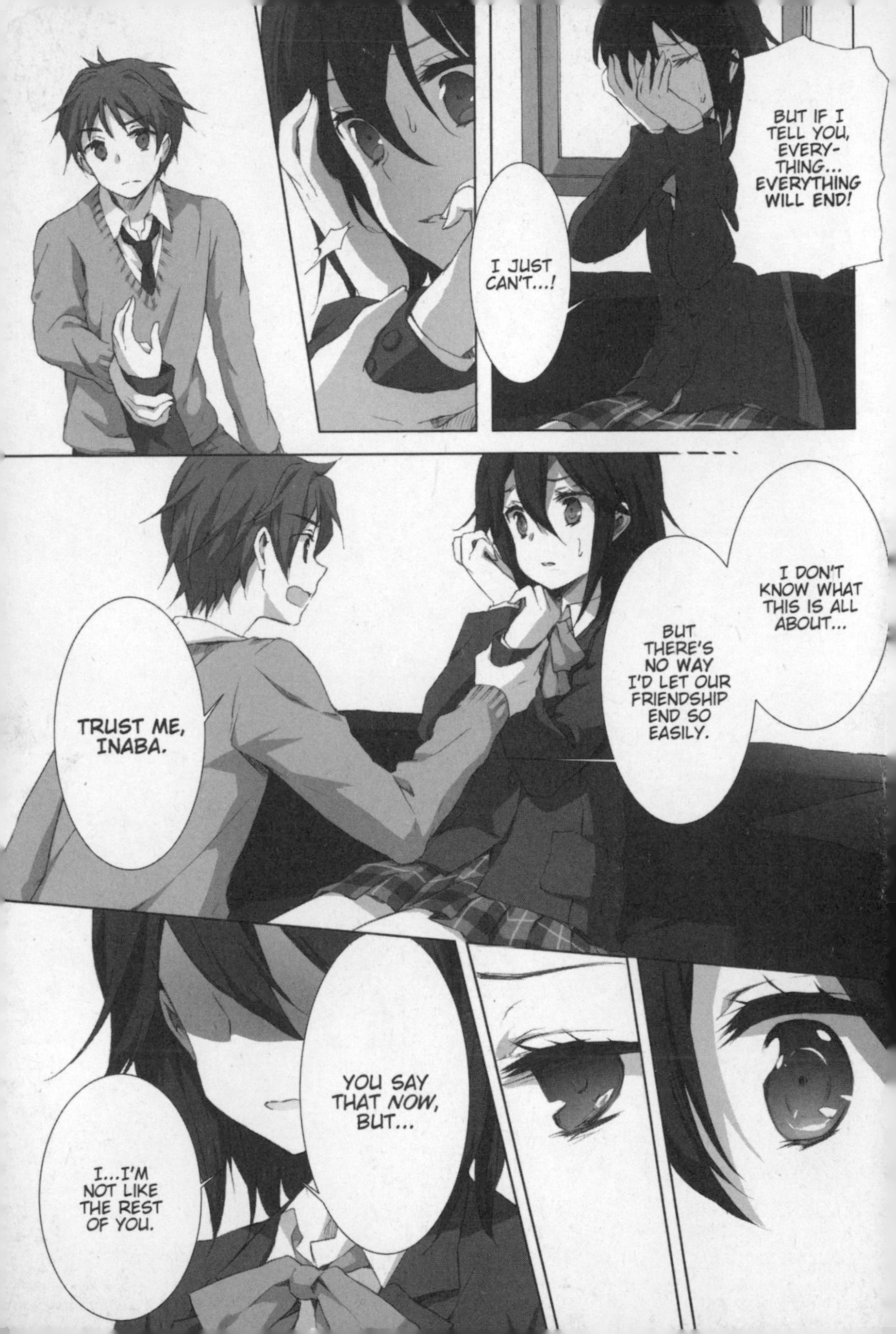
BUT IF I TELL YOU, EVERY-THING... EVERYTHING WILL END!
I JUST CAN'T...!
I DON'T KNOW WHAT THIS IS ALL ABOUT...
BUT THERE'S NO WAY I'D LET OUR FRIENDSHIP END SO EASILY.
TRUST ME, INABA.
YOU SAY THAT NOW, BUT...
I...I'M NOT LIKE THE REST OF YOU.

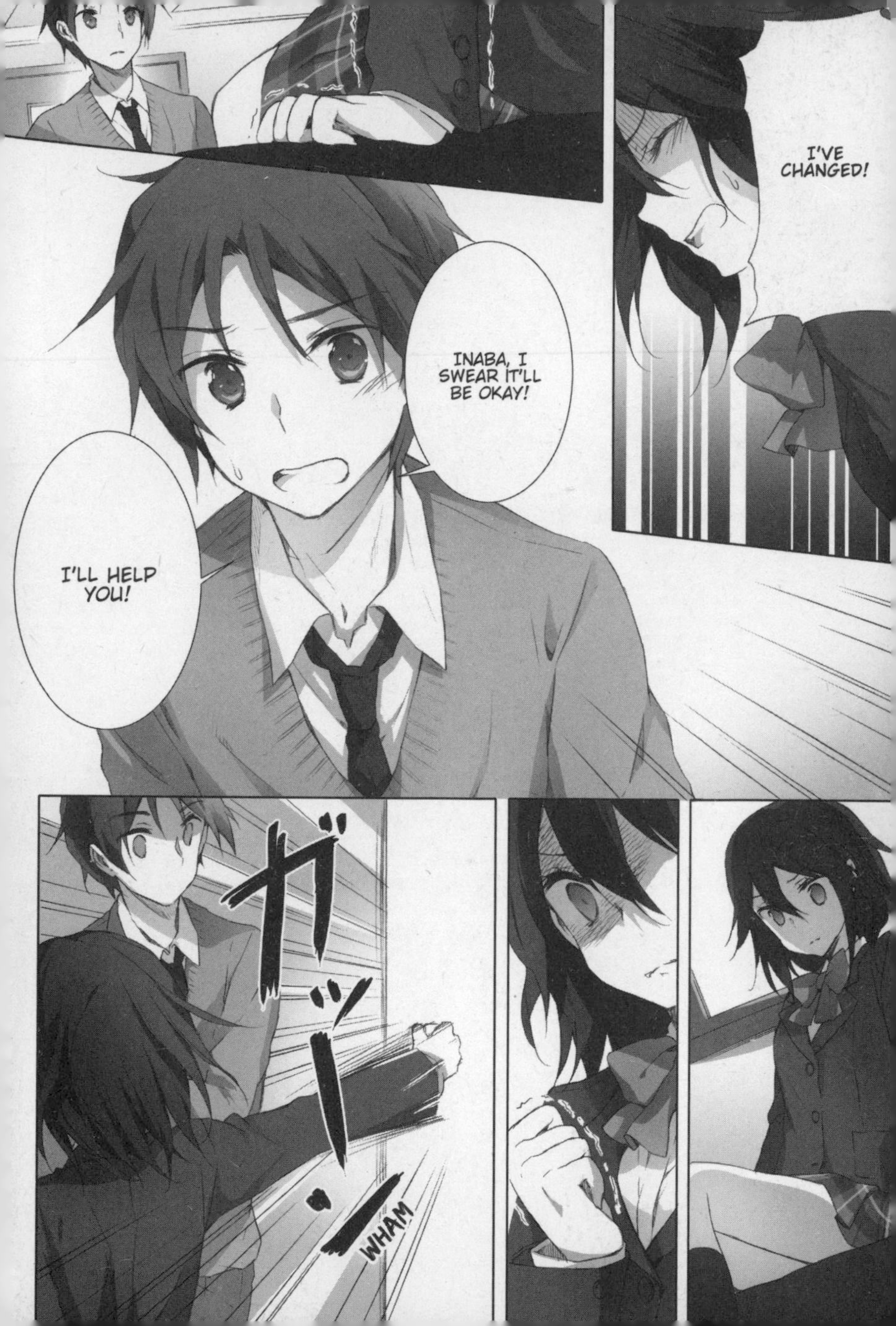
I'VE CHANGED!
INABA, I SWEAR IT'LL BE OKAY!
I'LL HELP YOU!
WHAM

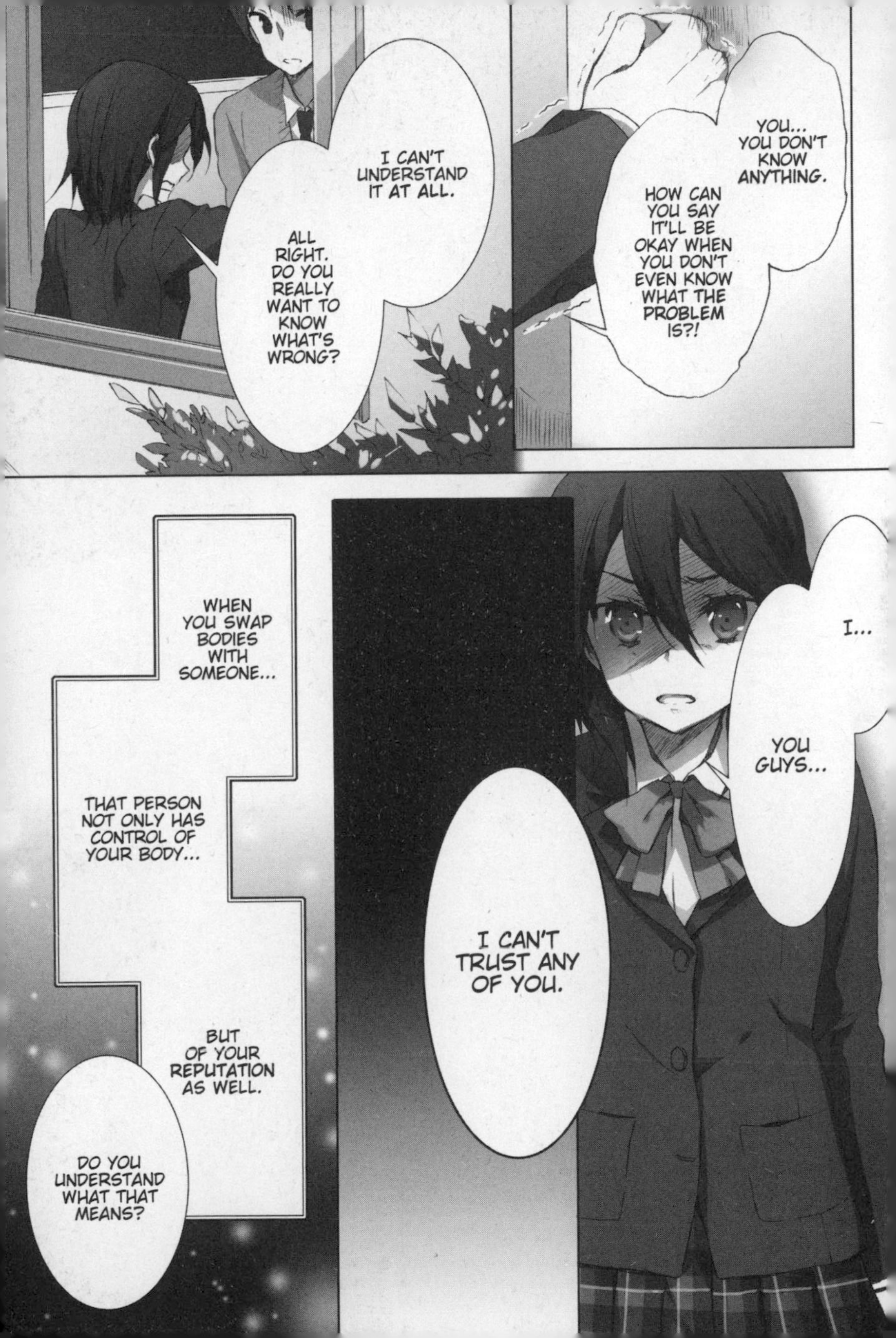
YOU... YOU DON'T KNOW ANYTHING.
HOW CAN YOU SAY IT'LL BE OKAY WHEN YOU DON'T EVEN KNOW WHAT THE PROBLEM IS?!
I CAN'T UNDERSTAND IT AT ALL.
ALL RIGHT. DO YOU REALLY WANT TO KNOW WHAT'S WRONG?
I...
YOU GUYS...
I CAN'T TRUST ANY OF YOU.
WHEN YOU SWAP BODIES WITH SOMEONE...
THAT PERSON NOT ONLY HAS CONTROL OF YOUR BODY...
BUT OF YOUR REPUTATION AS WELL.
DO YOU UNDERSTAND WHAT THAT MEANS?

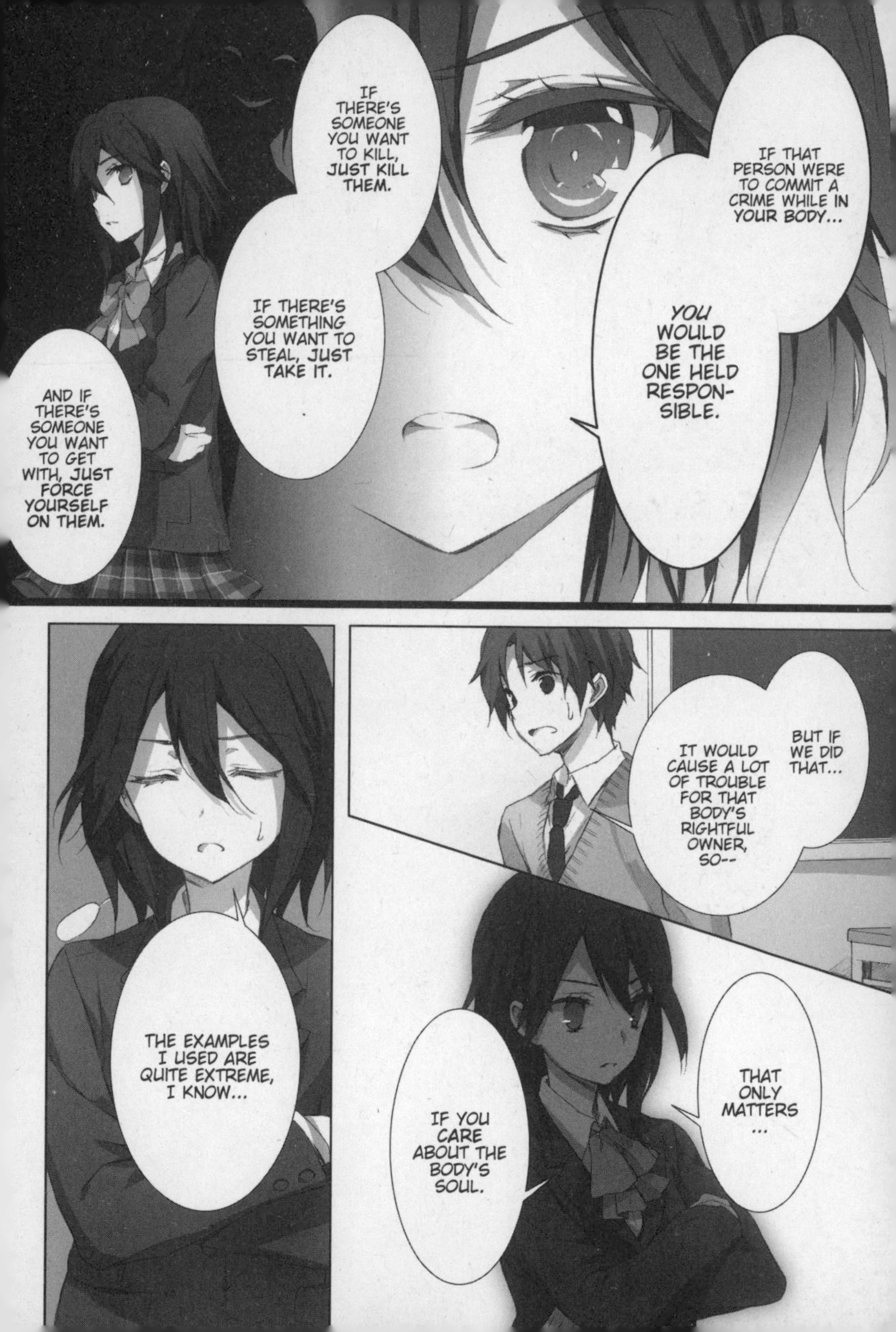
IF THAT PERSON WERE TO COMMIT A CRIME WHILE IN YOUR BODY...
YOU WOULD BE THE ONE HELD RESPONSIBLE.
IF THERE'S SOMEONE YOU WANT TO KILL, JUST KILL THEM.
IF THERE'S SOMETHING YOU WANT TO STEAL, JUST TAKE IT.
AND IF THERE'S SOMEONE YOU WANT TO GET WITH, JUST FORCE YOURSELF ON THEM.
BUT IF WE DID THAT...
IT WOULD CAUSE A LOT OF TROUBLE FOR THAT BODY'S RIGHTFUL OWNER, SO--
THAT ONLY MATTERS...
IF YOU CARE ABOUT THE BODY'S SOUL.
THE EXAMPLES I USED ARE QUITE EXTREME, I KNOW...

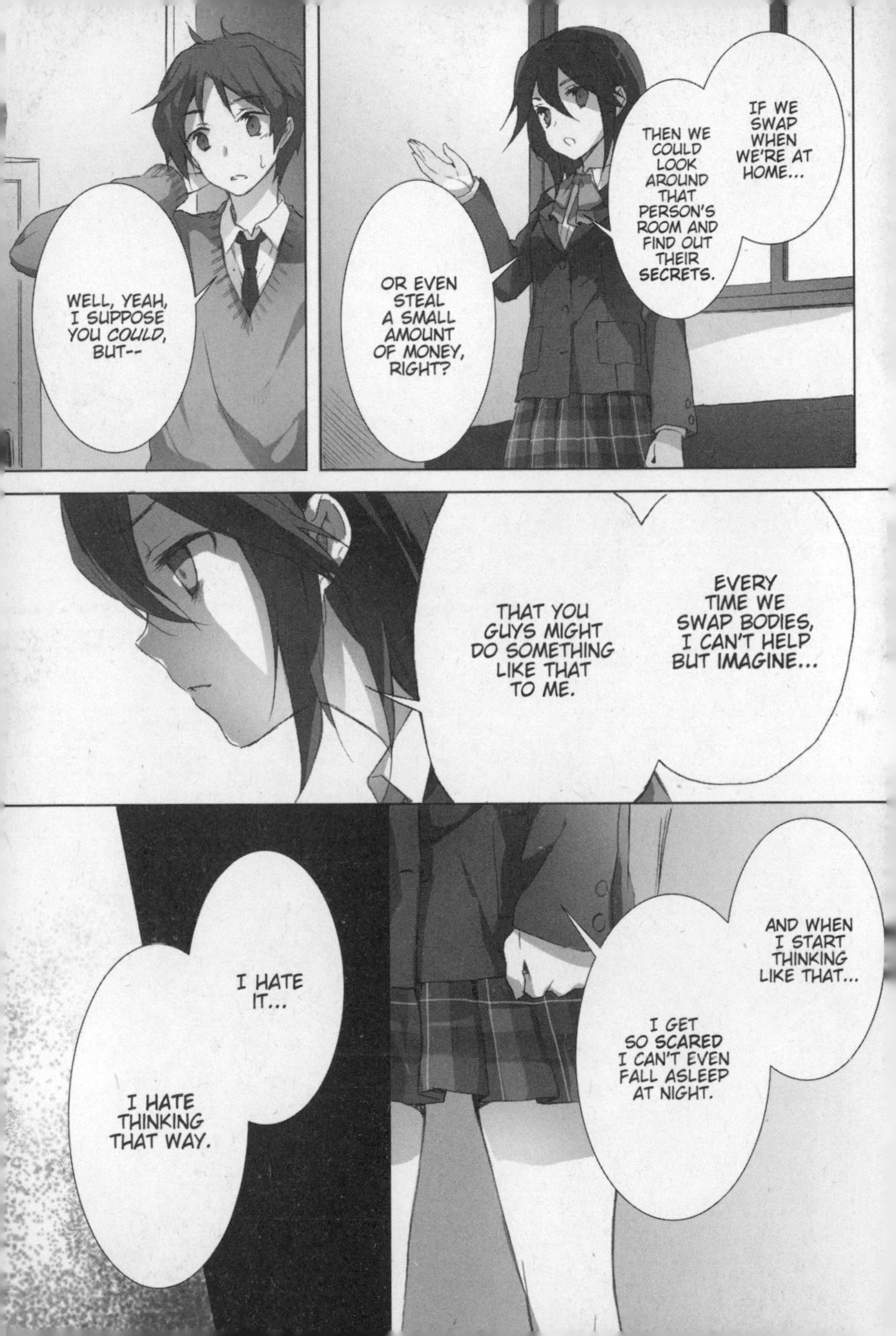
IF WE SWAP WHEN WE'RE AT HOME...
THEN WE COULD LOOK AROUND THAT PERSON'S ROOM AND FIND OUT THEIR SECRETS.
OR EVEN STEAL A SMALL AMOUNT OF MONEY, RIGHT?
WELL, YEAH, I SUPPOSE YOU *COULD*, BUT--
EVERY TIME WE SWAP BODIES, I CAN'T HELP BUT IMAGINE...
THAT YOU GUYS MIGHT DO SOMETHING LIKE THAT TO ME.
AND WHEN I START THINKING LIKE THAT...
I GET SO SCARED I CAN'T EVEN FALL ASLEEP AT NIGHT.
I HATE IT...
I HATE THINKING THAT WAY.

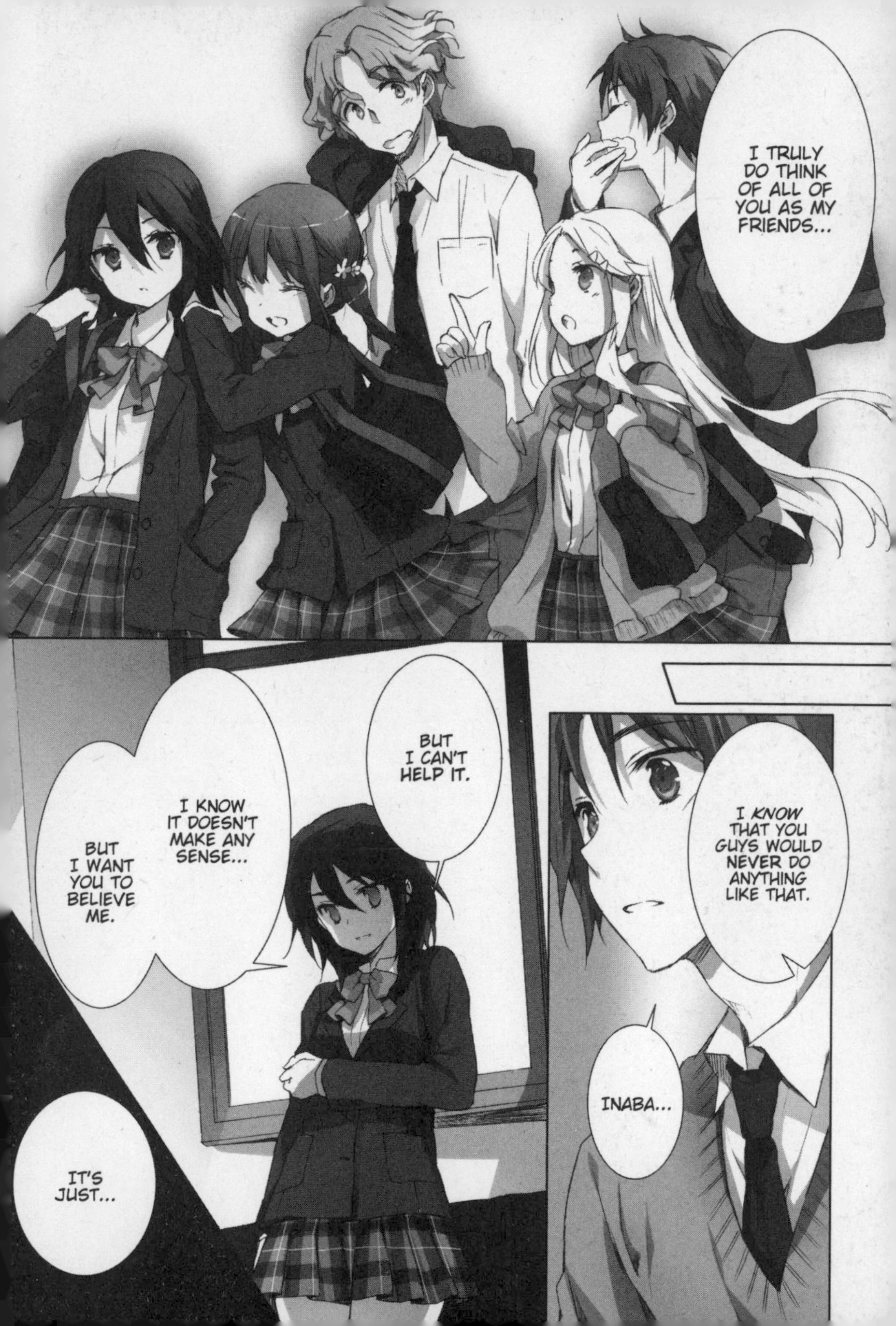
I TRULY DO THINK OF ALL OF YOU AS MY FRIENDS...
I KNOW THAT YOU GUYS WOULD NEVER DO ANYTHING LIKE THAT.
INABA...
BUT I CAN'T HELP IT.
I KNOW IT DOESN'T MAKE ANY SENSE...
BUT I WANT YOU TO BELIEVE ME.
IT'S JUST...

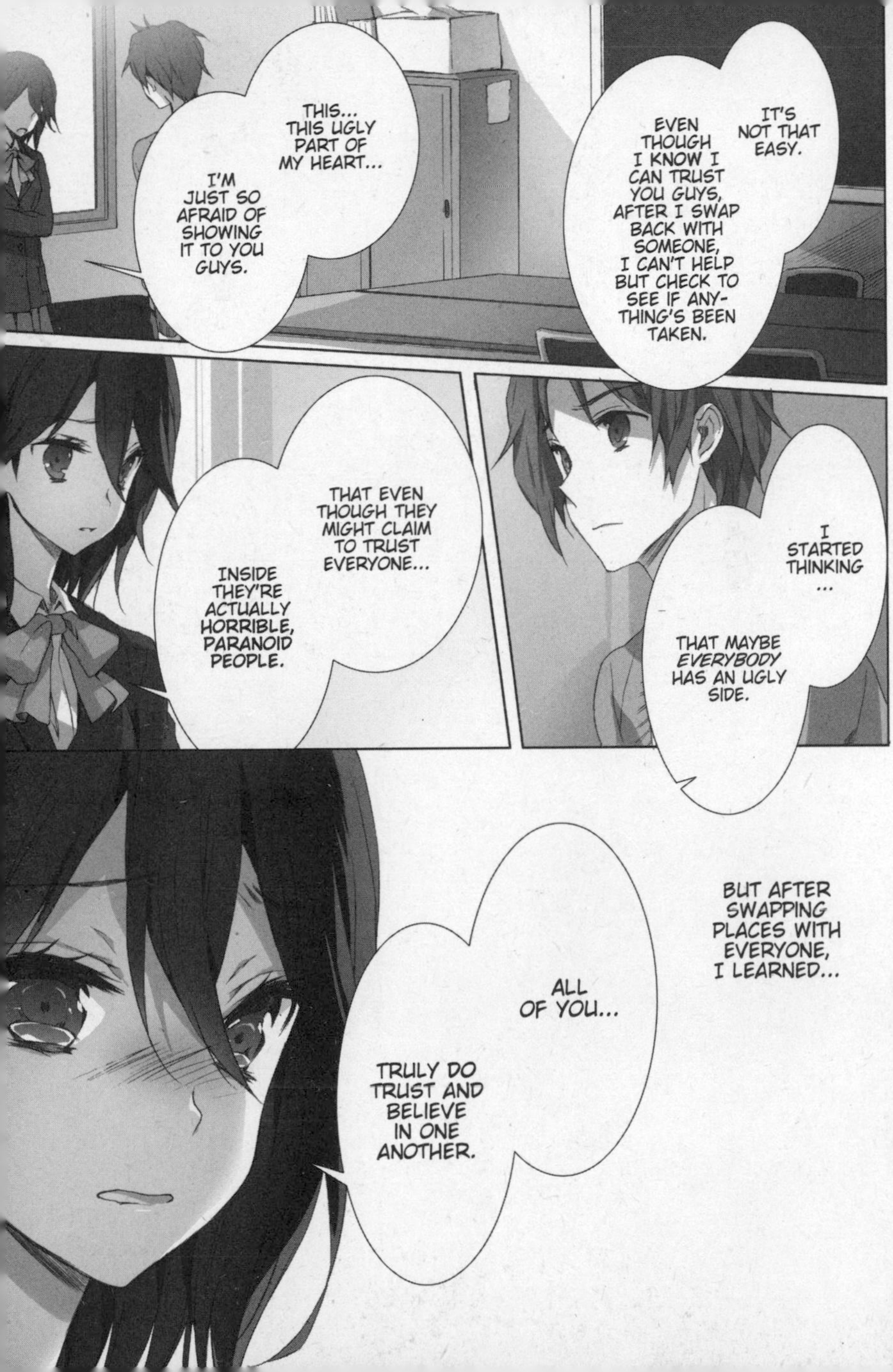
IT'S NOT THAT EASY.
EVEN THOUGH I KNOW I CAN TRUST YOU GUYS, AFTER I SWAP BACK WITH SOMEONE, I CAN'T HELP BUT CHECK TO SEE IF ANY-THING'S BEEN TAKEN.
THIS... THIS UGLY PART OF MY HEART...
I'M JUST SO AFRAID OF SHOWING IT TO YOU GUYS.
I STARTED THINKING ...
THAT MAYBE *EVERYBODY* HAS AN UGLY SIDE.
THAT EVEN THOUGH THEY MIGHT CLAIM TO TRUST EVERYONE...
INSIDE THEY'RE ACTUALLY HORRIBLE, PARANOID PEOPLE.
BUT AFTER SWAPPING PLACES WITH EVERYONE, I LEARNED...
ALL OF YOU...
TRULY DO TRUST AND BELIEVE IN ONE ANOTHER.

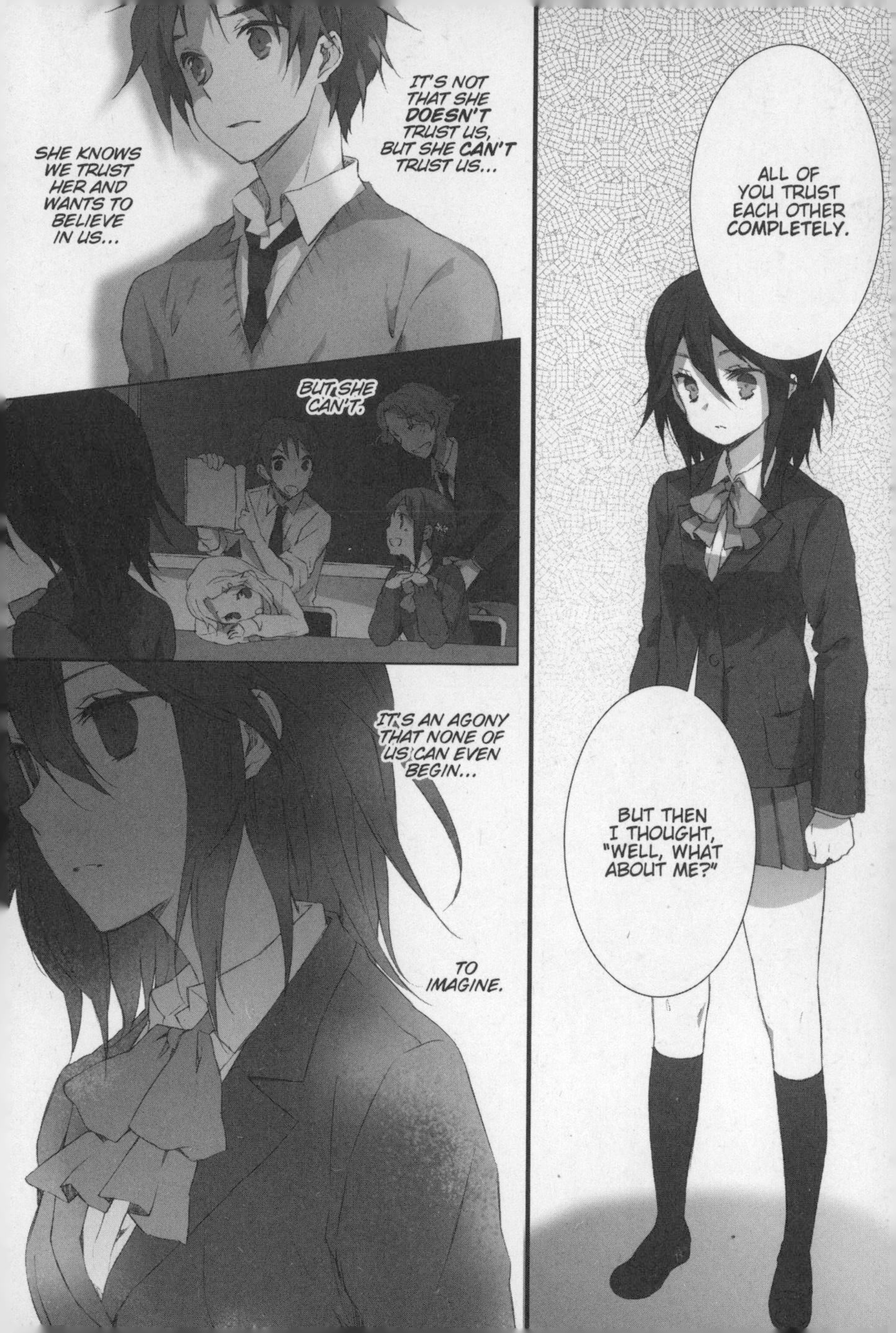
ALL OF YOU TRUST EACH OTHER COMPLETELY.
BUT THEN I THOUGHT, "WELL, WHAT ABOUT ME?"
IT'S NOT THAT SHE DOESN'T TRUST US, BUT SHE CAN'T TRUST US...
SHE KNOWS WE TRUST HER AND WANTS TO BELIEVE IN US...
BUT SHE CAN'T.
IT'S AN AGONY THAT NONE OF US CAN EVEN BEGIN...
TO IMAGINE.

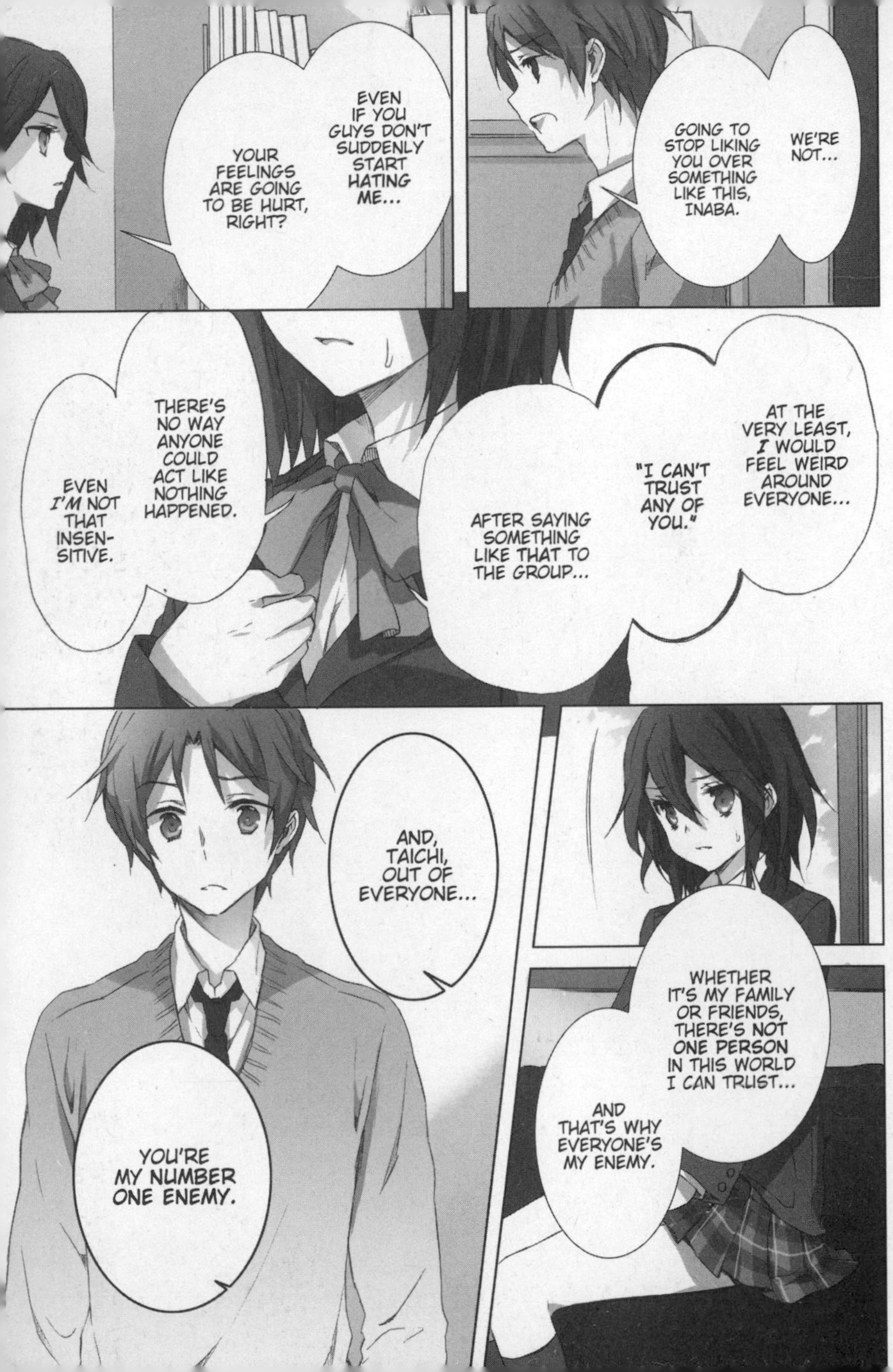
WE'RE NOT...
GOING TO STOP LIKING YOU OVER SOMETHING LIKE THIS, INABA.
EVEN IF YOU GUYS DON'T SUDDENLY START HATING ME...
YOUR FEELINGS ARE GOING TO BE HURT, RIGHT?
AT THE VERY LEAST, *I* WOULD FEEL WEIRD AROUND EVERYONE...
"I CAN'T TRUST ANY OF YOU."
AFTER SAYING SOMETHING LIKE THAT TO THE GROUP...
THERE'S NO WAY ANYONE COULD ACT LIKE NOTHING HAPPENED.
EVEN *I'M* NOT THAT INSEN-SITIVE.
WHETHER IT'S MY FAMILY OR FRIENDS, THERE'S NOT ONE PERSON IN THIS WORLD I CAN TRUST...
AND THAT'S WHY EVERYONE'S MY ENEMY.
AND, TAICHI, OUT OF EVERYONE...
YOU'RE MY NUMBER ONE ENEMY.

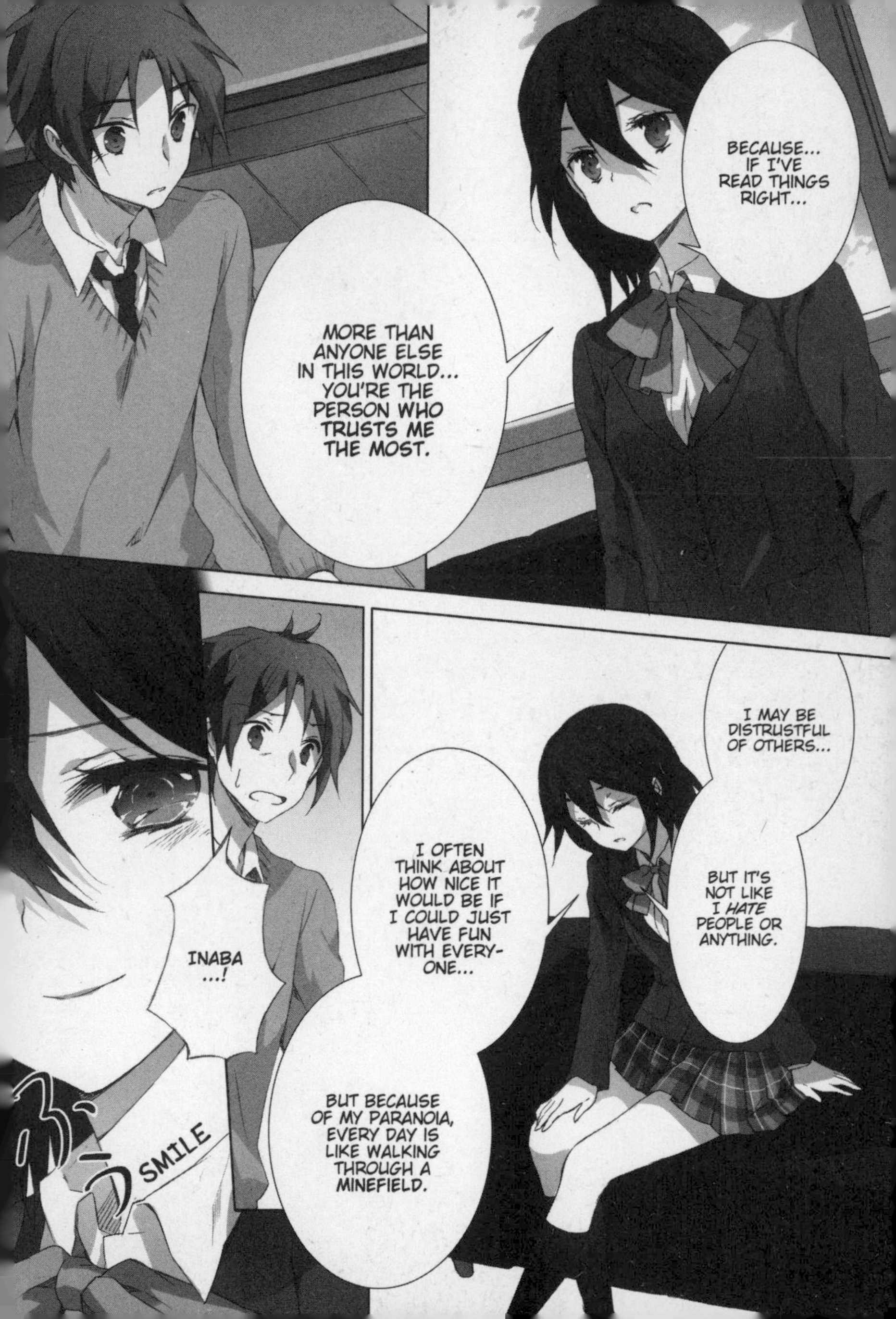
BECAUSE... IF I'VE READ THINGS RIGHT...
MORE THAN ANYONE ELSE IN THIS WORLD... YOU'RE THE PERSON WHO TRUSTS ME THE MOST.
I MAY BE DISTRUSTFUL OF OTHERS...
BUT IT'S NOT LIKE I *HATE* PEOPLE OR ANYTHING.
I OFTEN THINK ABOUT HOW NICE IT WOULD BE IF I COULD JUST HAVE FUN WITH EVERY-ONE...
BUT BECAUSE OF MY PARANOIA, EVERY DAY IS LIKE WALKING THROUGH A MINEFIELD.
INABA ...!
SMILE

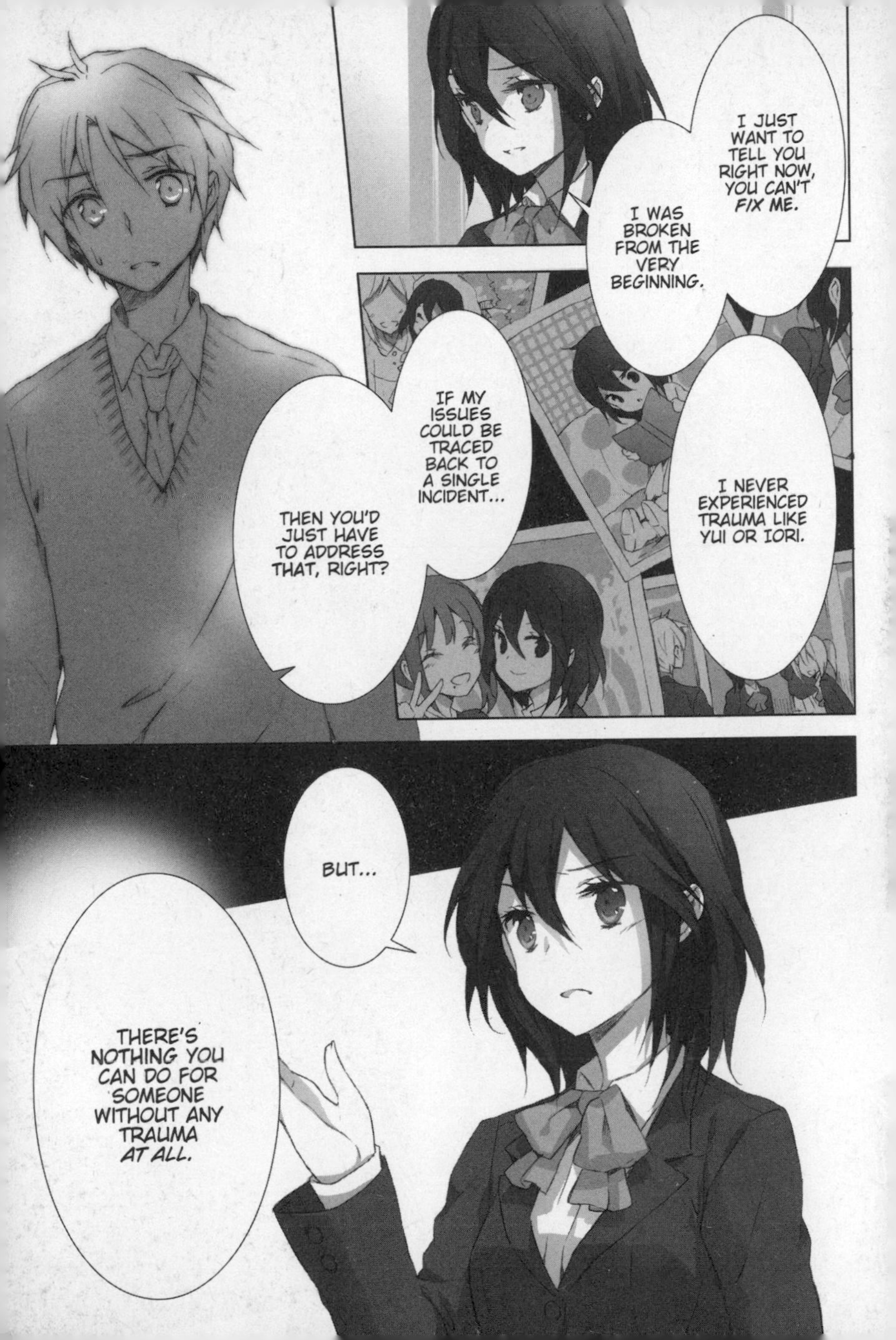
I JUST WANT TO TELL YOU RIGHT NOW, YOU CAN'T FIX ME.
I WAS BROKEN FROM THE VERY BEGINNING.
I NEVER EXPERIENCED TRAUMA LIKE YUI OR IORI.
IF MY ISSUES COULD BE TRACED BACK TO A SINGLE INCIDENT...
THEN YOU'D JUST HAVE TO ADDRESS THAT, RIGHT?
BUT...
THERE'S NOTHING YOU CAN DO FOR SOMEONE WITHOUT ANY TRAUMA AT ALL.

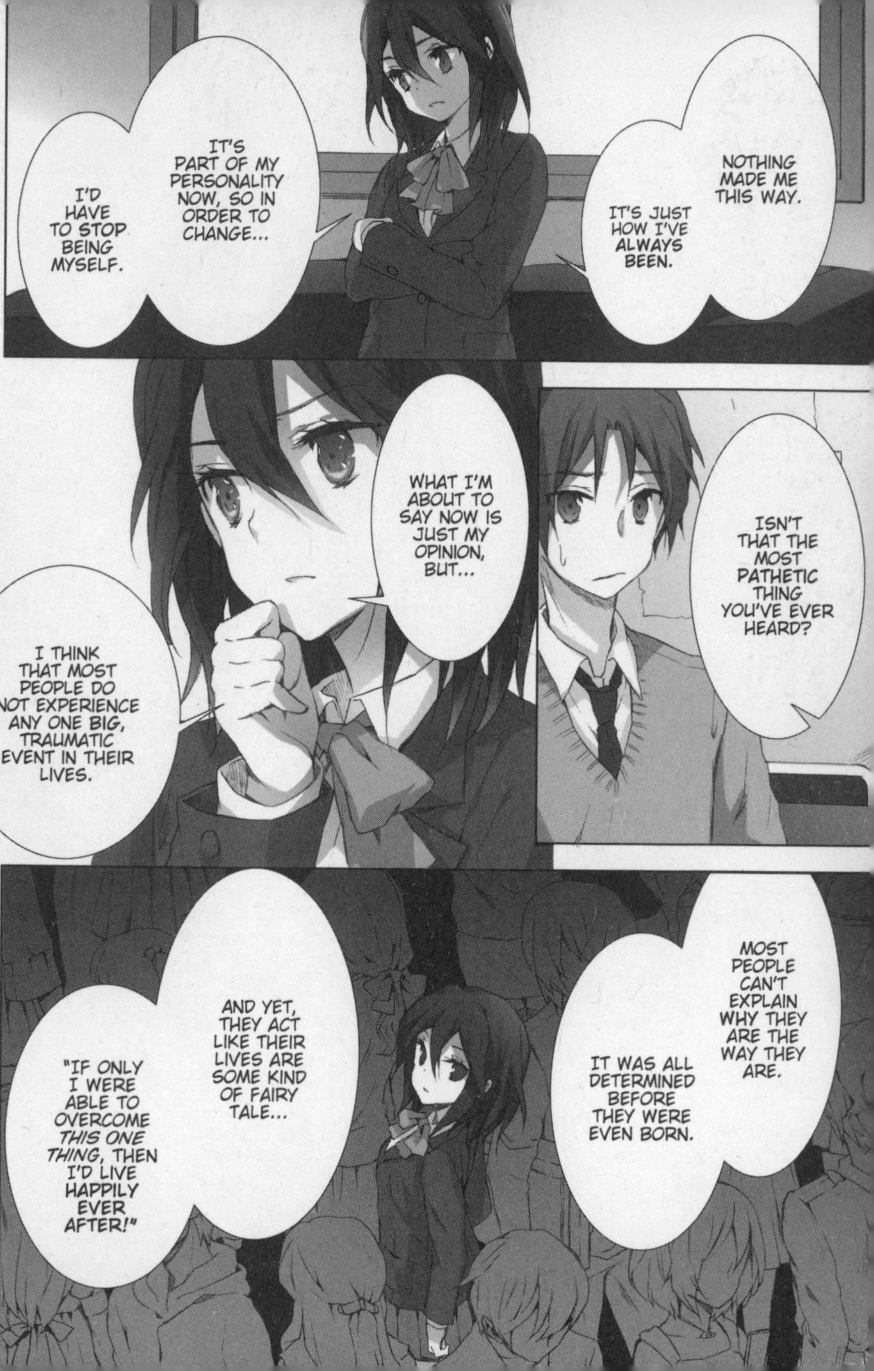
NOTHING MADE ME THIS WAY.
IT'S JUST HOW I'VE ALWAYS BEEN.
IT'S PART OF MY PERSONALITY NOW, SO IN ORDER TO CHANGE...
I'D HAVE TO STOP BEING MYSELF.
ISN'T THAT THE MOST PATHETIC THING YOU'VE EVER HEARD?
WHAT I'M ABOUT TO SAY NOW IS JUST MY OPINION, BUT...
I THINK THAT MOST PEOPLE DO NOT EXPERIENCE ANY ONE BIG, TRAUMATIC EVENT IN THEIR LIVES.
MOST PEOPLE CAN'T EXPLAIN WHY THEY ARE THE WAY THEY ARE.
IT WAS ALL DETERMINED BEFORE THEY WERE EVEN BORN.
AND YET, THEY ACT LIKE THEIR LIVES ARE SOME KIND OF FAIRY TALE...
"IF ONLY I WERE ABLE TO OVERCOME *THIS ONE THING*, THEN I'D LIVE HAPPILY EVER AFTER!"

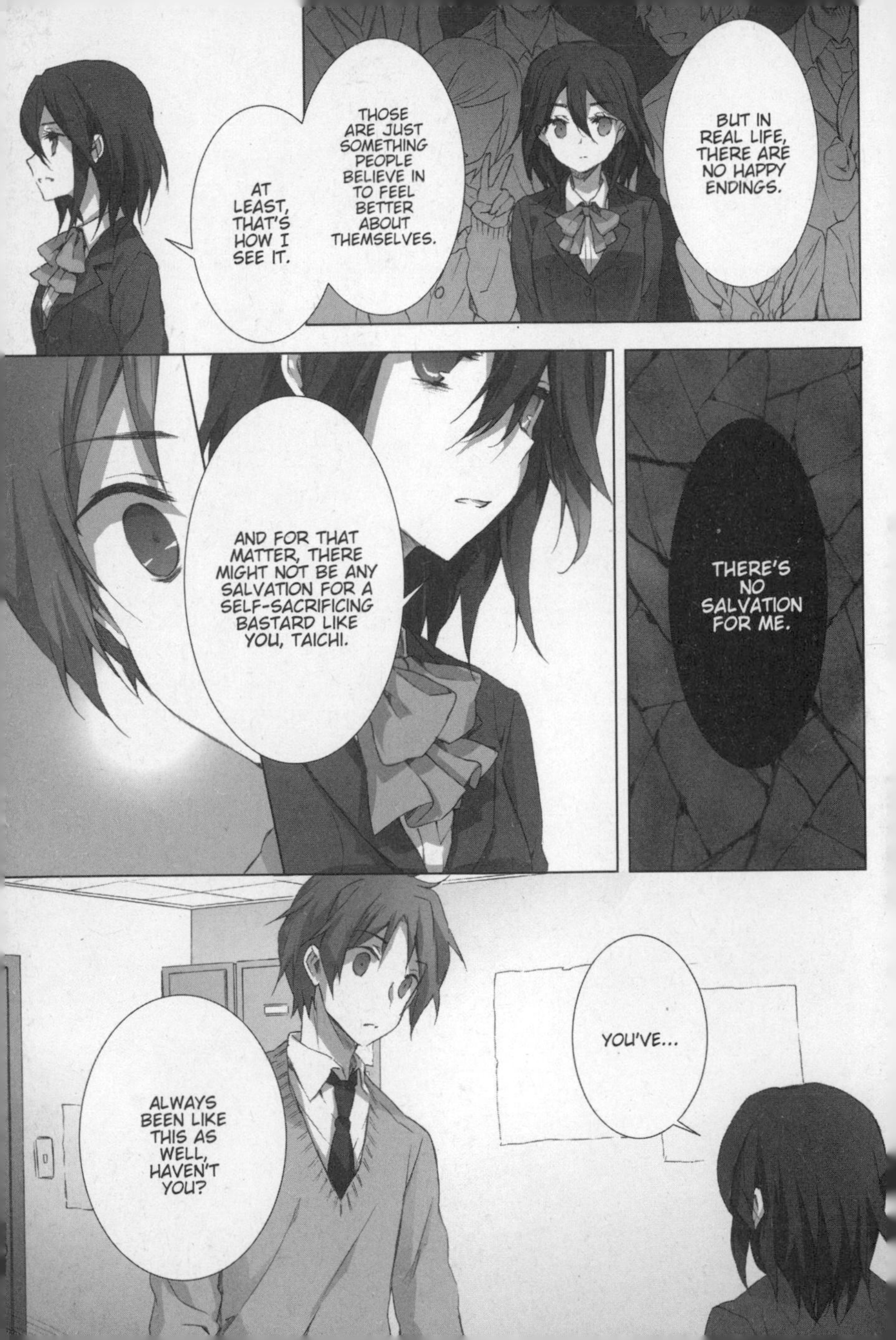
BUT IN REAL LIFE, THERE ARE NO HAPPY ENDINGS.
THOSE ARE JUST SOMETHING PEOPLE BELIEVE IN TO FEEL BETTER ABOUT THEMSELVES.
AT LEAST, THAT'S HOW I SEE IT.
THERE'S NO SALVATION FOR ME.
AND FOR THAT MATTER, THERE MIGHT NOT BE ANY SALVATION FOR A SELF-SACRIFICING BASTARD LIKE YOU, TAICHI.
YOU'VE...
ALWAYS BEEN LIKE THIS AS WELL, HAVEN'T YOU?

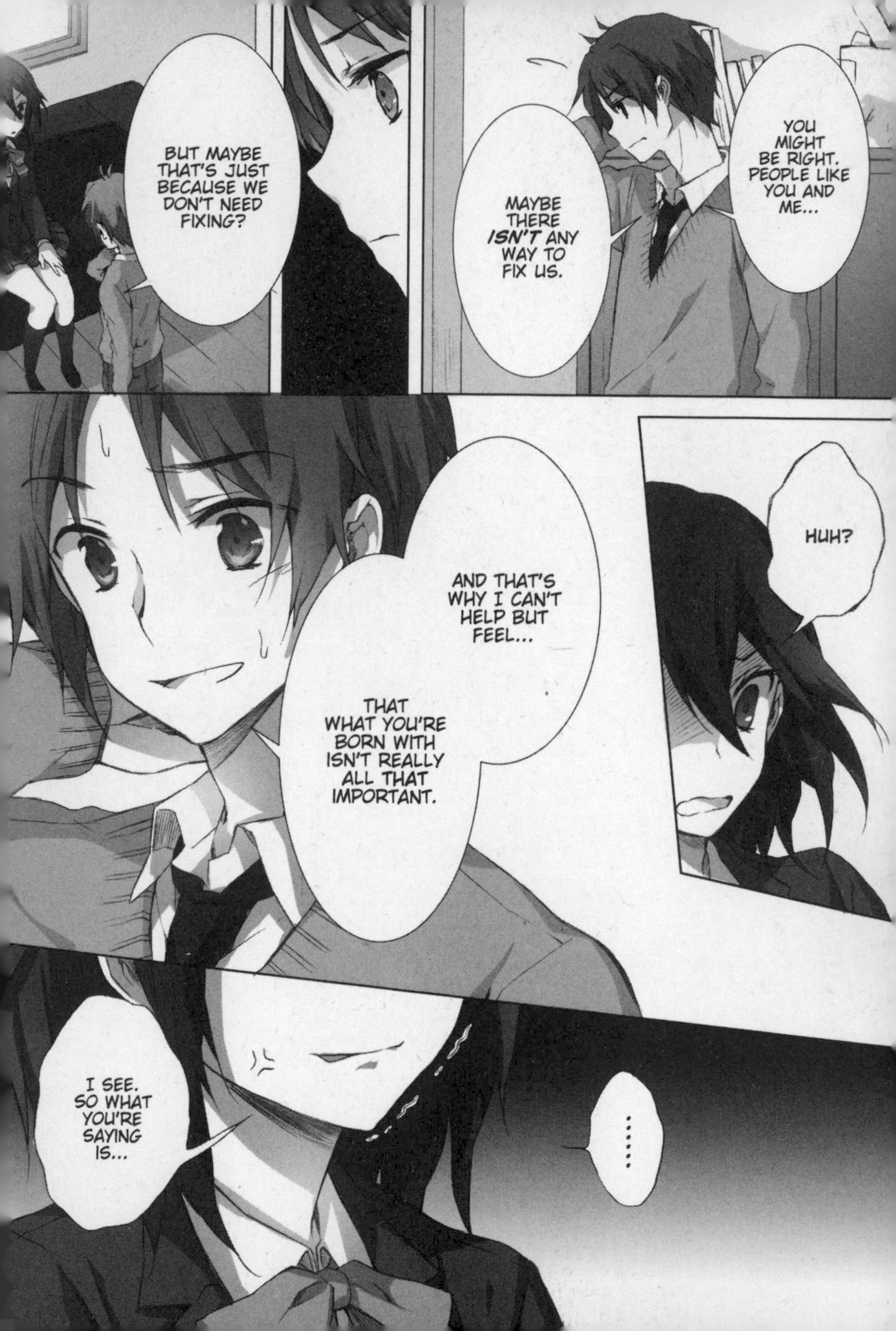
YOU MIGHT BE RIGHT. PEOPLE LIKE YOU AND ME...
MAYBE THERE *ISN'T* ANY WAY TO FIX US.
BUT MAYBE THAT'S JUST BECAUSE WE DON'T NEED FIXING?
HUH?
AND THAT'S WHY I CAN'T HELP BUT FEEL...
THAT WHAT YOU'RE BORN WITH ISN'T REALLY ALL THAT IMPORTANT.
......
I SEE. SO WHAT YOU'RE SAYING IS...

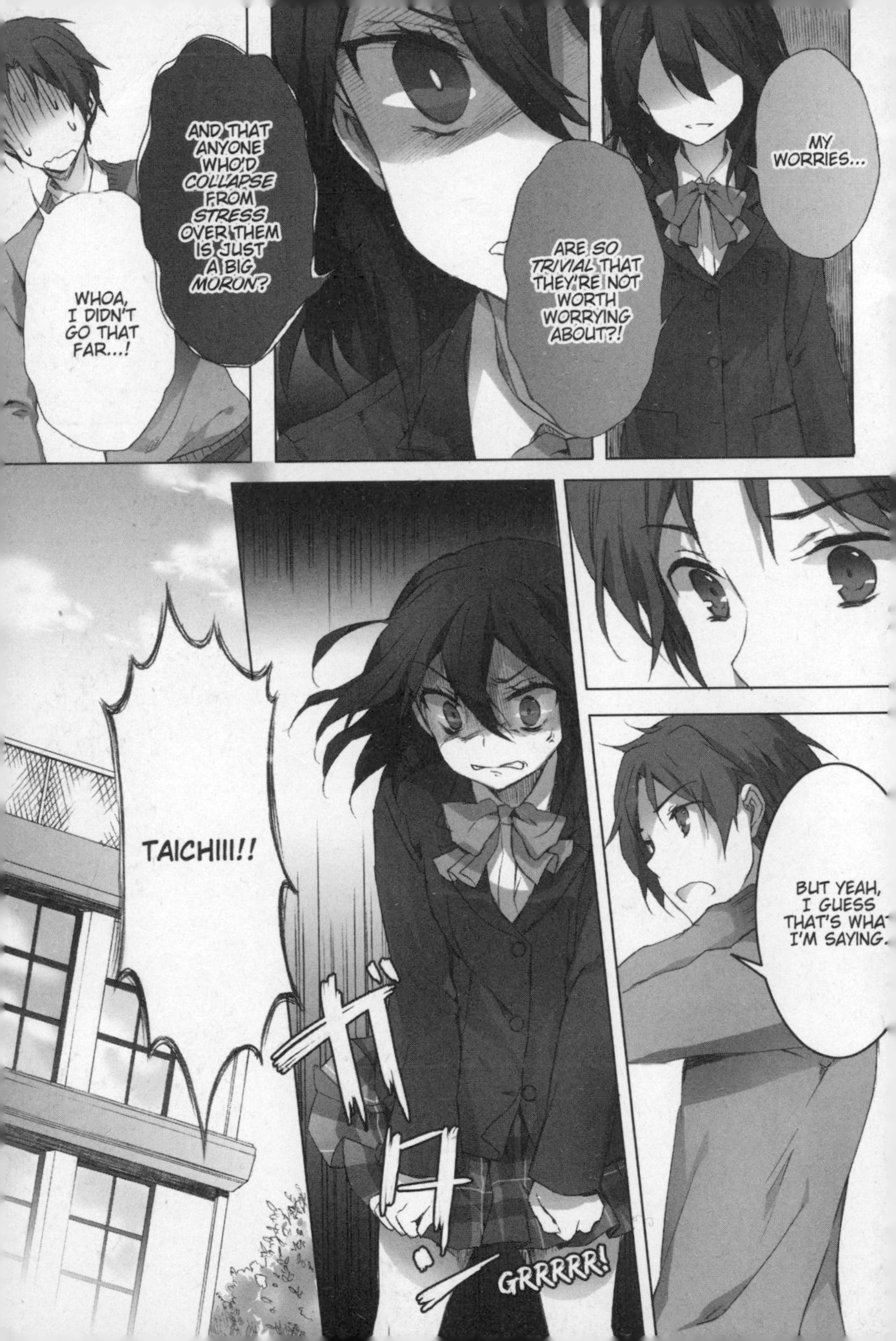

MY WORRIES...
ARE SO TRIVIAL THAT THEY'RE NOT WORTH WORRYING ABOUT?!
AND THAT ANYONE WHO'D COLLAPSE FROM STRESS OVER THEM IS JUST A BIG MORON?
WHOA, I DIDN'T GO THAT FAR...!
BUT YEAH, I GUESS THAT'S WHAT I'M SAYING.
GRRRRR!
TAICHIIII!!

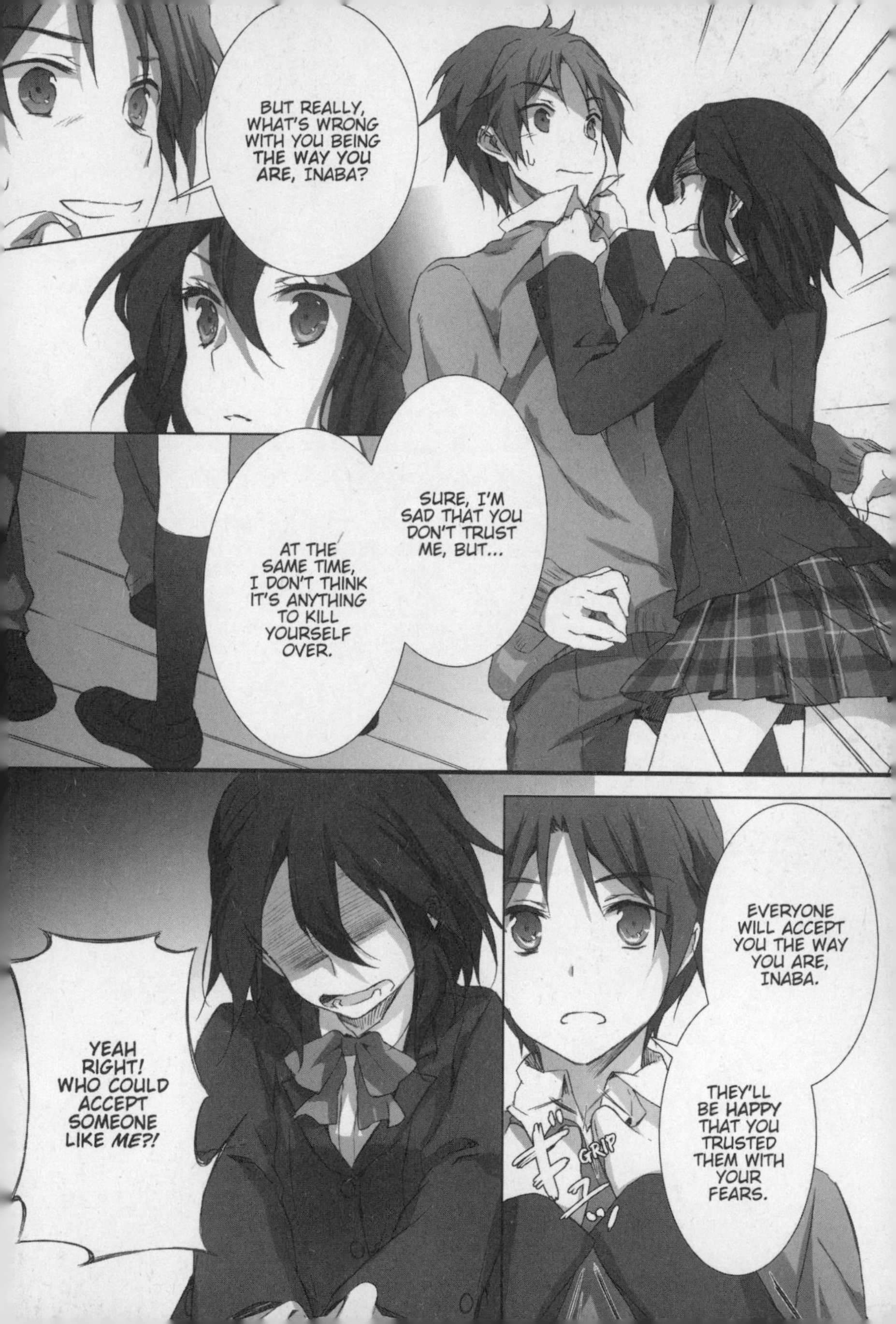
BUT REALLY, WHAT'S WRONG WITH YOU BEING THE WAY YOU ARE, INABA?
SURE, I'M SAD THAT YOU DON'T TRUST ME, BUT...
AT THE SAME TIME, I DON'T THINK IT'S ANYTHING TO KILL YOURSELF OVER.
EVERYONE WILL ACCEPT YOU THE WAY YOU ARE, INABA.
THEY'LL BE HAPPY THAT YOU TRUSTED THEM WITH YOUR FEARS.
GRIP
YEAH RIGHT! WHO COULD ACCEPT SOMEONE LIKE *ME*?!

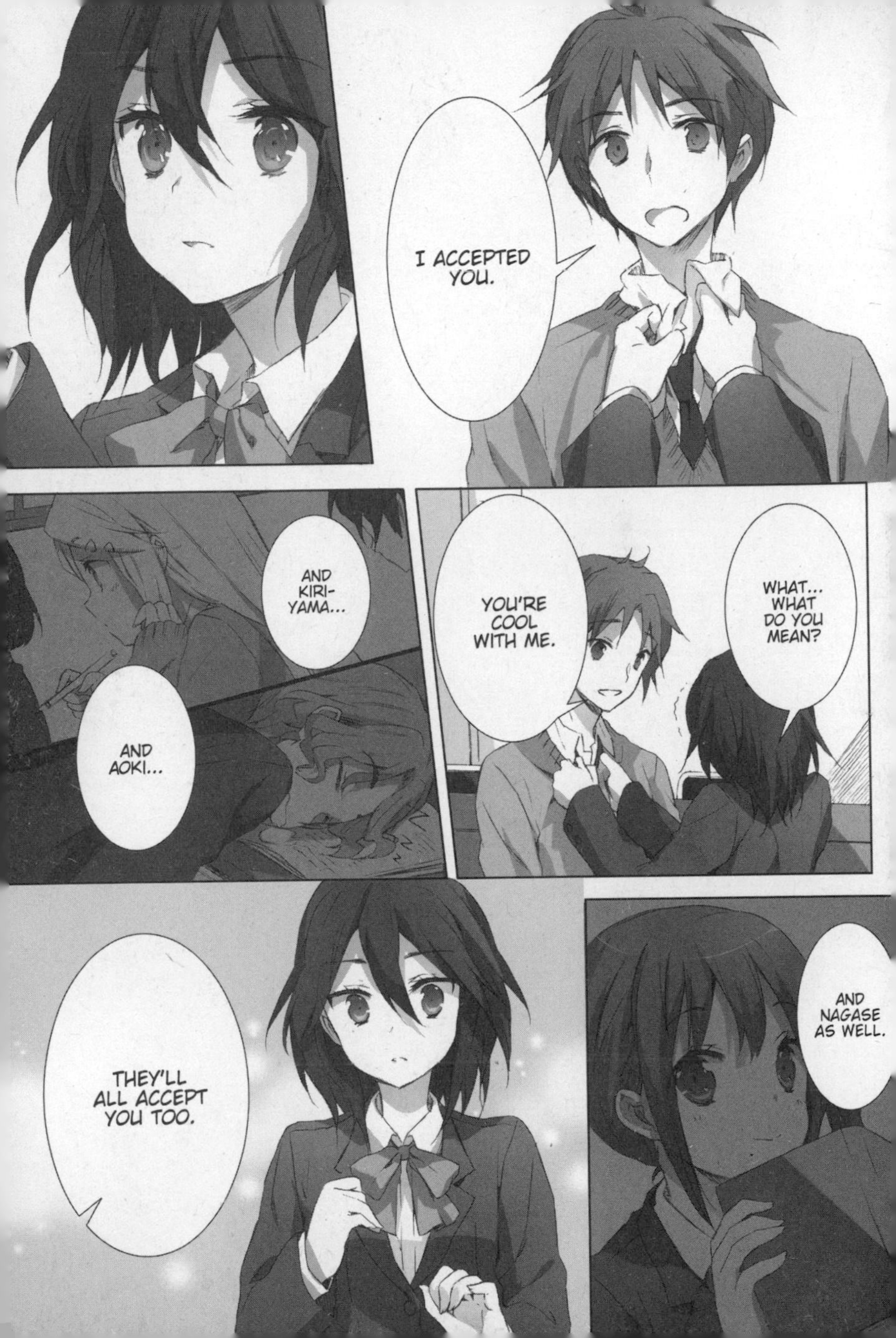
I ACCEPTED YOU.
WHAT... WHAT DO YOU MEAN?
YOU'RE COOL WITH ME.
AND KIRI-YAMA...
AND AOKI...
AND NAGASE AS WELL.
THEY'LL ALL ACCEPT YOU TOO.

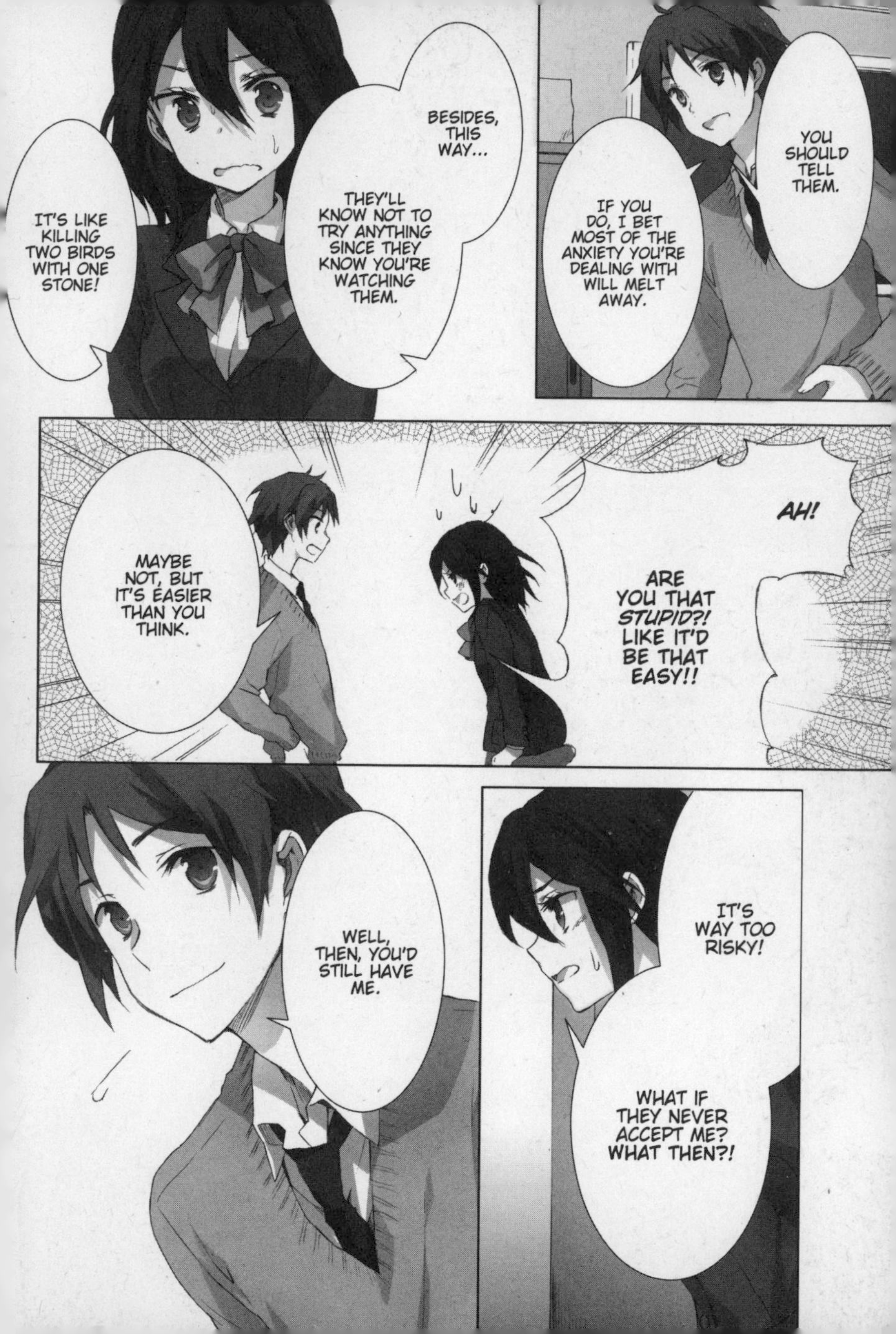
YOU SHOULD TELL THEM.
IF YOU DO, I BET MOST OF THE ANXIETY YOU'RE DEALING WITH WILL MELT AWAY.
BESIDES, THIS WAY...
THEY'LL KNOW NOT TO TRY ANYTHING SINCE THEY KNOW YOU'RE WATCHING THEM.
IT'S LIKE KILLING TWO BIRDS WITH ONE STONE!
AH!
ARE YOU THAT *STUPID*?! LIKE IT'D BE THAT EASY!!
MAYBE NOT, BUT IT'S EASIER THAN YOU THINK.
IT'S WAY TOO RISKY!
WHAT IF THEY NEVER ACCEPT ME? WHAT THEN?!
WELL, THEN, YOU'D STILL HAVE ME.

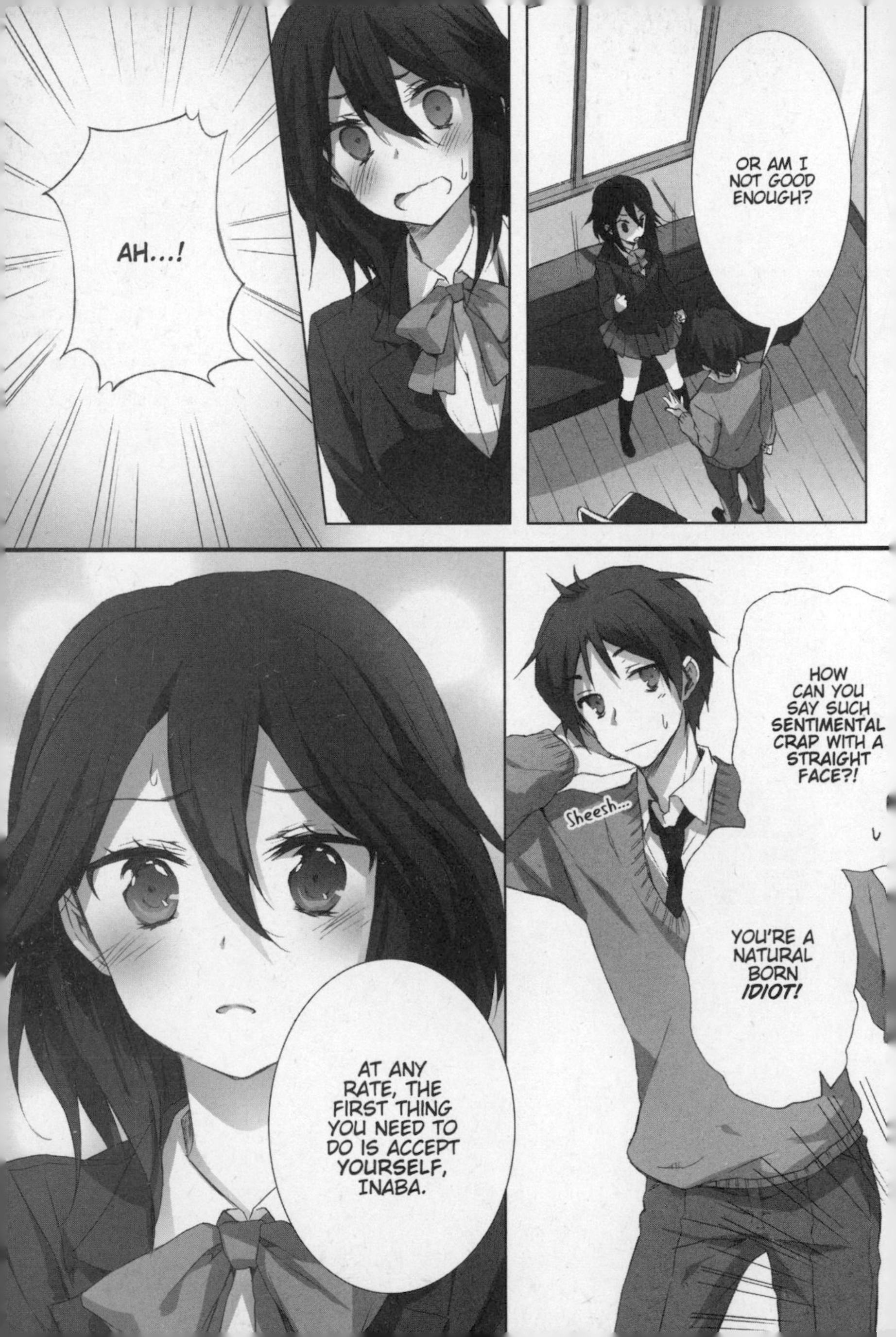
OR AM I NOT GOOD ENOUGH?
AH...!
HOW CAN YOU SAY SUCH SENTIMENTAL CRAP WITH A STRAIGHT FACE?!
Sheesh...
YOU'RE A NATURAL BORN IDIOT!
AT ANY RATE, THE FIRST THING YOU NEED TO DO IS ACCEPT YOURSELF, INABA.

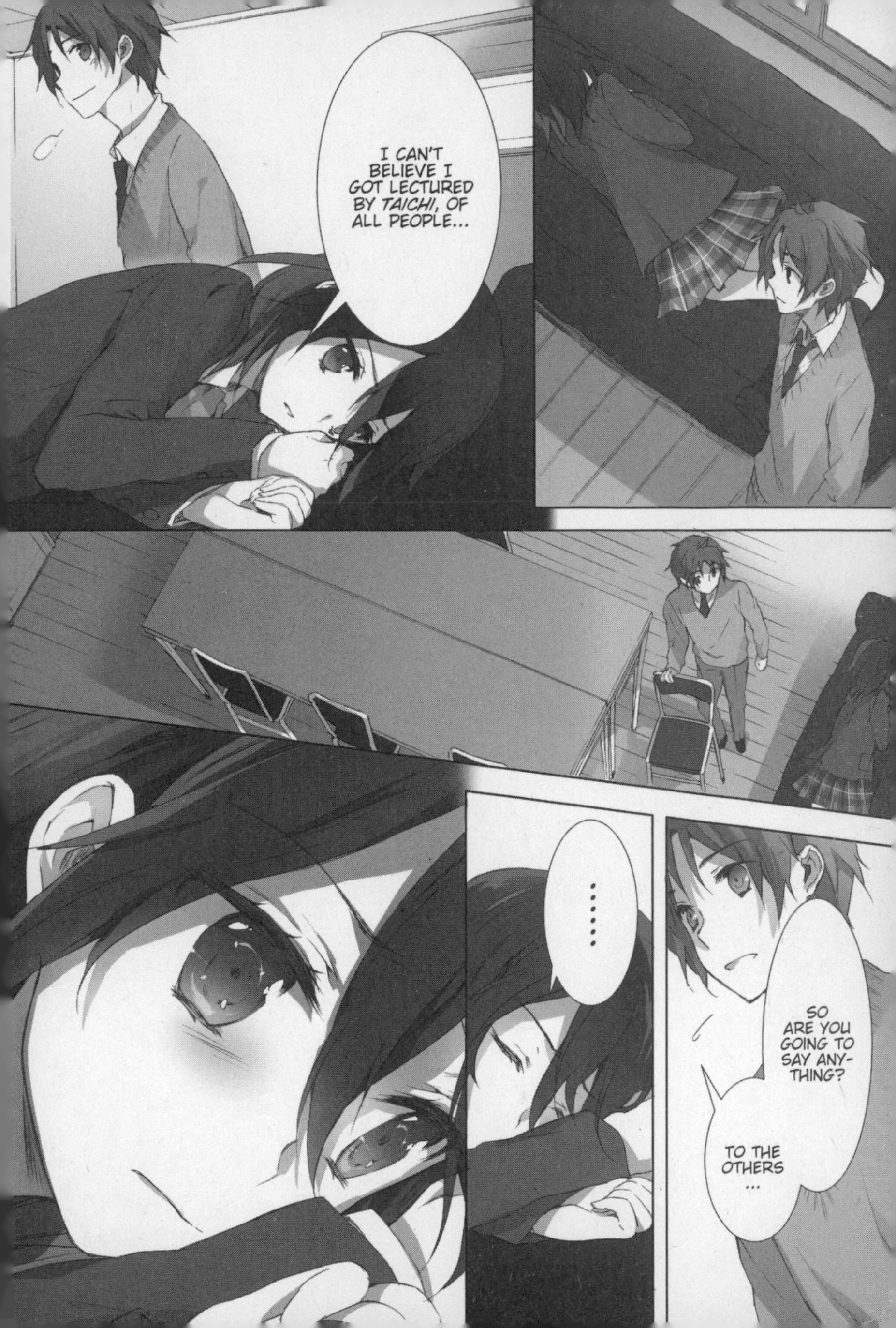
I CAN'T BELIEVE I GOT LECTURED BY *TAICHI*, OF ALL PEOPLE...
SO ARE YOU GOING TO SAY ANY-THING?
TO THE OTHERS ...
......

KOKORO CONNECT

Man the springtime of our lives shouldn't be this complicated...

KOKORO CONNECT

Chapter 10

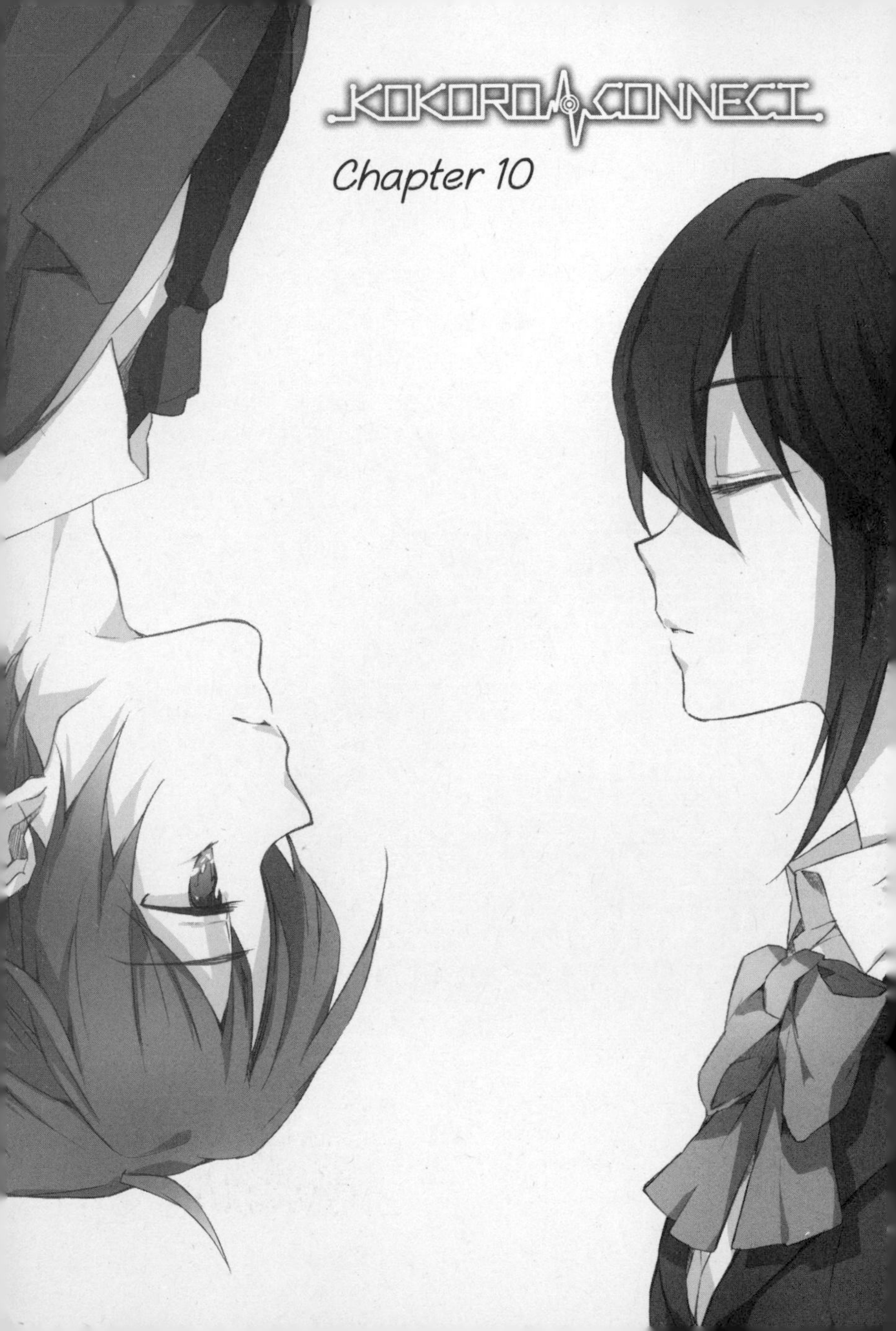

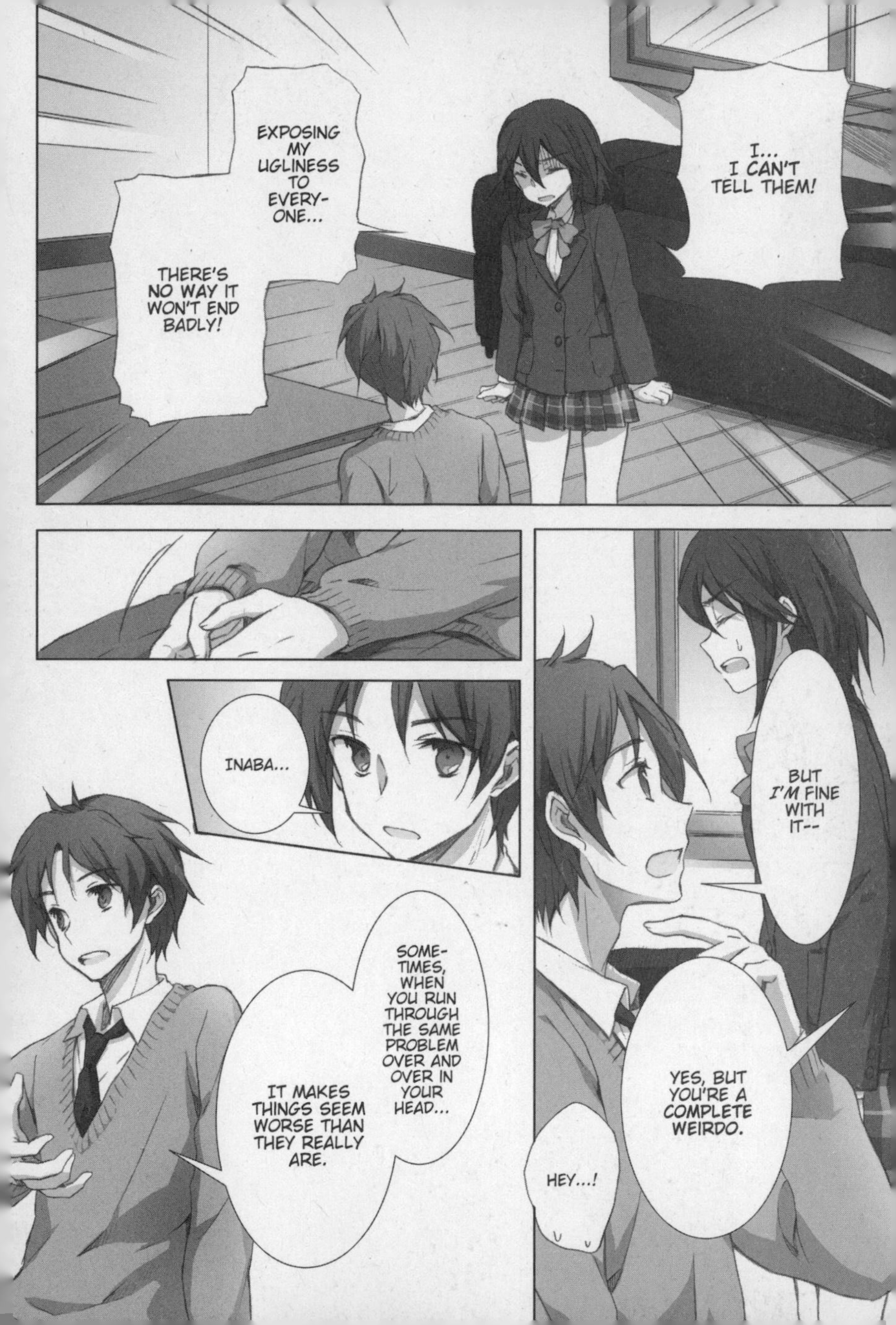
I... I CAN'T TELL THEM!
EXPOSING MY UGLINESS TO EVERYONE...
THERE'S NO WAY IT WON'T END BADLY!
BUT I'M FINE WITH IT--
YES, BUT YOU'RE A COMPLETE WEIRDO.
HEY...!
INABA...
SOMETIMES, WHEN YOU RUN THROUGH THE SAME PROBLEM OVER AND OVER IN YOUR HEAD...
IT MAKES THINGS SEEM WORSE THAN THEY REALLY ARE.

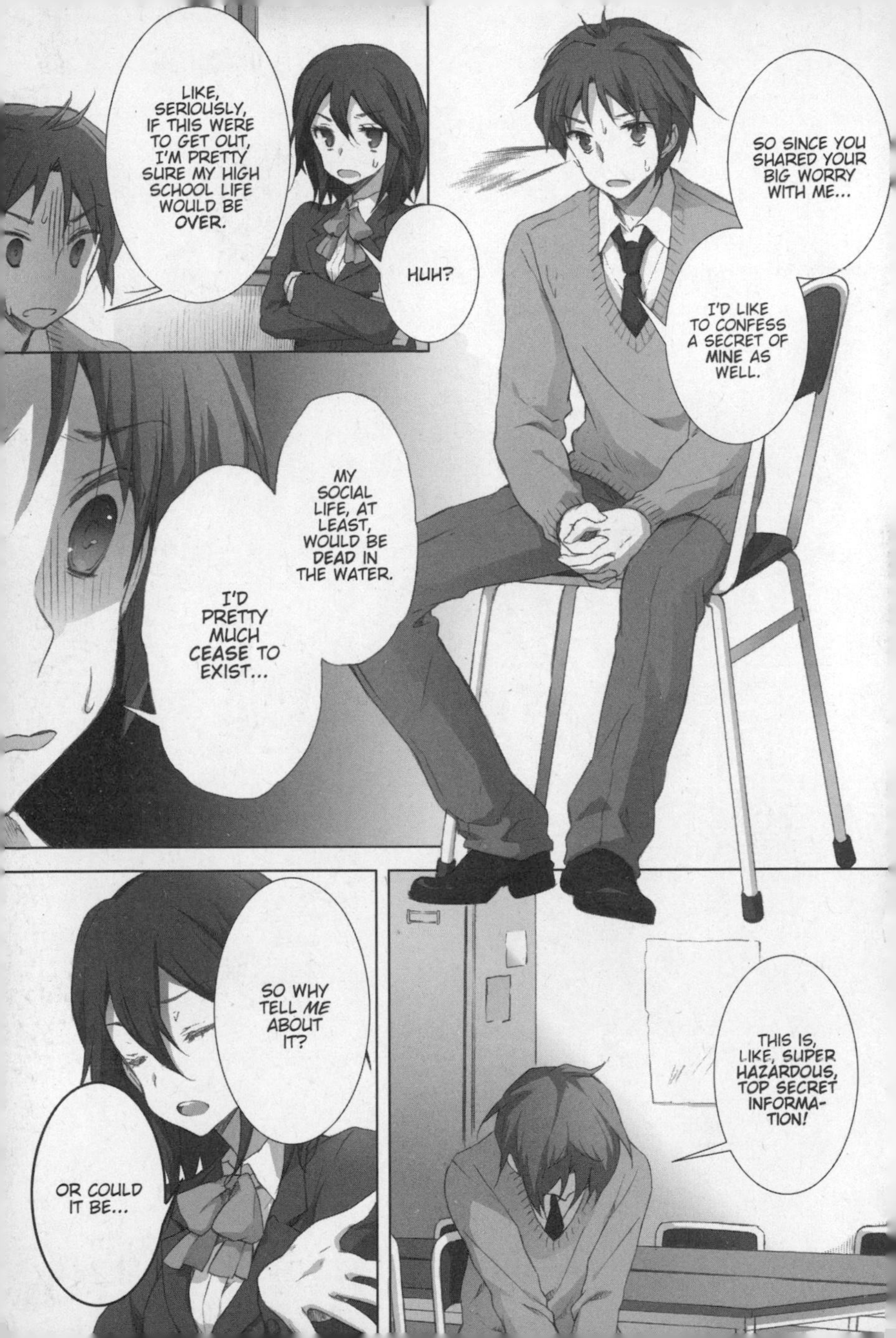
SO SINCE YOU SHARED YOUR BIG WORRY WITH ME...
I'D LIKE TO CONFESS A SECRET OF MINE AS WELL.
HUH?
LIKE, SERIOUSLY, IF THIS WERE TO GET OUT, I'M PRETTY SURE MY HIGH SCHOOL LIFE WOULD BE OVER.
MY SOCIAL LIFE, AT LEAST, WOULD BE DEAD IN THE WATER.
I'D PRETTY MUCH CEASE TO EXIST...
THIS IS, LIKE, SUPER HAZARDOUS, TOP SECRET INFORMA-TION!
SO WHY TELL *ME* ABOUT IT?
OR COULD IT BE...

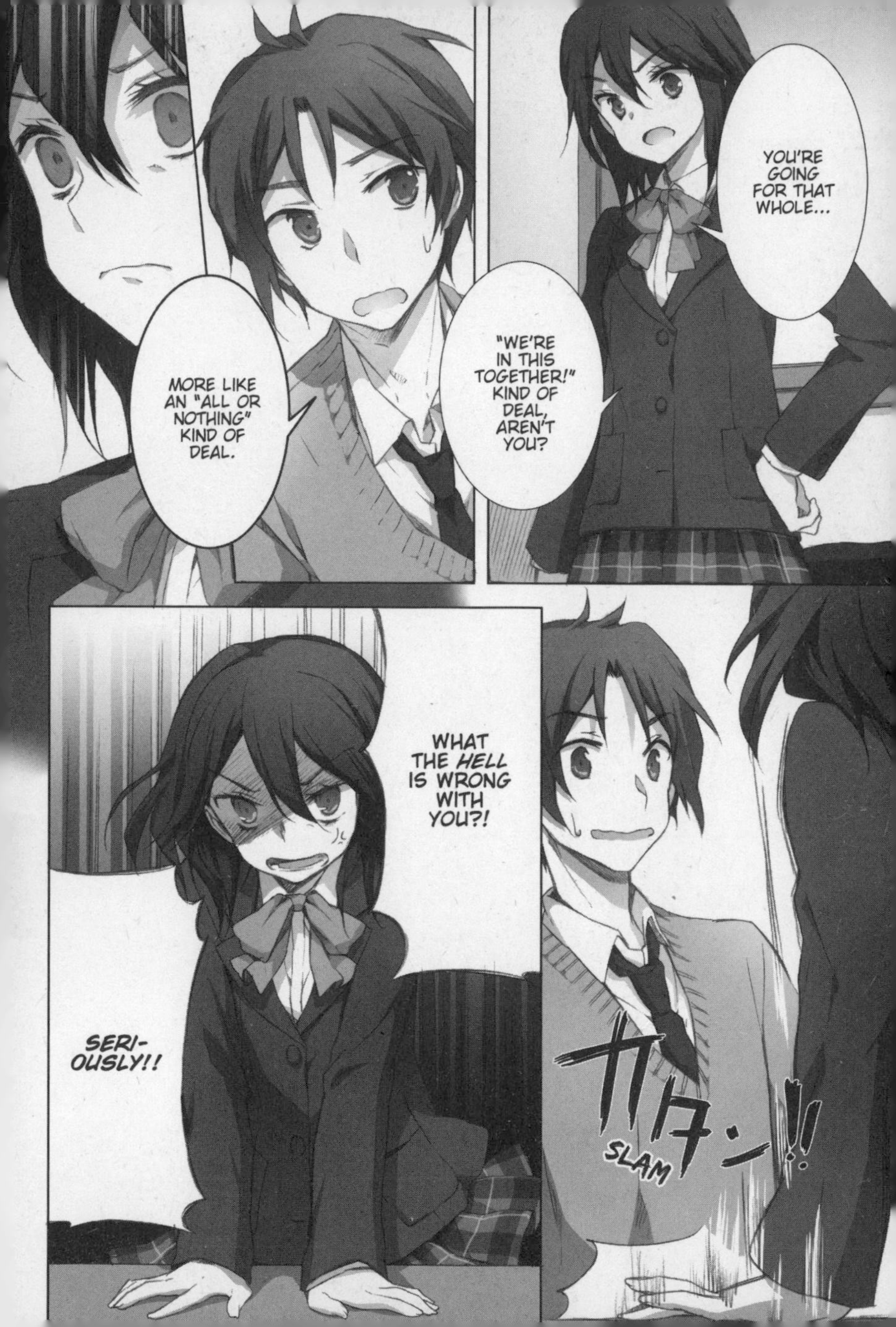
YOU'RE GOING FOR THAT WHOLE...
"WE'RE IN THIS TOGETHER!" KIND OF DEAL, AREN'T YOU?
MORE LIKE AN "ALL OR NOTHING" KIND OF DEAL.
SLAM
WHAT THE *HELL* IS WRONG WITH YOU?!
SERI-OUSLY!!

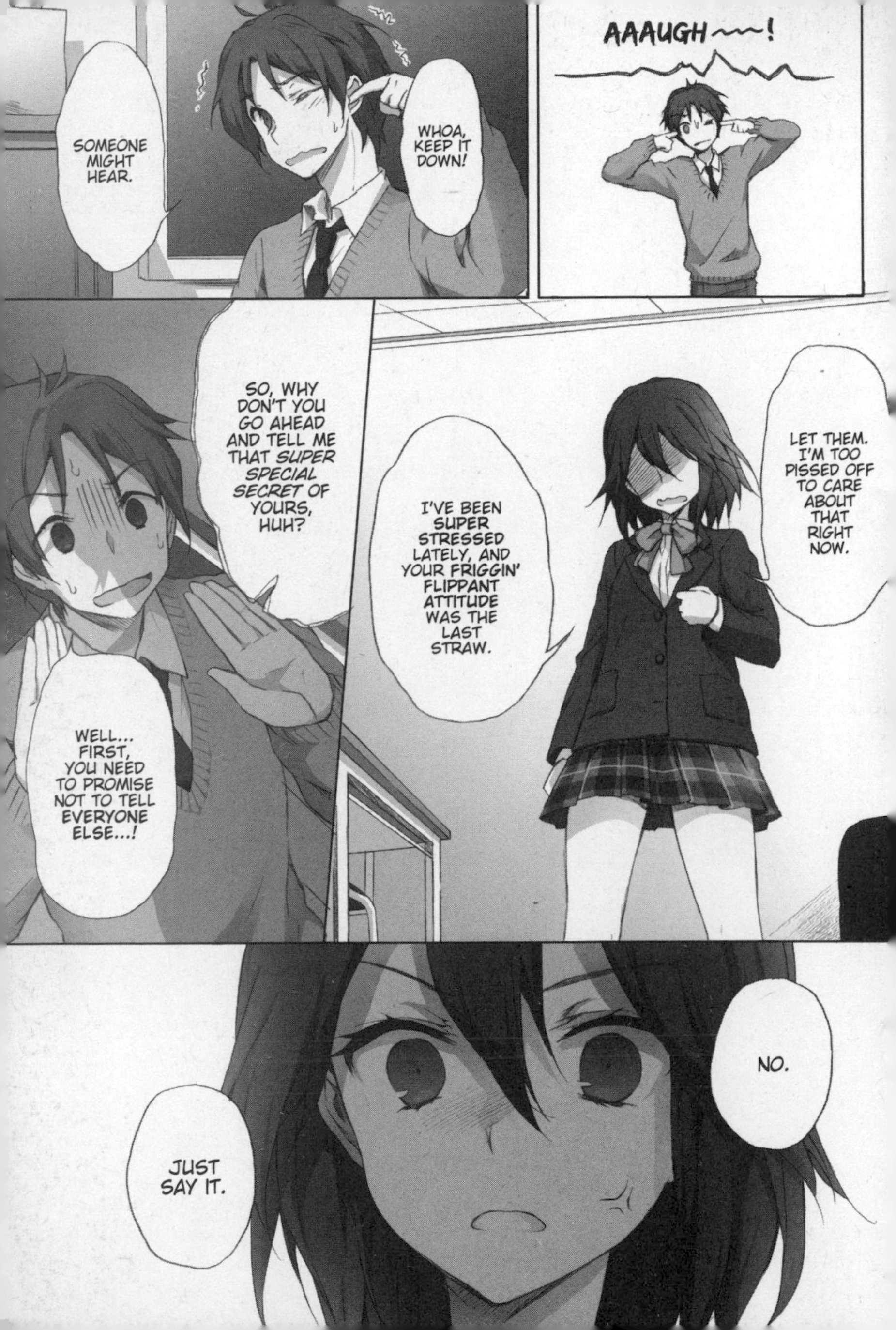
AAAUGH~~~!
WHOA, KEEP IT DOWN!
SOMEONE MIGHT HEAR.
LET THEM. I'M TOO PISSED OFF TO CARE ABOUT THAT RIGHT NOW.
I'VE BEEN SUPER STRESSED LATELY, AND YOUR FRIGGIN' FLIPPANT ATTITUDE WAS THE LAST STRAW.
SO, WHY DON'T YOU GO AHEAD AND TELL ME THAT *SUPER SPECIAL SECRET* OF YOURS, HUH?
WELL... FIRST, YOU NEED TO PROMISE NOT TO TELL EVERYONE ELSE...!
NO.
JUST SAY IT.

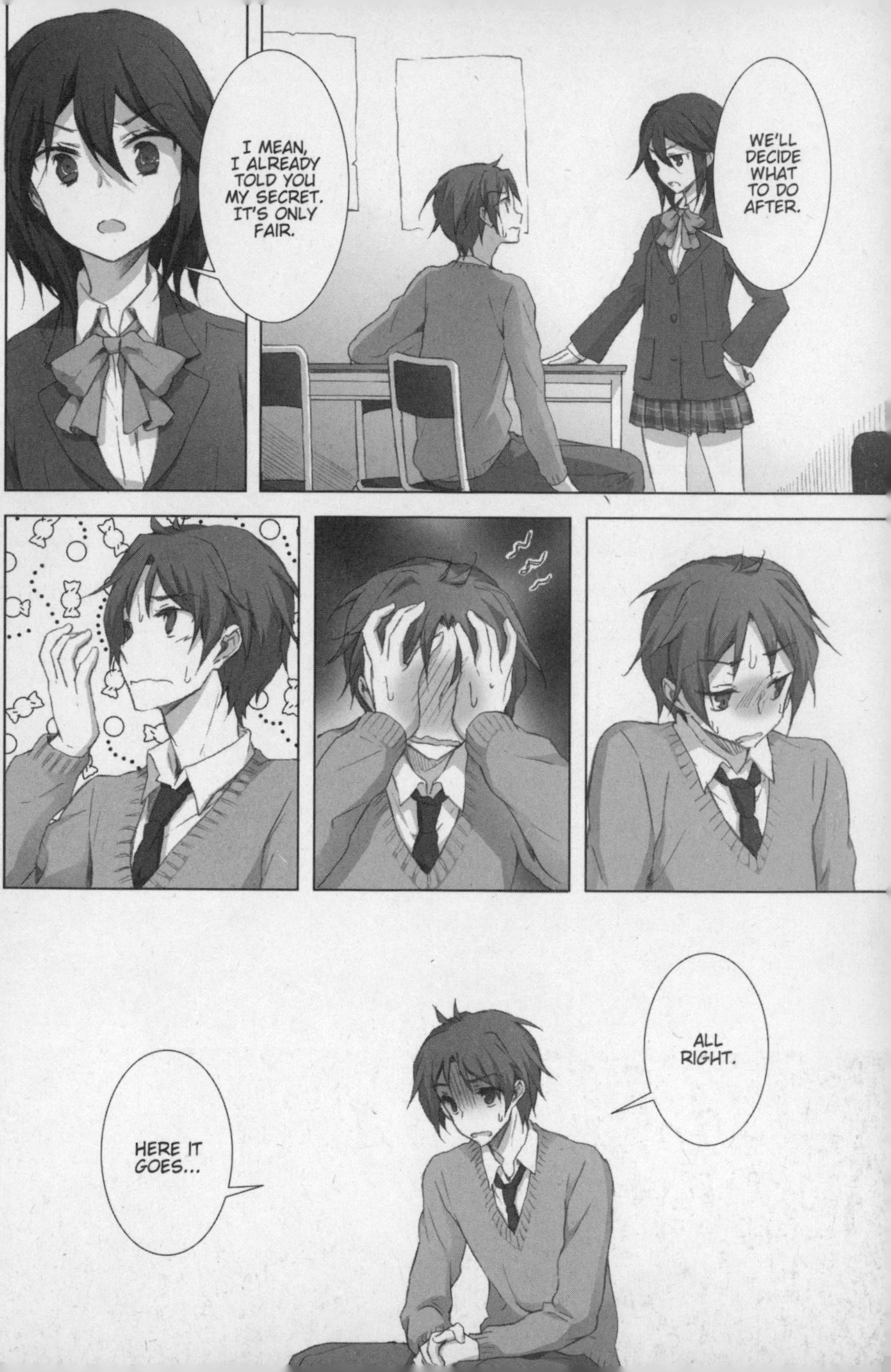
WE'LL DECIDE WHAT TO DO AFTER.
I MEAN, I ALREADY TOLD YOU MY SECRET. IT'S ONLY FAIR.
ALL RIGHT.
HERE IT GOES...

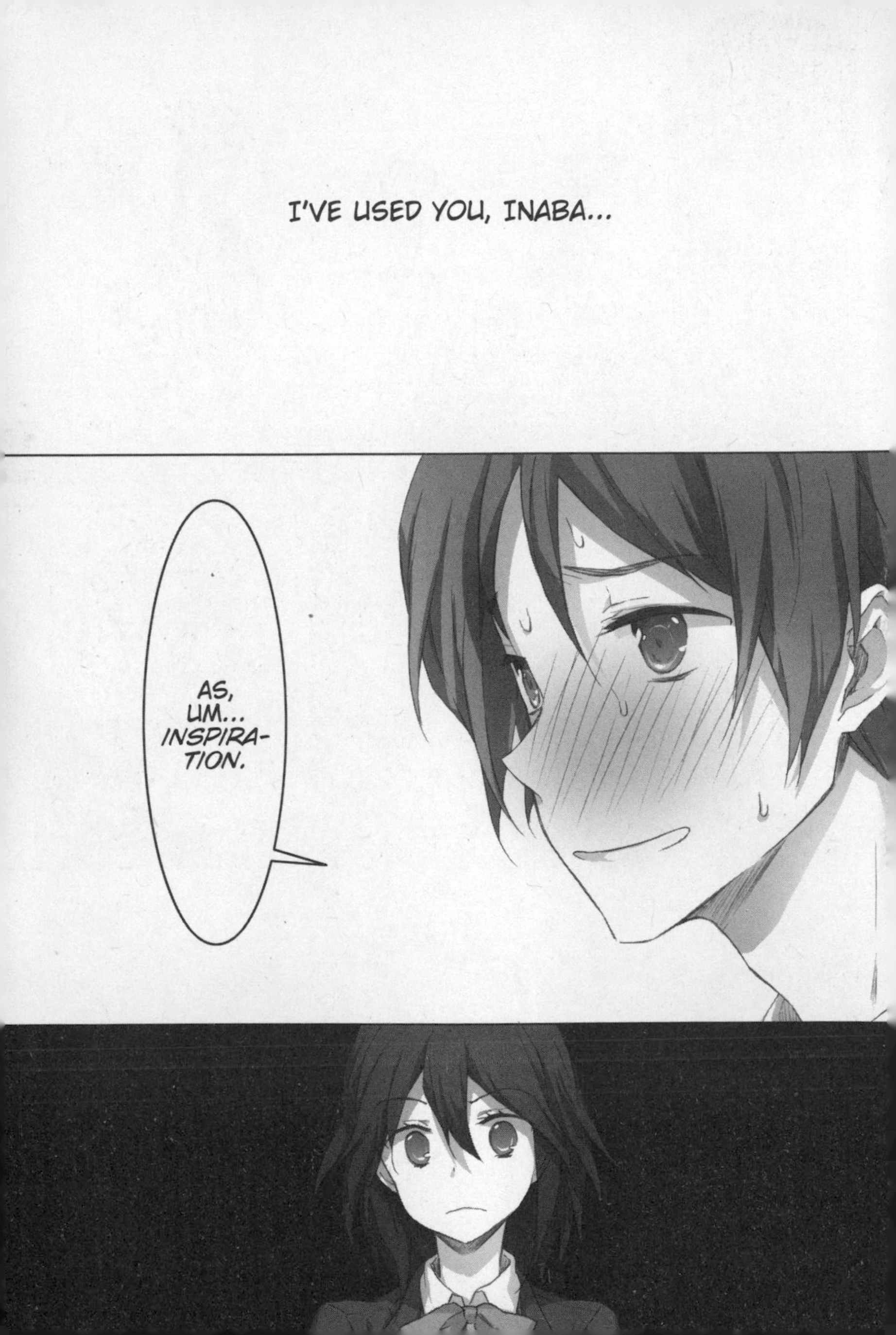
I'VE USED YOU, INABA...
AS, UM... INSPIRATION.

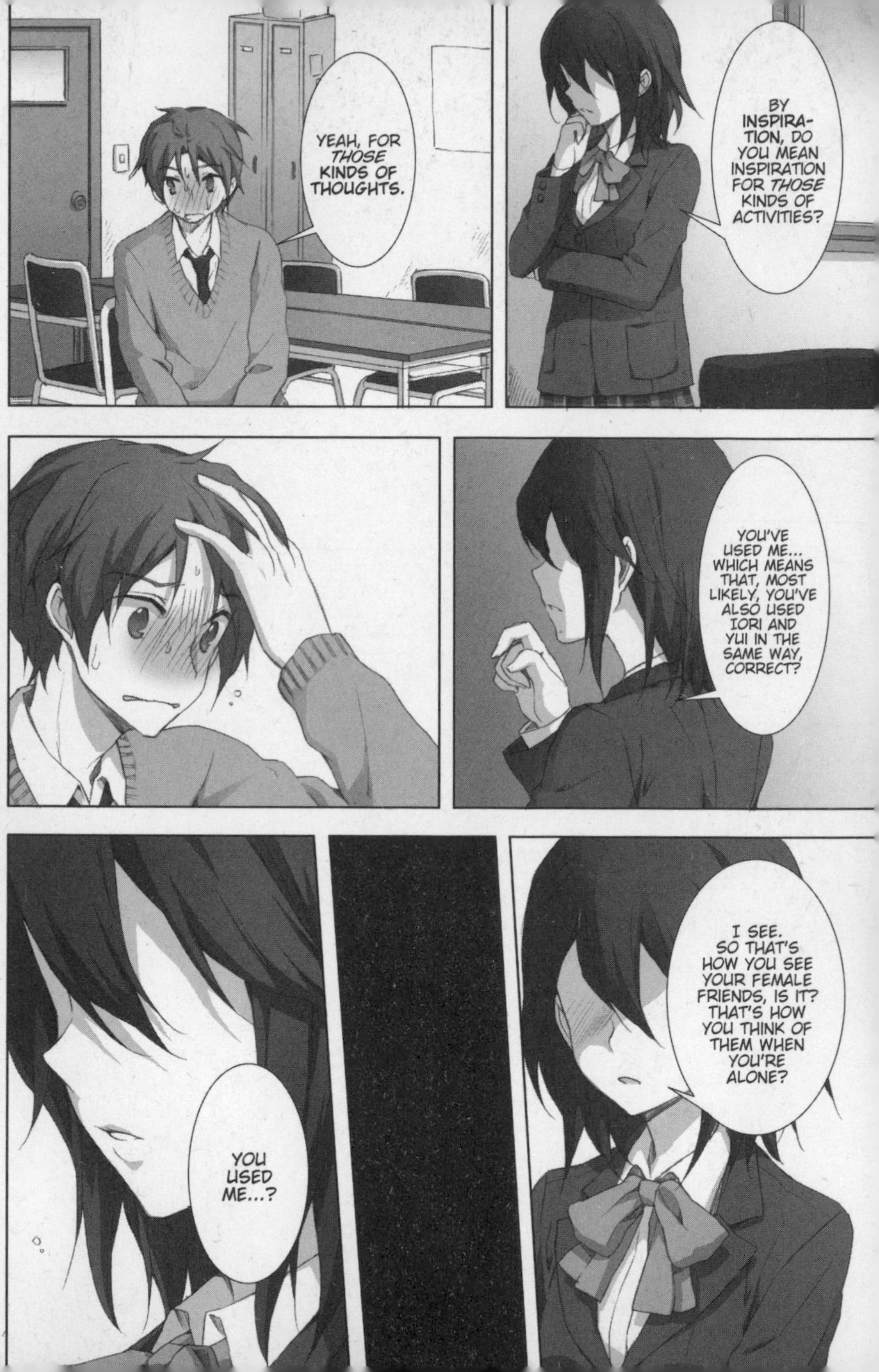
BY INSPIRA-TION, DO YOU MEAN INSPIRATION FOR *THOSE* KINDS OF ACTIVITIES?
YEAH, FOR *THOSE* KINDS OF THOUGHTS.
YOU'VE USED ME... WHICH MEANS THAT, MOST LIKELY, YOU'VE ALSO USED IORI AND YUI IN THE SAME WAY, CORRECT?
I SEE. SO THAT'S HOW YOU SEE YOUR FEMALE FRIENDS, IS IT? THAT'S HOW YOU THINK OF THEM WHEN YOU'RE ALONE?
YOU USED ME...?

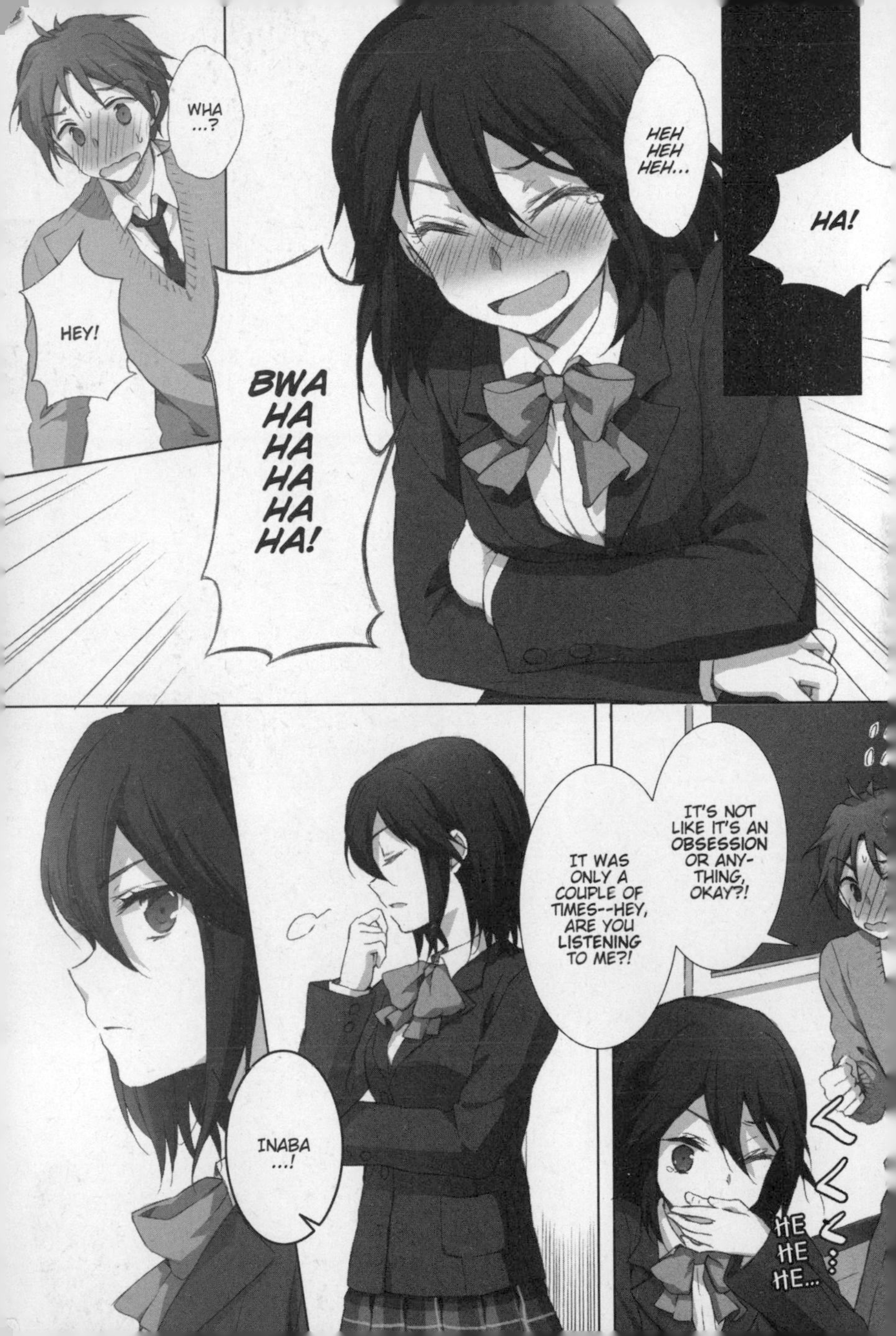
HEH HEH HEH...
HA!
BWA HA HA HA HA HA!
WHA ...?
HEY!
IT'S NOT LIKE IT'S AN OBSESSION OR ANY-THING, OKAY?!
IT WAS ONLY A COUPLE OF TIMES--HEY, ARE YOU LISTENING TO ME?!
HE HE HE...
INABA ...!

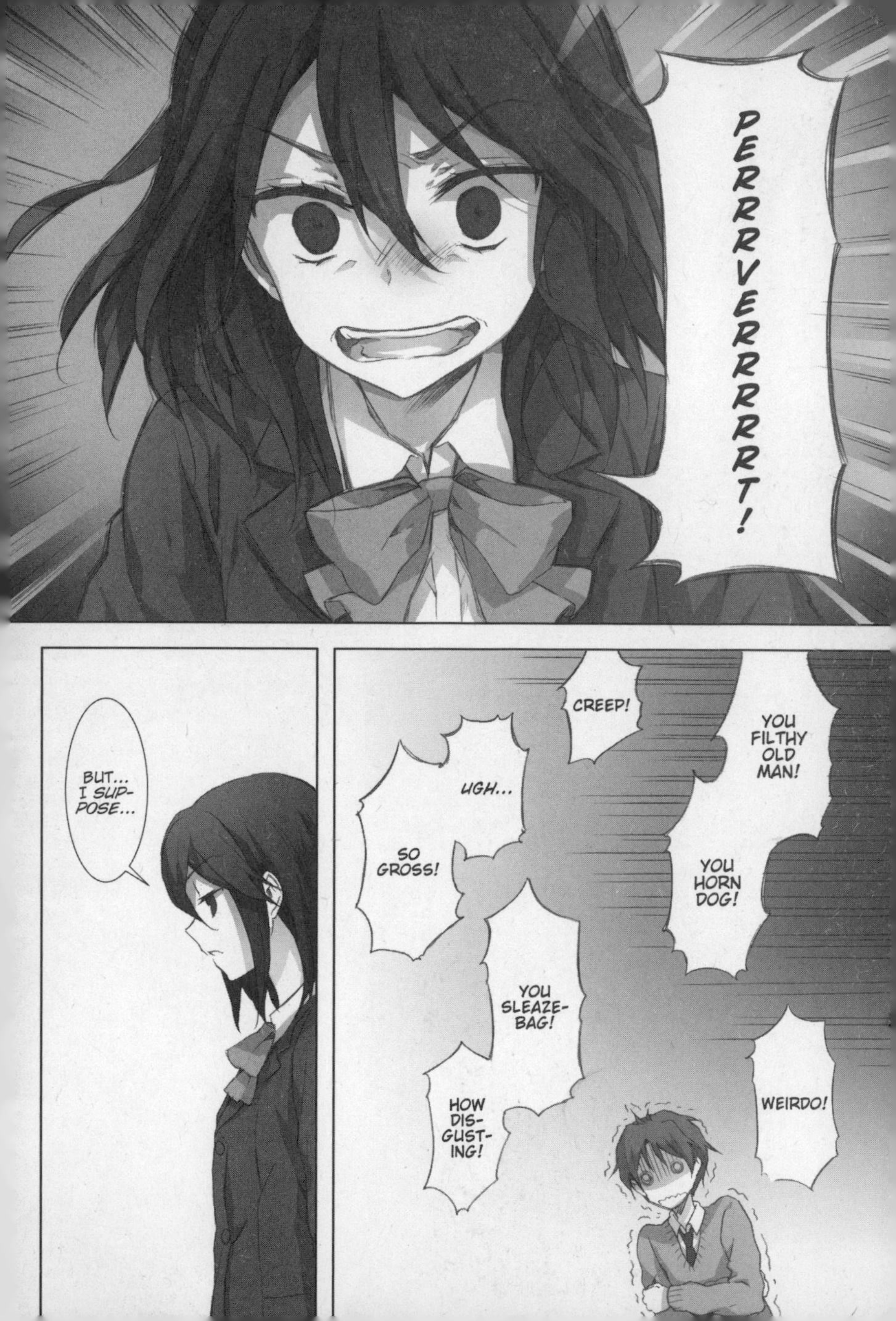
PERRRVERRRRRT!
CREEP!
YOU FILTHY OLD MAN!
UGH...
SO GROSS!
YOU HORN DOG!
YOU SLEAZE-BAG!
WEIRDO!
HOW DIS-GUST-ING!
BUT... I SUP-POSE...

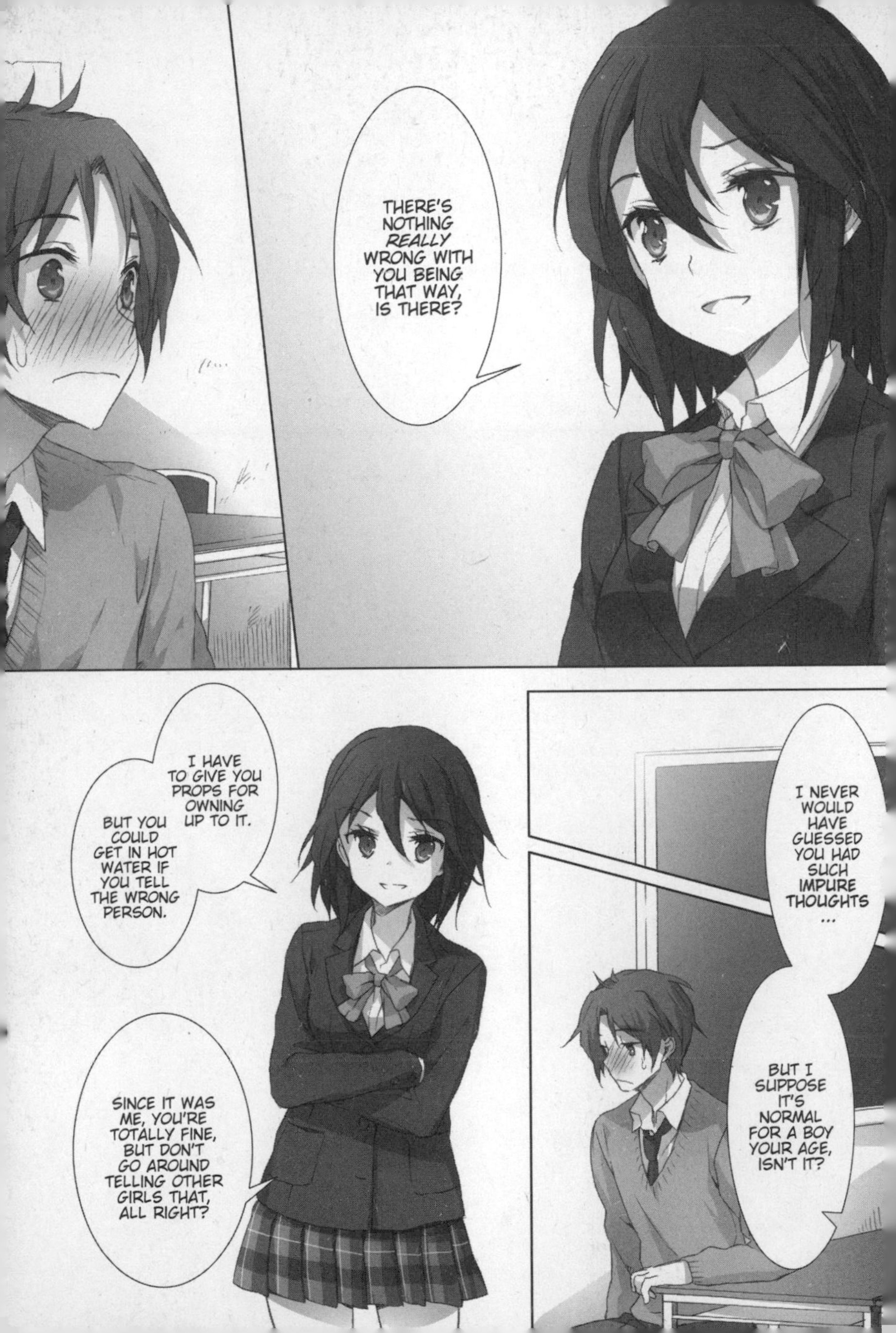
THERE'S NOTHING *REALLY* WRONG WITH YOU BEING THAT WAY, IS THERE?
I NEVER WOULD HAVE GUESSED YOU HAD SUCH IMPURE THOUGHTS ...
BUT I SUPPOSE IT'S NORMAL FOR A BOY YOUR AGE, ISN'T IT?
I HAVE TO GIVE YOU PROPS FOR OWNING UP TO IT.
BUT YOU COULD GET IN HOT WATER IF YOU TELL THE WRONG PERSON.
SINCE IT WAS ME, YOU'RE TOTALLY FINE, BUT DON'T GO AROUND TELLING OTHER GIRLS THAT, ALL RIGHT?

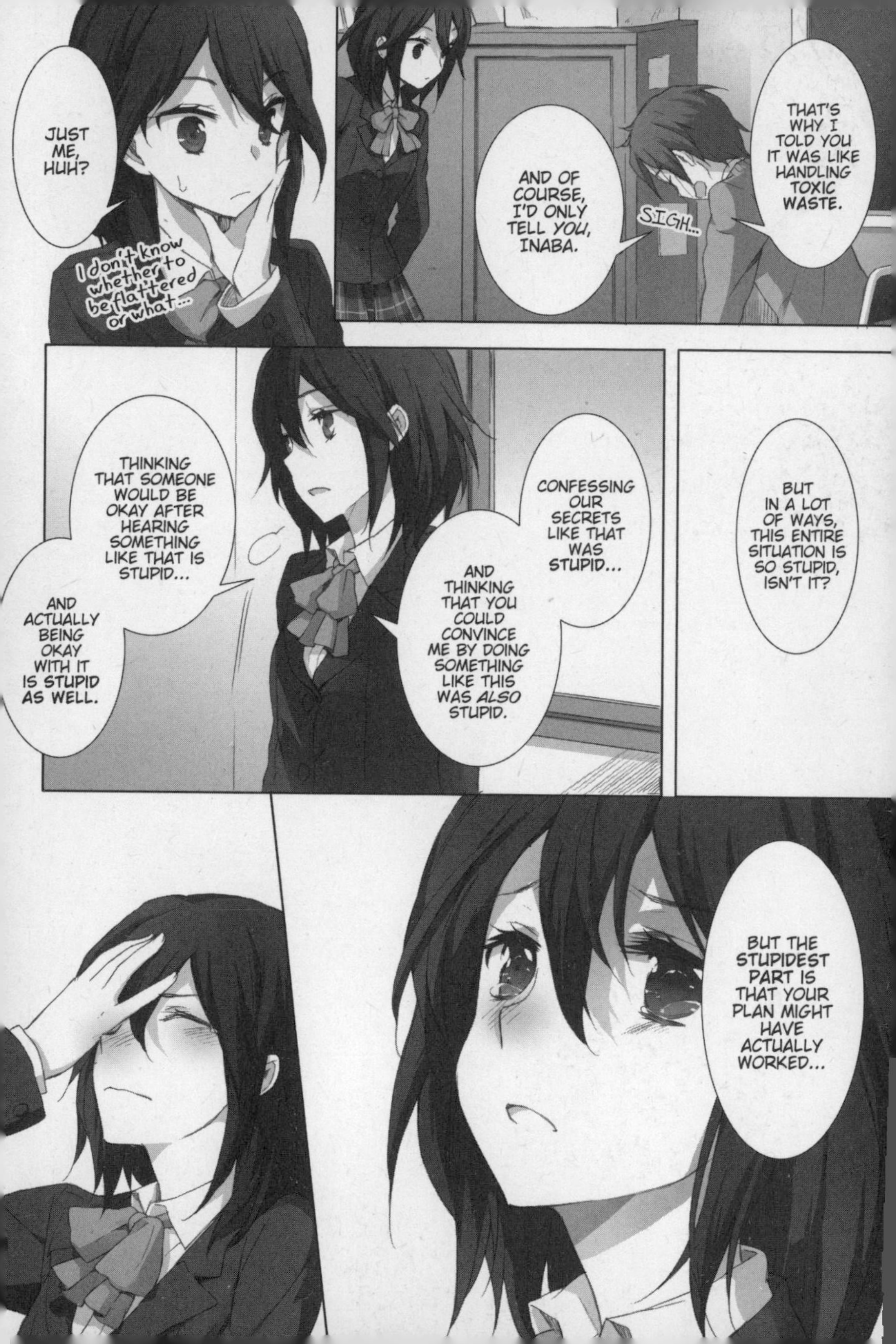
THAT'S WHY I TOLD YOU IT WAS LIKE HANDLING TOXIC WASTE.
SIGH...
AND OF COURSE, I'D ONLY TELL *YOU*, INABA.
JUST ME, HUH?
I don't know whether to be flattered or what...
BUT IN A LOT OF WAYS, THIS ENTIRE SITUATION IS SO STUPID, ISN'T IT?
CONFESSING OUR SECRETS LIKE THAT WAS STUPID...
AND THINKING THAT YOU COULD CONVINCE ME BY DOING SOMETHING LIKE THIS WAS *ALSO* STUPID.
THINKING THAT SOMEONE WOULD BE OKAY AFTER HEARING SOMETHING LIKE THAT IS STUPID...
AND ACTUALLY BEING OKAY WITH IT IS STUPID AS WELL.
BUT THE STUPIDEST PART IS THAT YOUR PLAN MIGHT HAVE ACTUALLY WORKED...

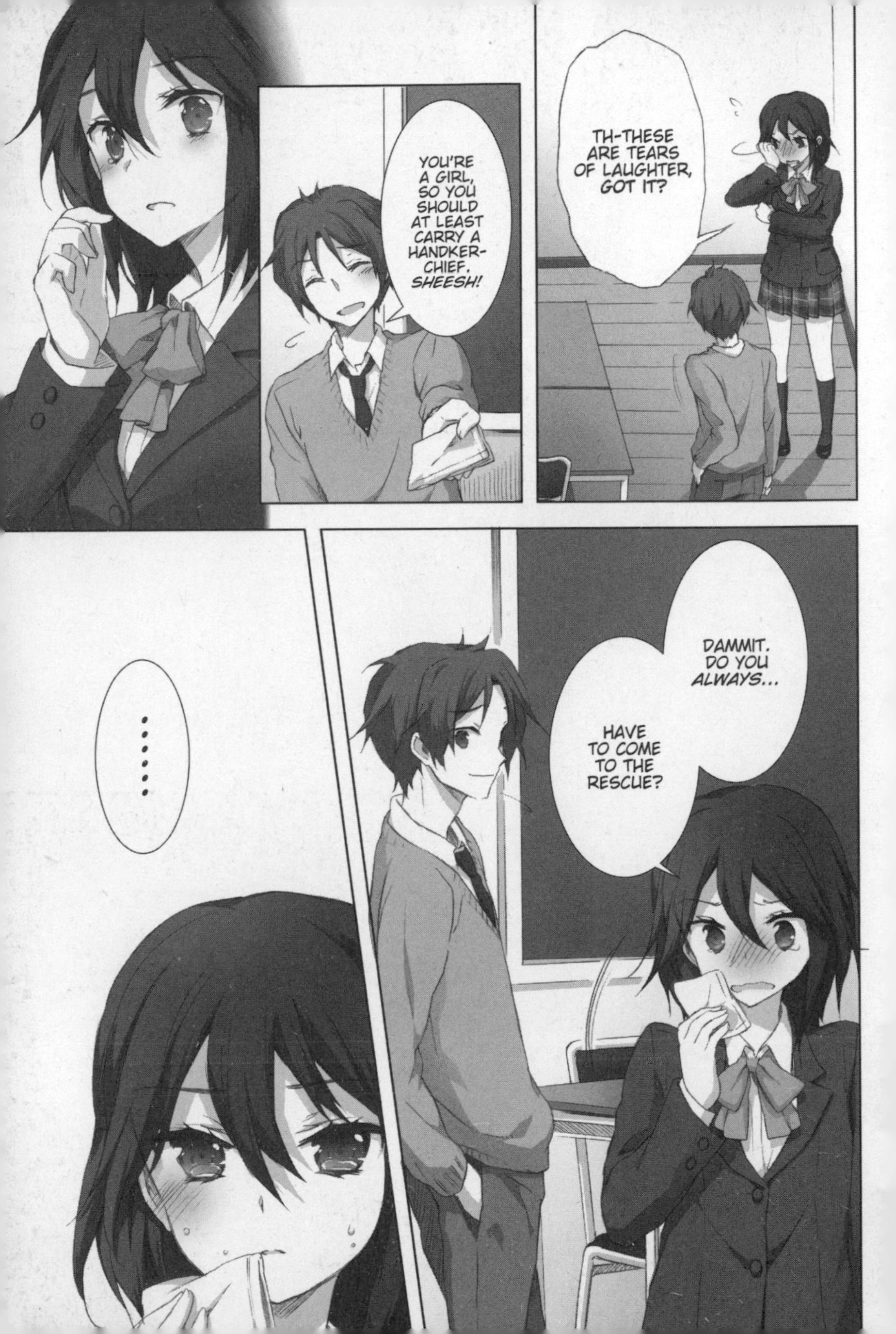
TH-THESE ARE TEARS OF LAUGHTER, GOT IT?
YOU'RE A GIRL, SO YOU SHOULD AT LEAST CARRY A HANDKERCHIEF. SHEESH!
DAMMIT. DO YOU ALWAYS...
HAVE TO COME TO THE RESCUE?
......

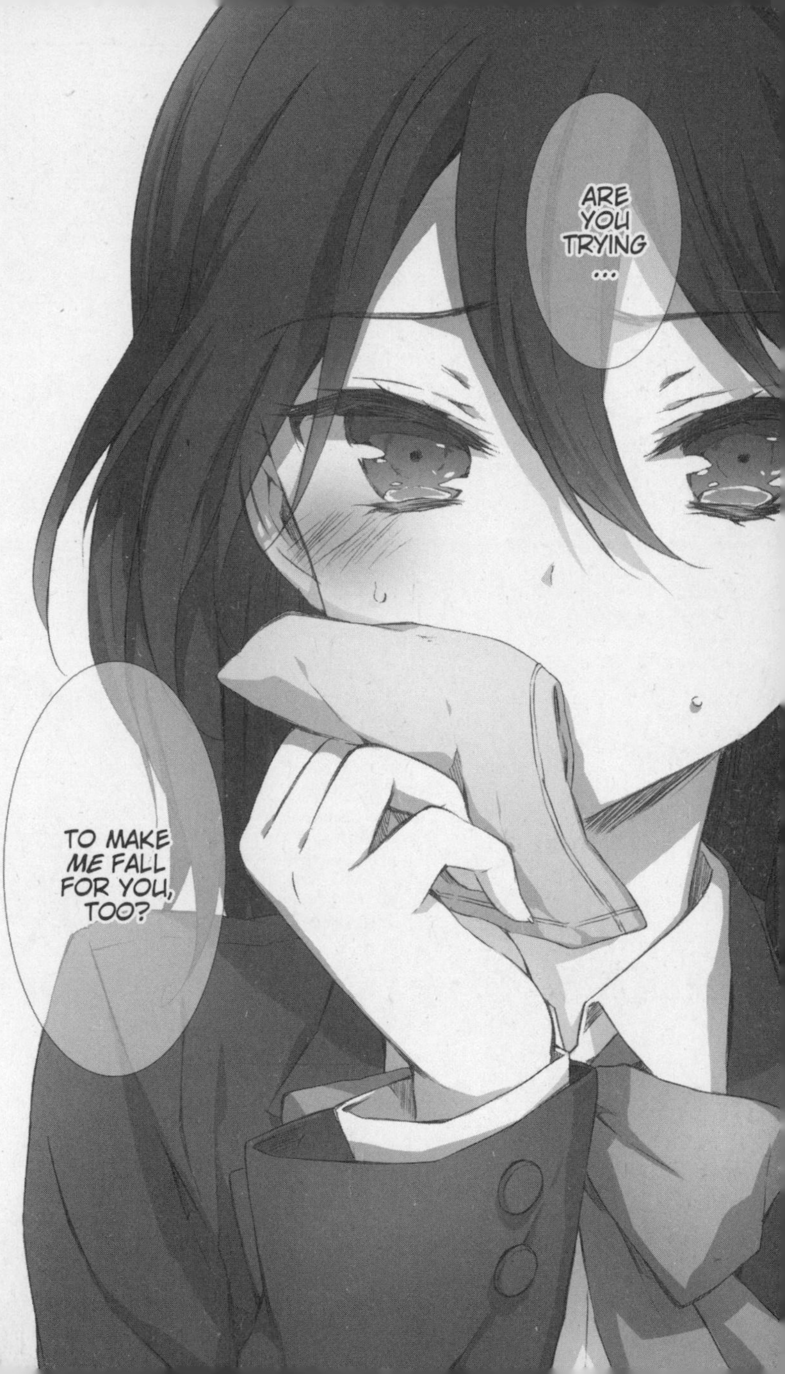
ARE YOU TRYING...
TO MAKE *ME* FALL FOR YOU, TOO?

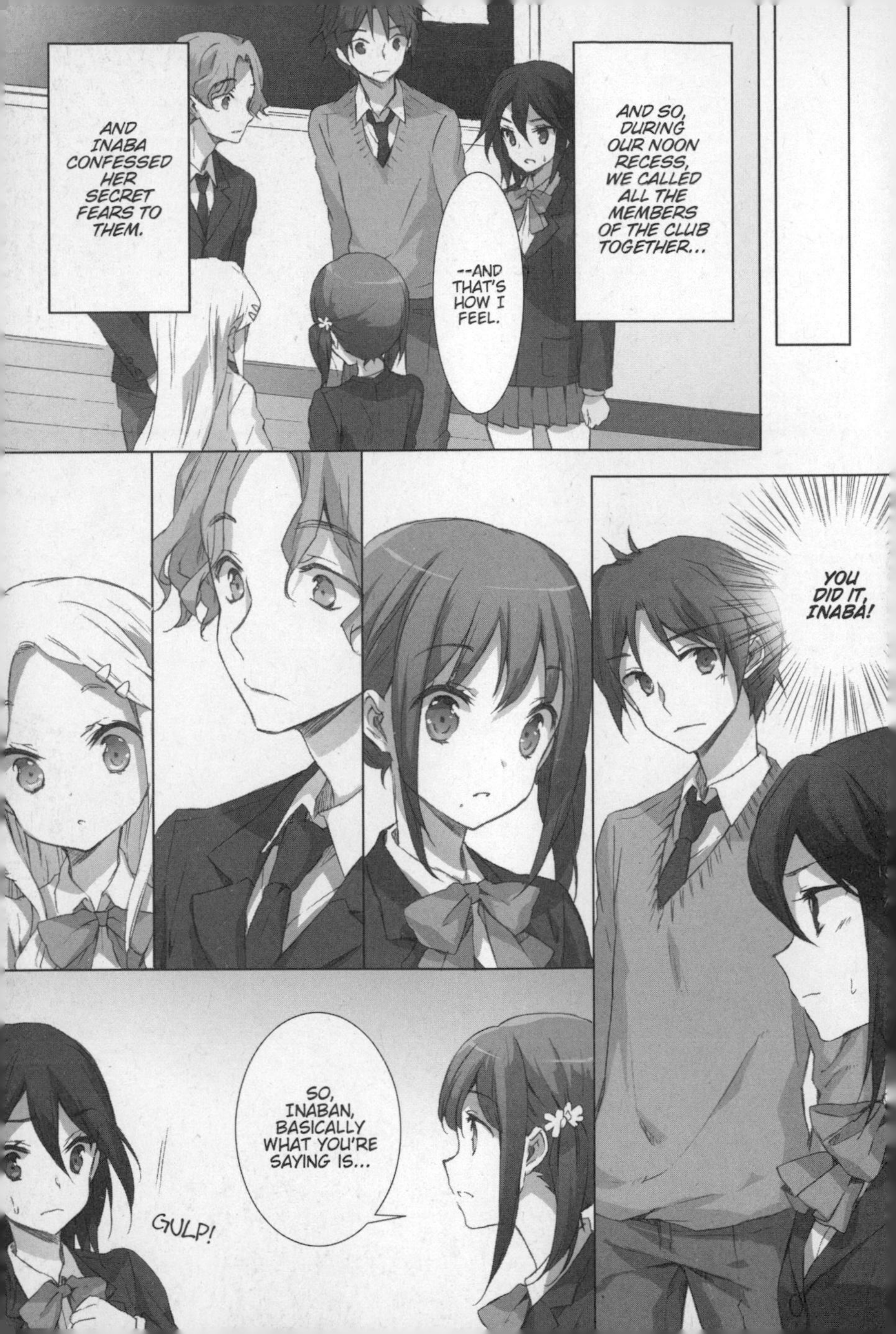

AND SO, DURING OUR NOON RECESS, WE CALLED ALL THE MEMBERS OF THE CLUB TOGETHER...
--AND THAT'S HOW I FEEL.
AND INABA CONFESSED HER SECRET FEARS TO THEM.
YOU DID IT, INABA!
SO, INABAN, BASICALLY WHAT YOU'RE SAYING IS...
GULP!

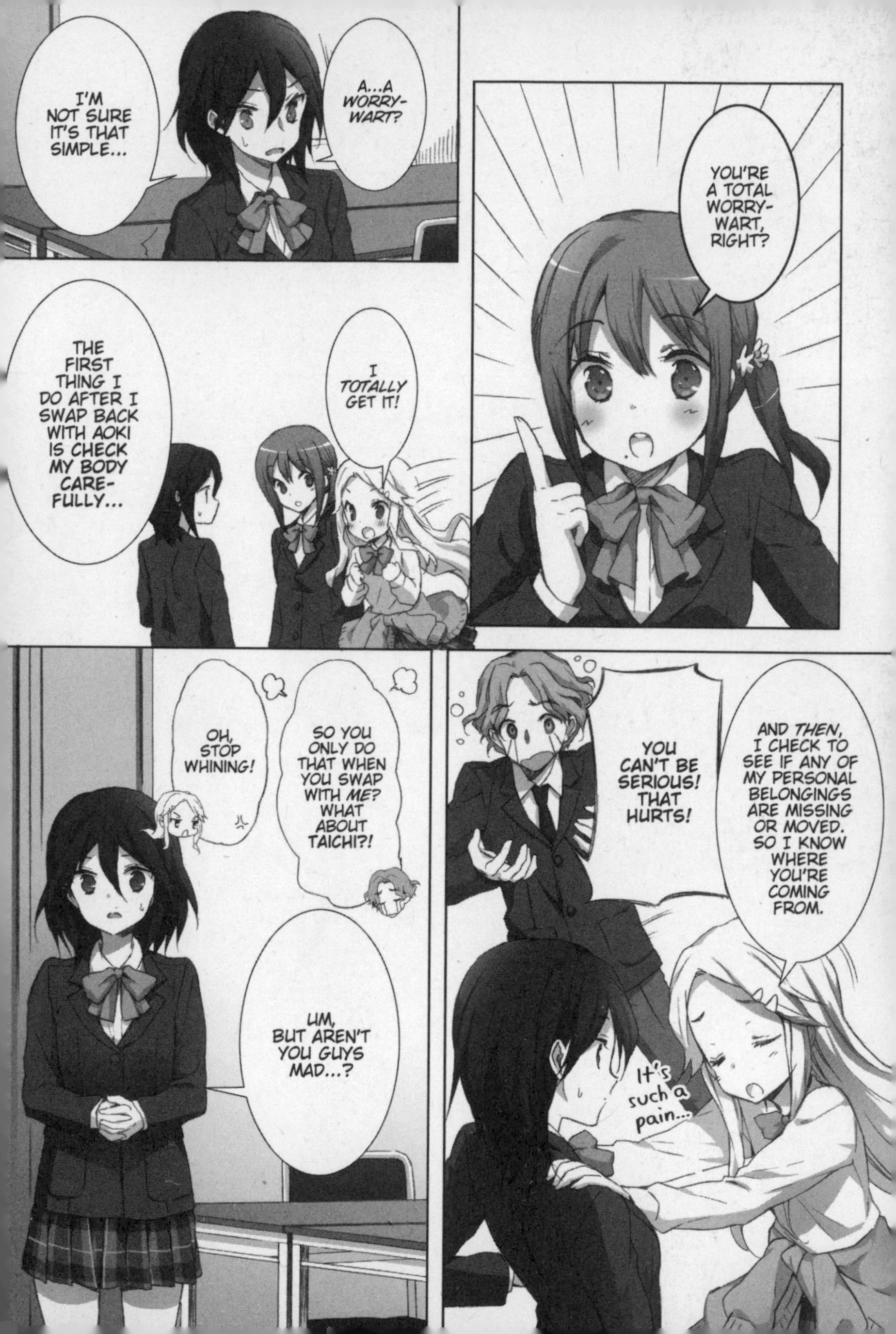
YOU'RE A TOTAL WORRY-WART, RIGHT?
A...A *WORRY-WART?*
I'M NOT SURE IT'S THAT SIMPLE...
I *TOTALLY* GET IT!
THE FIRST THING I DO AFTER I SWAP BACK WITH AOKI IS CHECK MY BODY CARE-FULLY...
AND *THEN*, I CHECK TO SEE IF ANY OF MY PERSONAL BELONGINGS ARE MISSING OR MOVED. SO I KNOW WHERE YOU'RE COMING FROM.
YOU CAN'T BE SERIOUS! THAT HURTS!
It's such a pain...
SO YOU ONLY DO THAT WHEN YOU SWAP WITH *ME?* WHAT ABOUT TAICHI?!
OH, STOP WHINING!
UM, BUT AREN'T YOU GUYS MAD...?

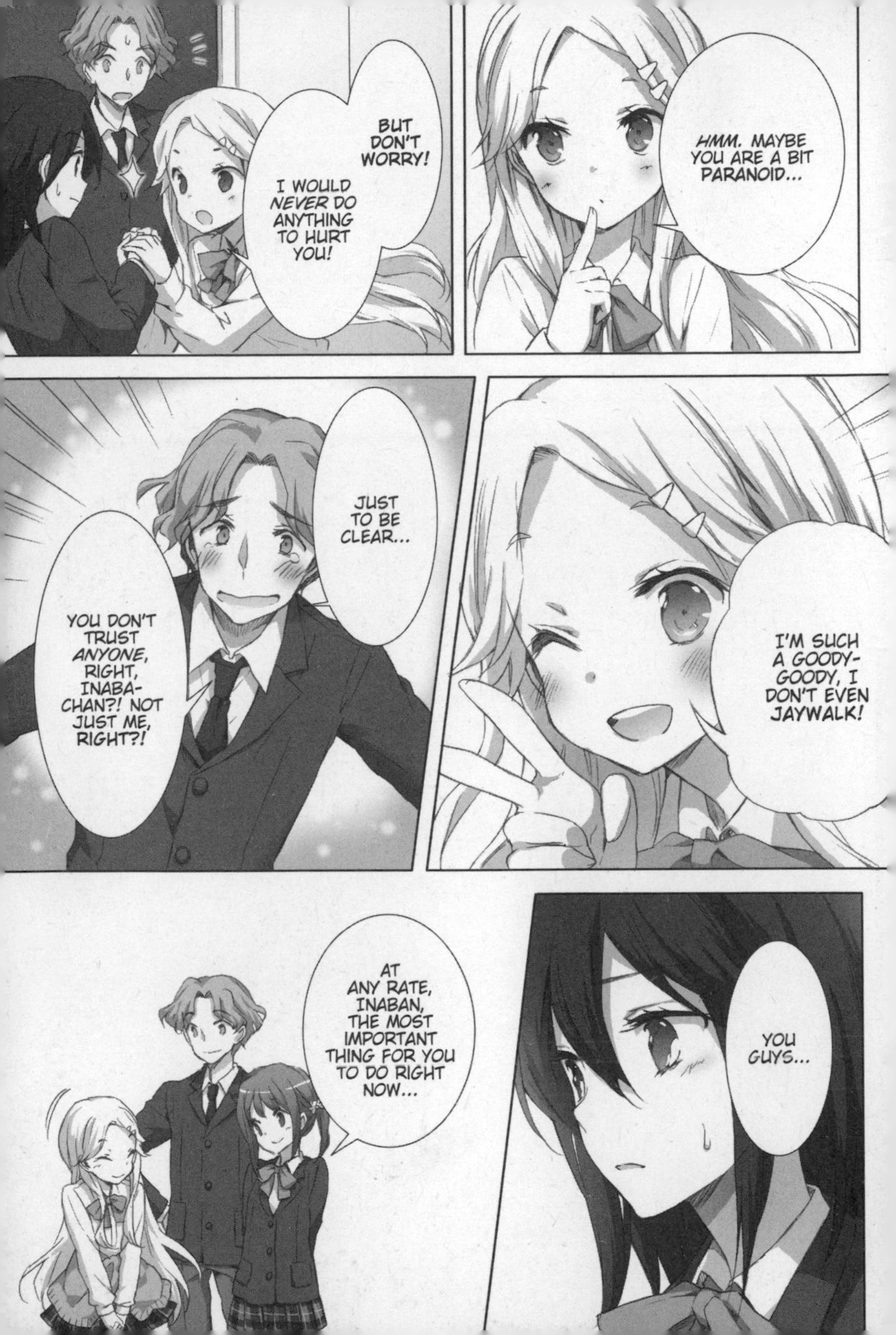
HMM. MAYBE YOU ARE A BIT PARANOID...
BUT DON'T WORRY!
I WOULD NEVER DO ANYTHING TO HURT YOU!
I'M SUCH A GOODY-GOODY, I DON'T EVEN JAYWALK!
JUST TO BE CLEAR...
YOU DON'T TRUST ANYONE, RIGHT, INABA-CHAN?! NOT JUST ME, RIGHT?!
YOU GUYS...
AT ANY RATE, INABAN, THE MOST IMPORTANT THING FOR YOU TO DO RIGHT NOW...

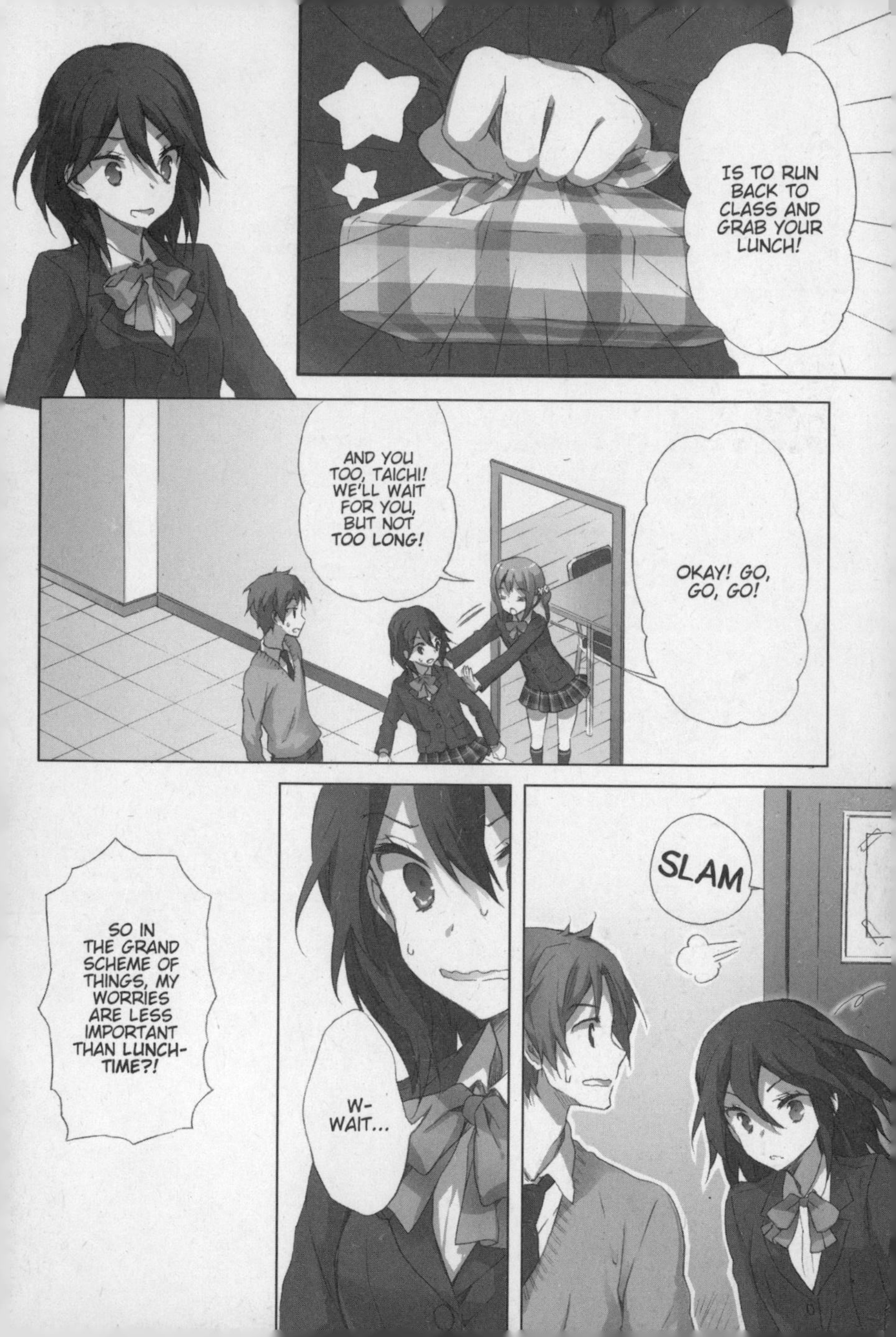
IS TO RUN BACK TO CLASS AND GRAB YOUR LUNCH!
OKAY! GO, GO, GO!
AND YOU TOO, TAICHI! WE'LL WAIT FOR YOU, BUT NOT TOO LONG!
SLAM
W- WAIT...
SO IN THE GRAND SCHEME OF THINGS, MY WORRIES ARE LESS IMPORTANT THAN LUNCH-TIME?!

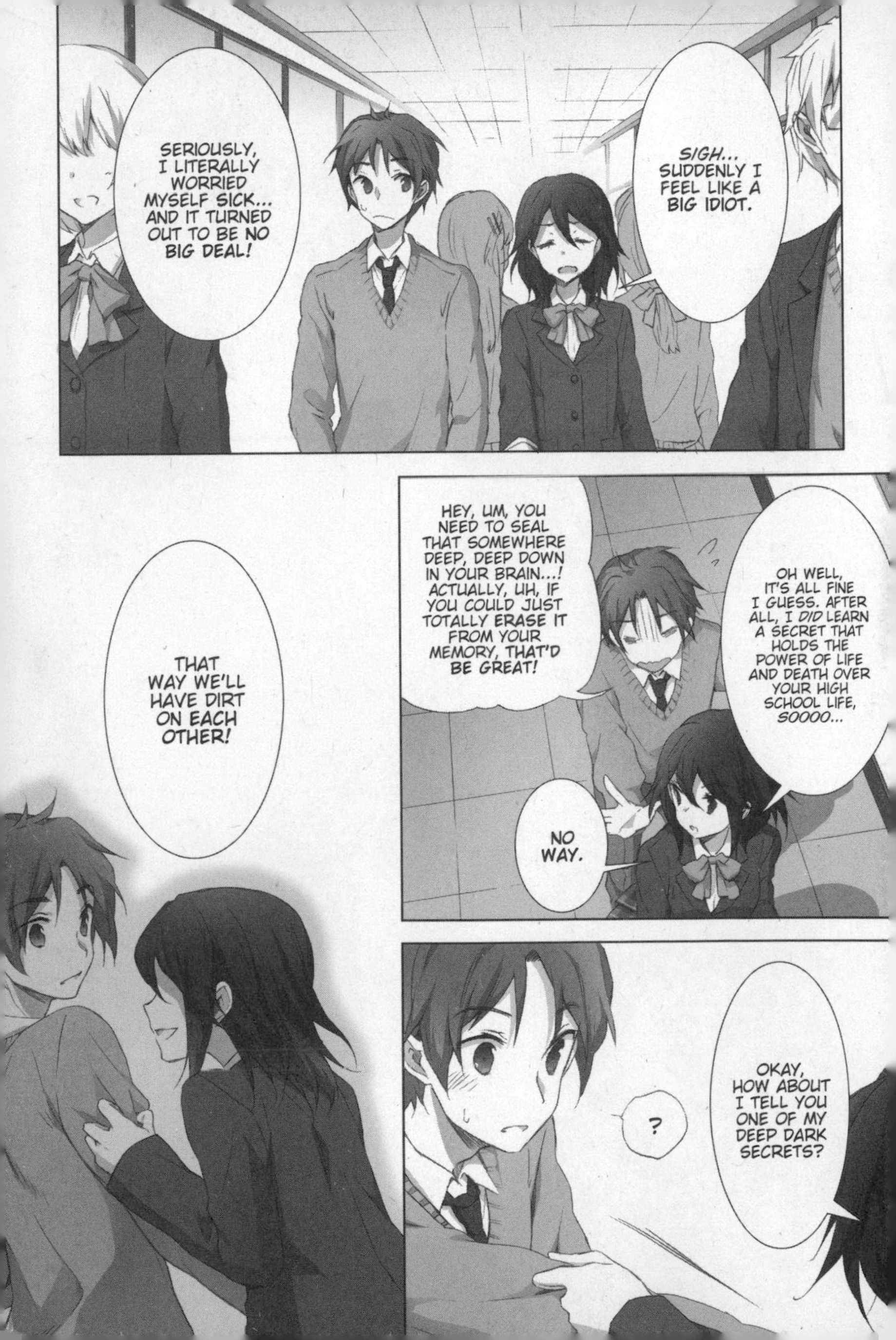
SIGH... SUDDENLY I FEEL LIKE A BIG IDIOT.
SERIOUSLY, I LITERALLY WORRIED MYSELF SICK... AND IT TURNED OUT TO BE NO BIG DEAL!
OH WELL, IT'S ALL FINE I GUESS. AFTER ALL, I DID LEARN A SECRET THAT HOLDS THE POWER OF LIFE AND DEATH OVER YOUR HIGH SCHOOL LIFE, SOOOO...
HEY, UM, YOU NEED TO SEAL THAT SOMEWHERE DEEP, DEEP DOWN IN YOUR BRAIN...! ACTUALLY, UH, IF YOU COULD JUST TOTALLY ERASE IT FROM YOUR MEMORY, THAT'D BE GREAT!
NO WAY.
OKAY, HOW ABOUT I TELL YOU ONE OF MY DEEP DARK SECRETS?
?
THAT WAY WE'LL HAVE DIRT ON EACH OTHER!

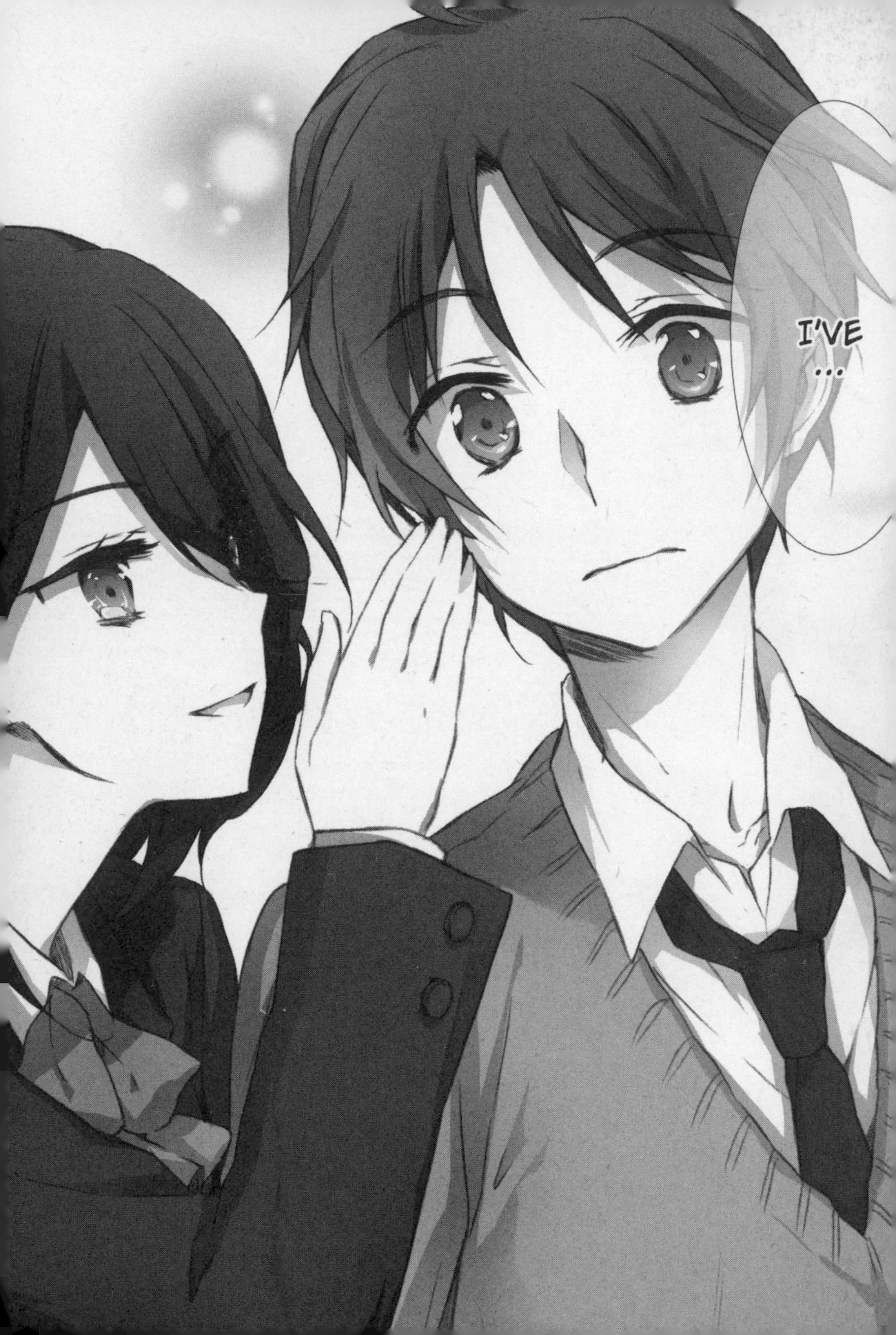
I'VE
...

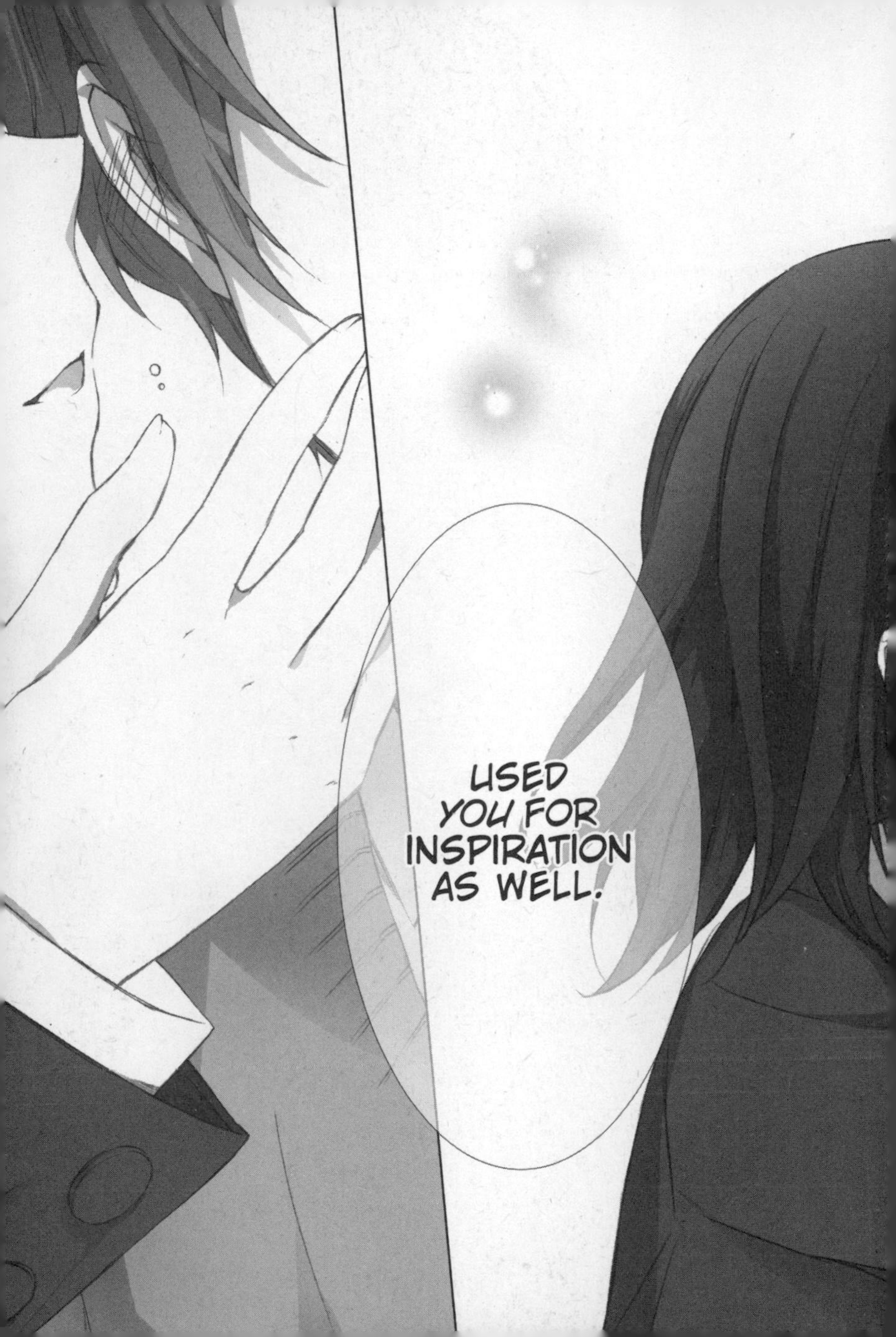
USED YOU FOR INSPIRATION AS WELL.

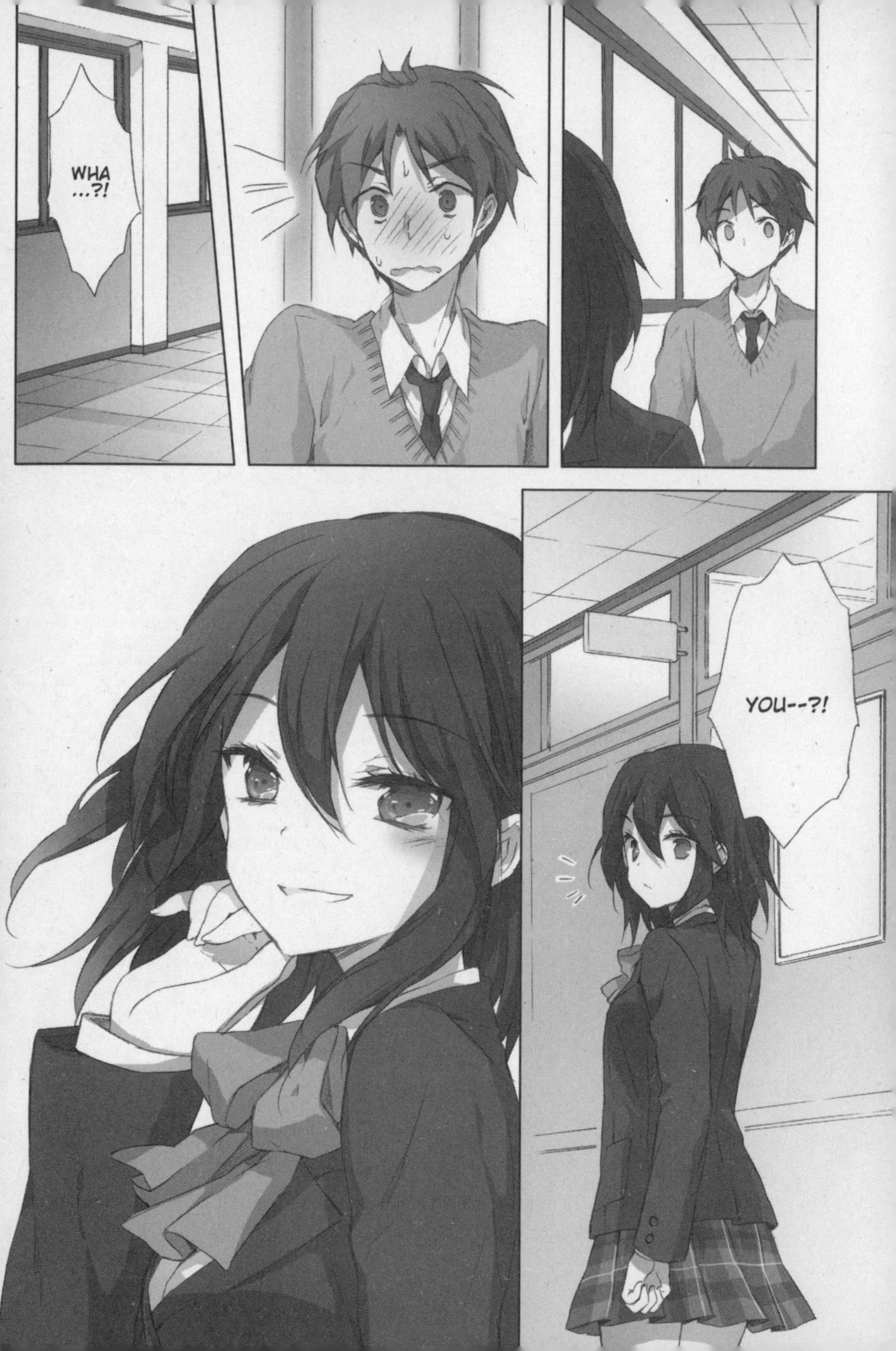
WHA ...?!
YOU--?!

KOKORO CONNECT

A Very Kokoro
Connect Animal
Crossing!

KOKORO CONNECT

Chapter 11

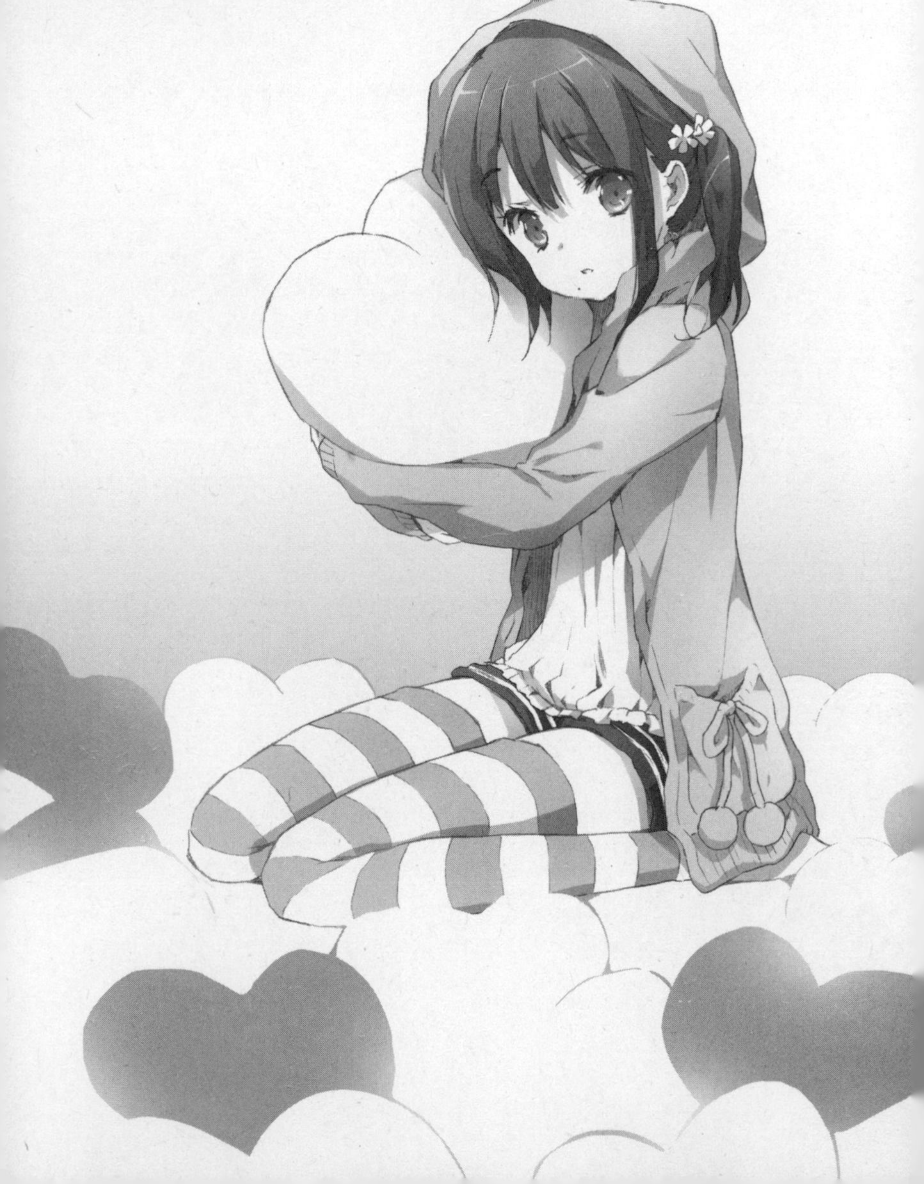

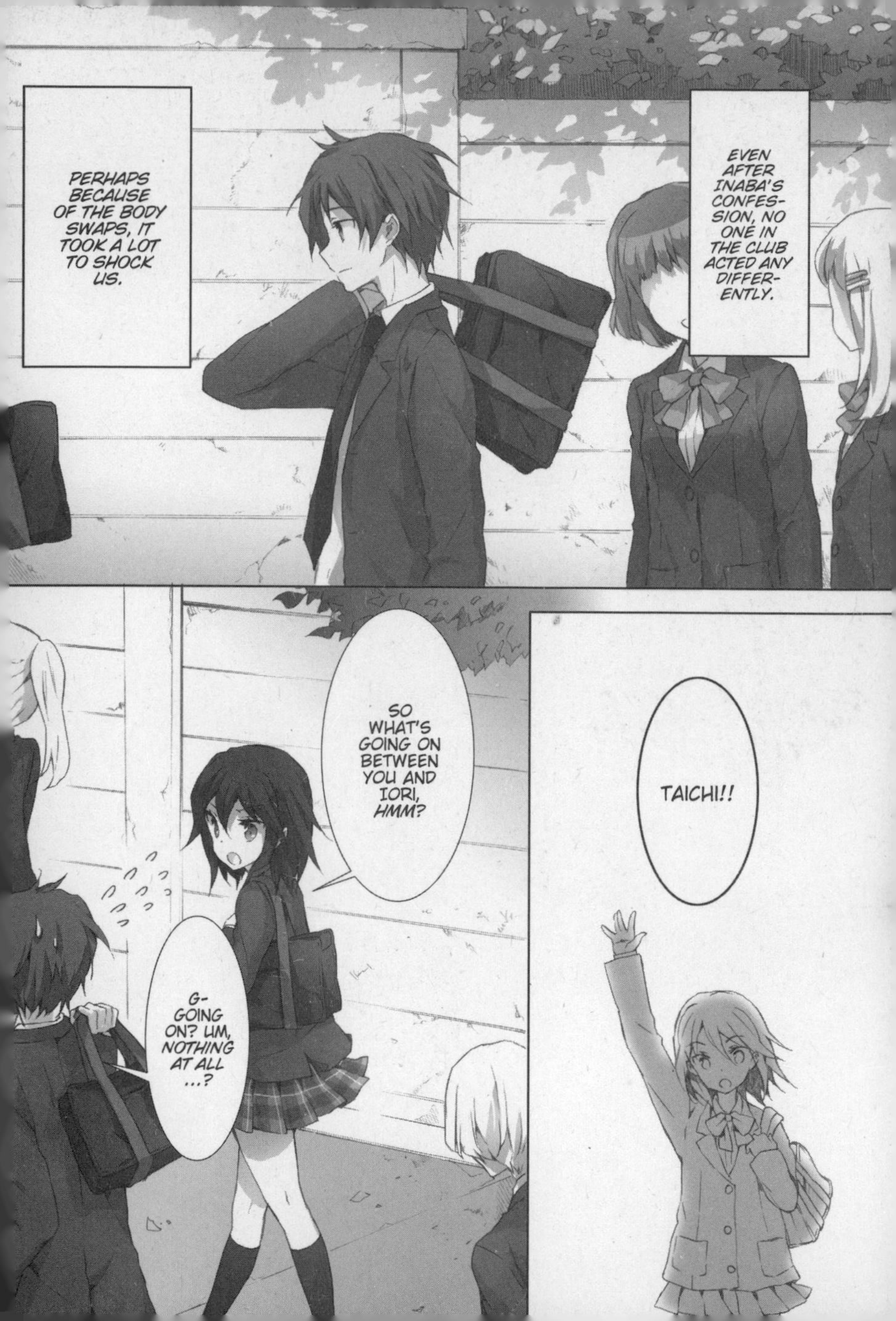
EVEN AFTER INABA'S CONFESSION, NO ONE IN THE CLUB ACTED ANY DIFFERENTLY.
PERHAPS BECAUSE OF THE BODY SWAPS, IT TOOK A LOT TO SHOCK US.
TAICHI!!
SO WHAT'S GOING ON BETWEEN YOU AND IORI, HMM?
G-GOING ON? UM, NOTHING AT ALL ...?

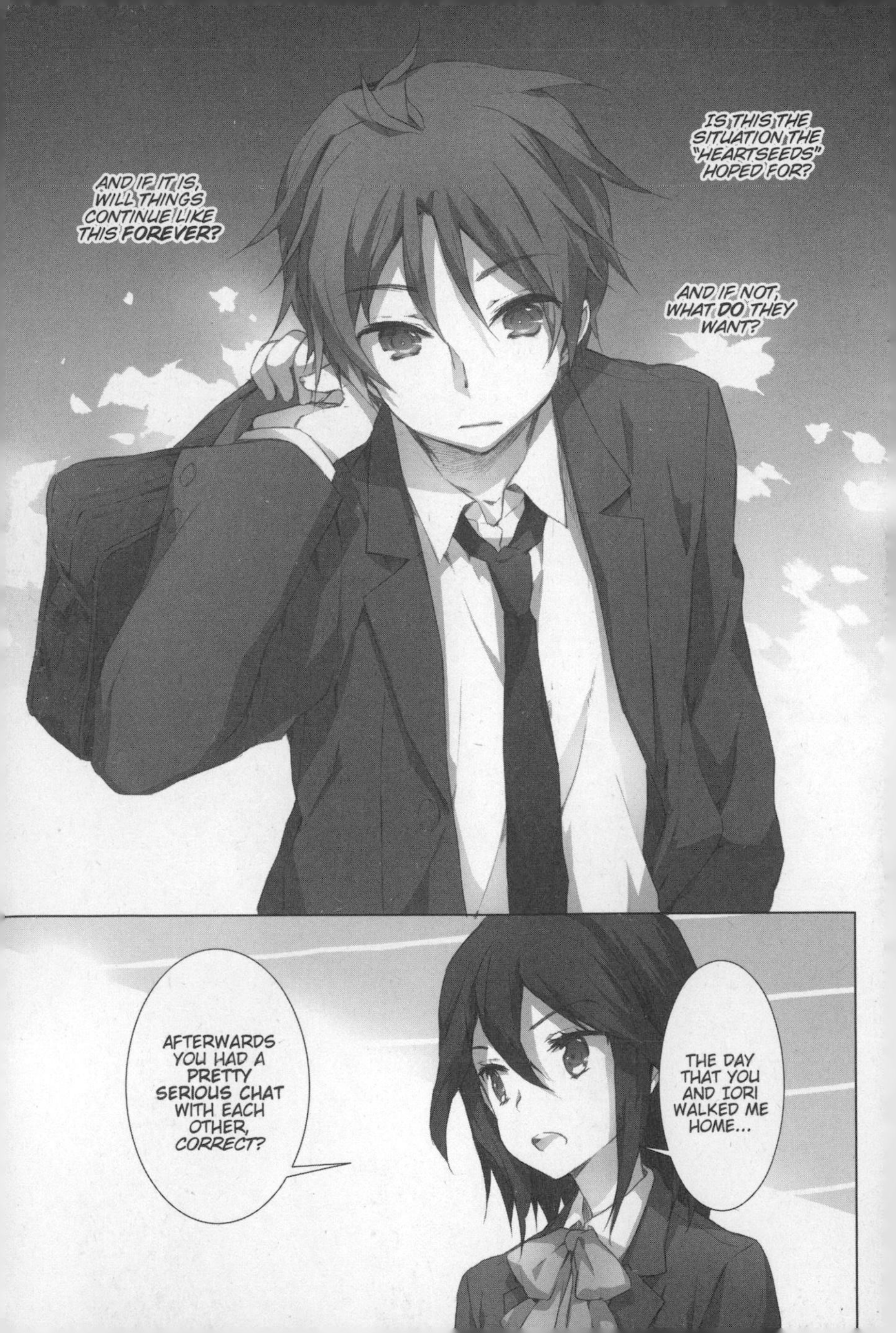
IS THIS THE SITUATION THE "HEARTSEEDS" HOPED FOR?
AND IF IT IS, WILL THINGS CONTINUE LIKE THIS FOREVER?
AND IF NOT, WHAT DO THEY WANT?
THE DAY THAT YOU AND IORI WALKED ME HOME...
AFTERWARDS YOU HAD A PRETTY SERIOUS CHAT WITH EACH OTHER, CORRECT?

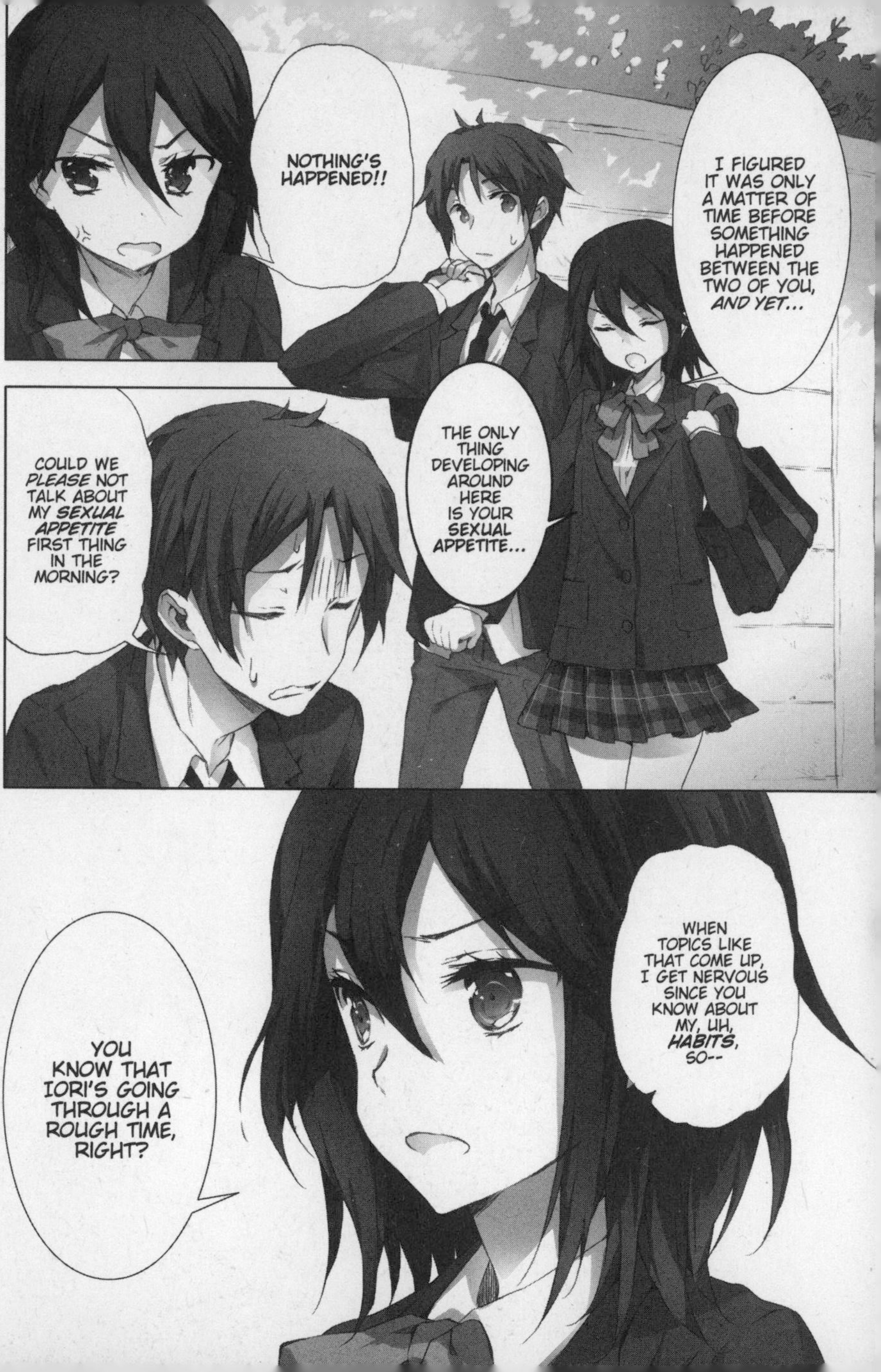
I FIGURED IT WAS ONLY A MATTER OF TIME BEFORE SOMETHING HAPPENED BETWEEN THE TWO OF YOU, *AND YET...*
NOTHING'S HAPPENED!!
THE ONLY THING DEVELOPING AROUND HERE IS YOUR SEXUAL APPETITE...
COULD WE *PLEASE* NOT TALK ABOUT MY ***SEXUAL APPETITE*** FIRST THING IN THE MORNING?
WHEN TOPICS LIKE THAT COME UP, I GET NERVOUS SINCE YOU KNOW ABOUT MY, UH, ***HABITS***, SO--
YOU KNOW THAT IORI'S GOING THROUGH A ROUGH TIME, RIGHT?

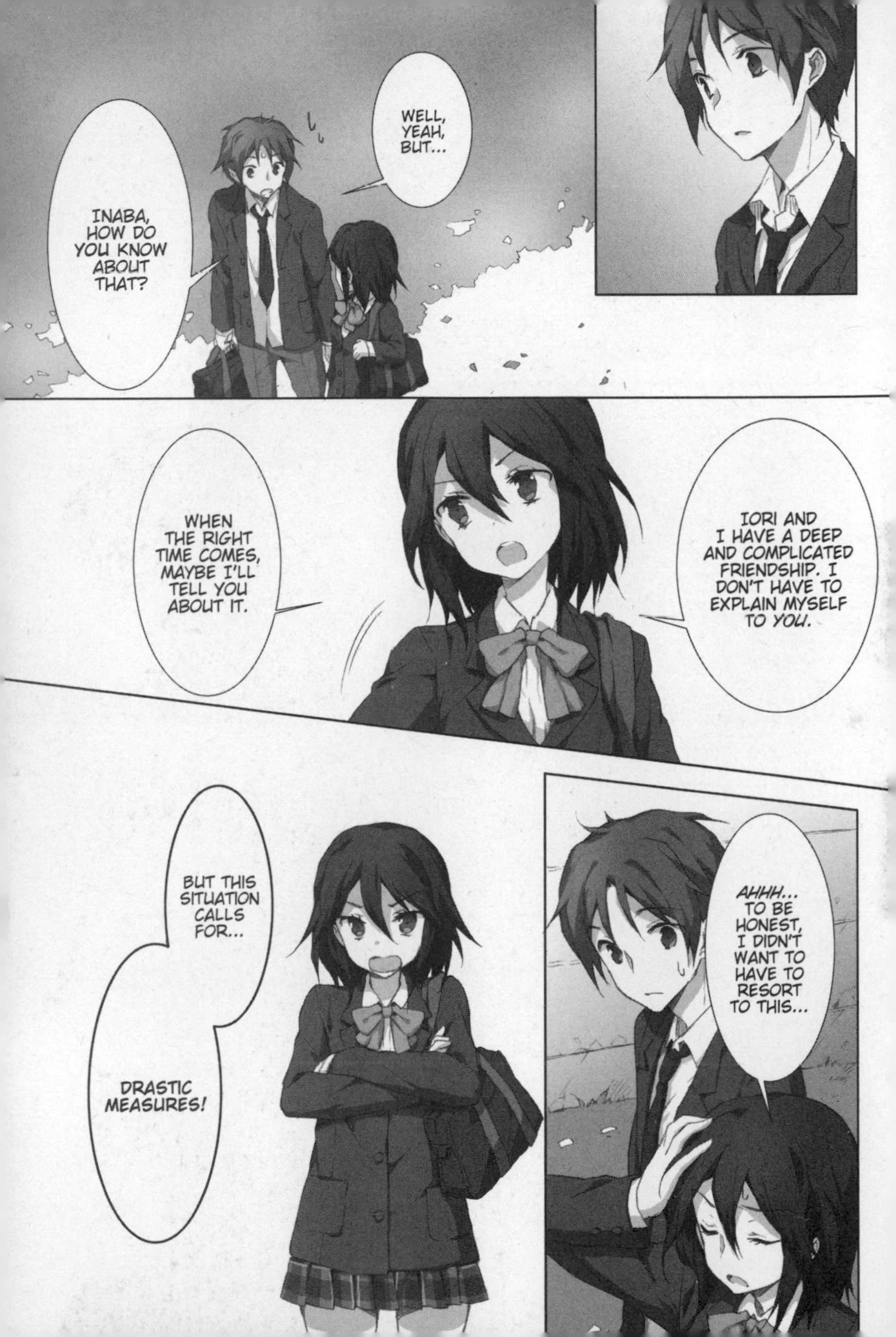
WELL, YEAH, BUT...
INABA, HOW DO YOU KNOW ABOUT THAT?
IORI AND I HAVE A DEEP AND COMPLICATED FRIENDSHIP. I DON'T HAVE TO EXPLAIN MYSELF TO *YOU*.
WHEN THE RIGHT TIME COMES, MAYBE I'LL TELL YOU ABOUT IT.
AHHH... TO BE HONEST, I DIDN'T WANT TO HAVE TO RESORT TO THIS...
BUT THIS SITUATION CALLS FOR...
DRASTIC MEASURES!

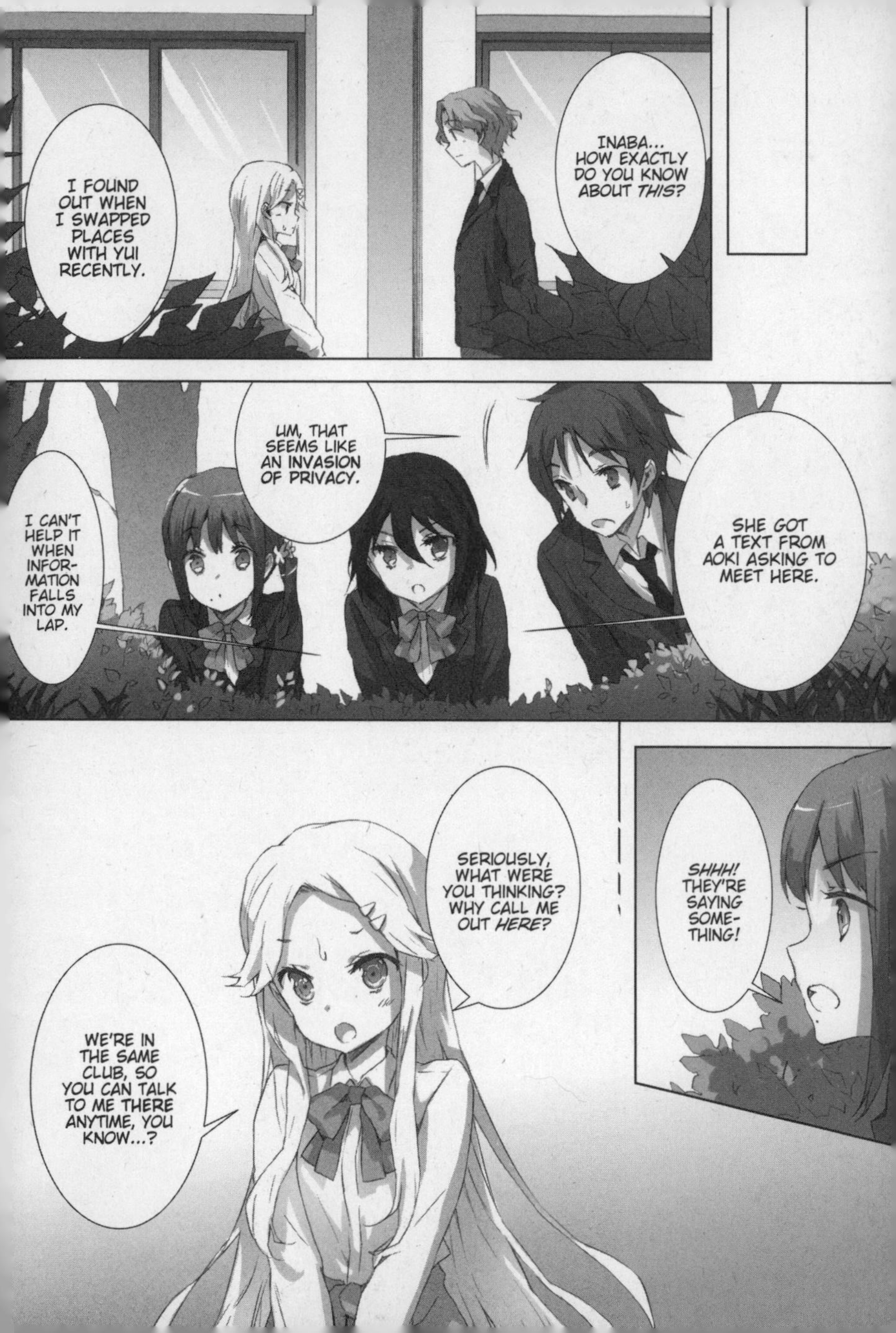
INABA... HOW EXACTLY DO YOU KNOW ABOUT *THIS*?
I FOUND OUT WHEN I SWAPPED PLACES WITH YUI RECENTLY.
SHE GOT A TEXT FROM AOKI ASKING TO MEET HERE.
UM, THAT SEEMS LIKE AN INVASION OF PRIVACY.
I CAN'T HELP IT WHEN INFORMATION FALLS INTO MY LAP.
SHHH! THEY'RE SAYING SOMETHING!
SERIOUSLY, WHAT WERE YOU THINKING? WHY CALL ME OUT *HERE*?
WE'RE IN THE SAME CLUB, SO YOU CAN TALK TO ME THERE ANYTIME, YOU KNOW...?

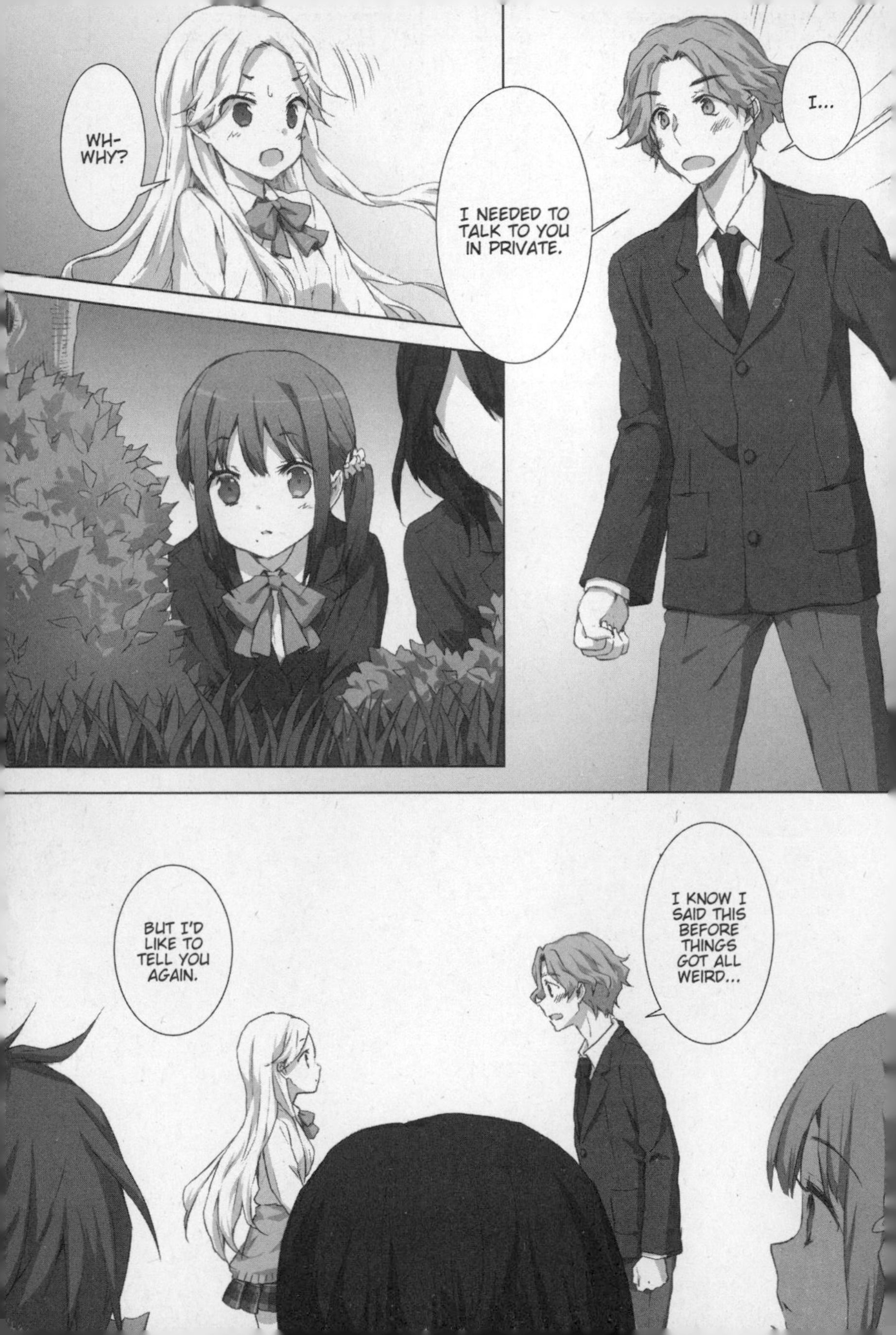
I...
I NEEDED TO TALK TO YOU IN PRIVATE.
WH- WHY?
I KNOW I SAID THIS BEFORE THINGS GOT ALL WEIRD...
BUT I'D LIKE TO TELL YOU AGAIN.

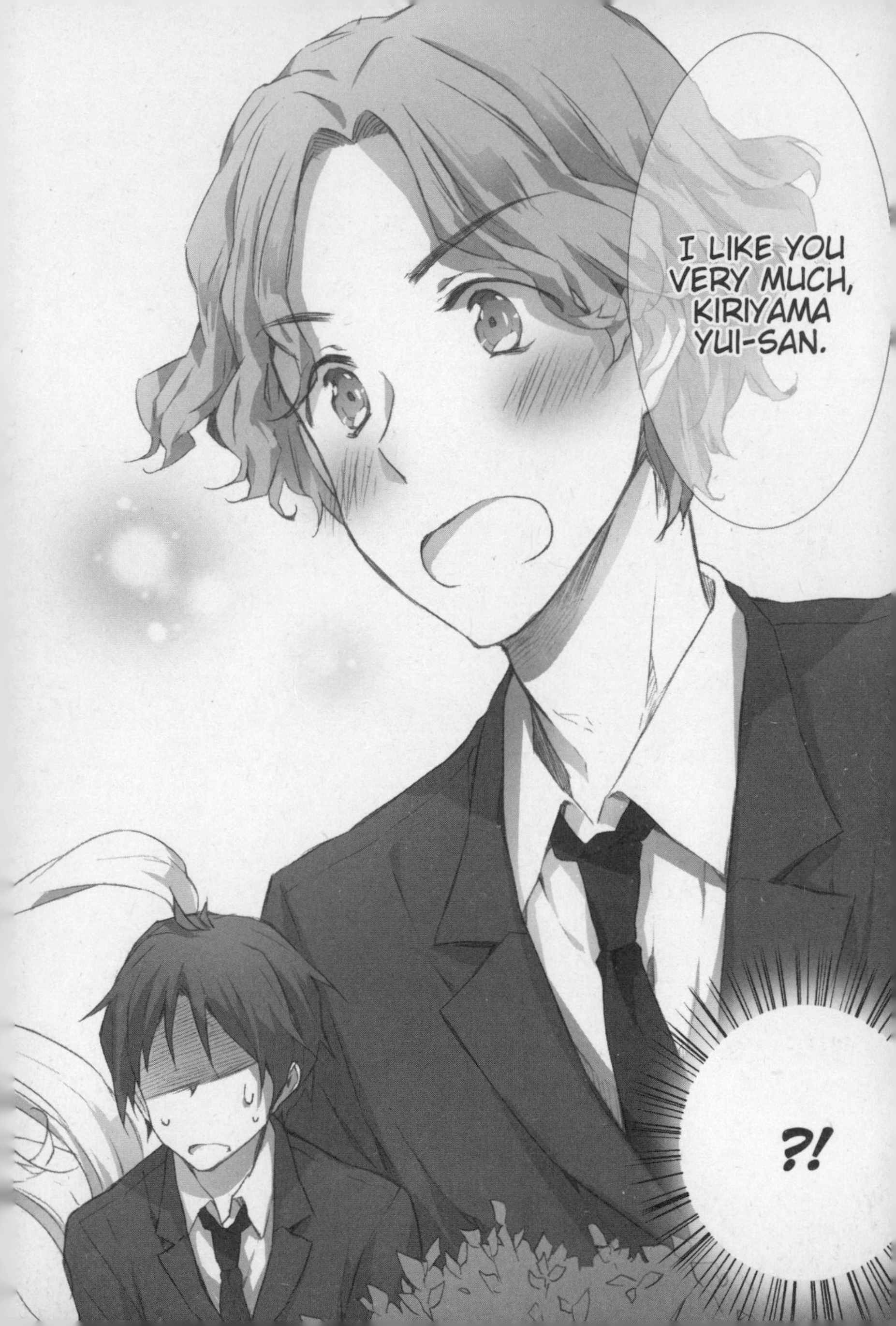
I LIKE YOU VERY MUCH, KIRIYAMA YUI-SAN.
?!

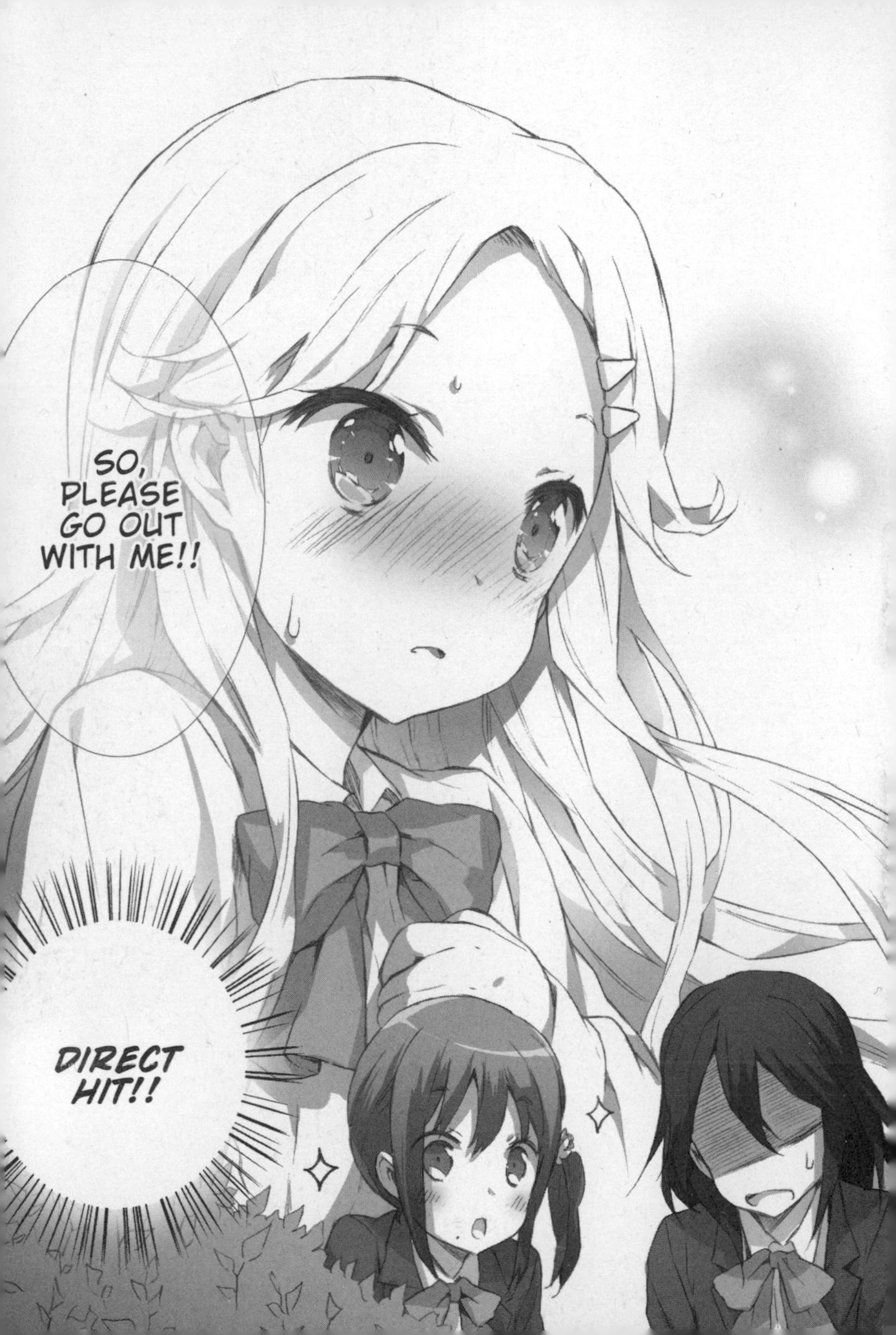
SO, PLEASE GO OUT WITH ME!!
DIRECT HIT!!

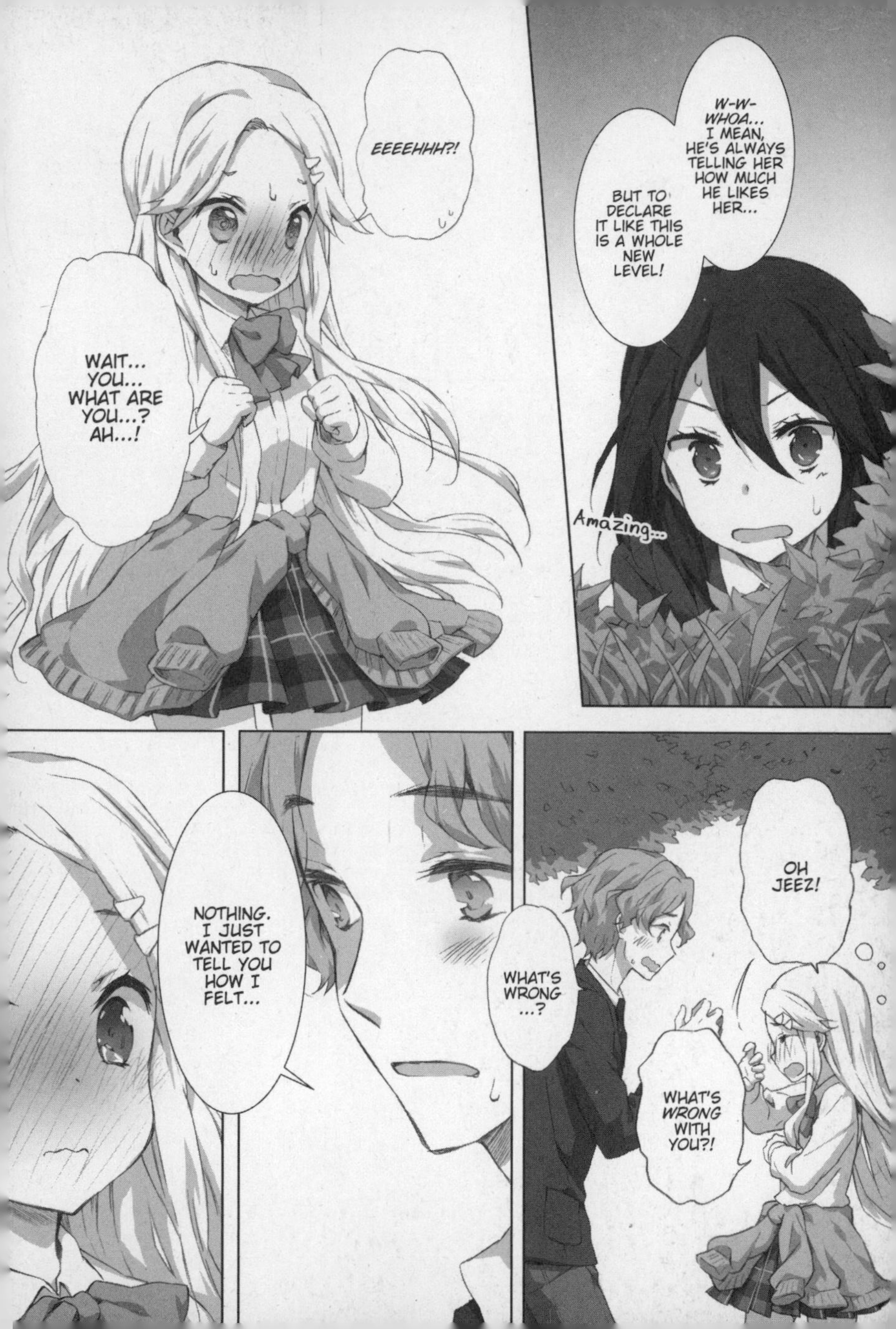
W-W-WHOA... I MEAN, HE'S ALWAYS TELLING HER HOW MUCH HE LIKES HER...
BUT TO DECLARE IT LIKE THIS IS A WHOLE NEW LEVEL!
Amazing...
EEEEHHH?!
WAIT... YOU... WHAT ARE YOU...? AH...!
OH JEEZ!
WHAT'S WRONG ...?
WHAT'S WRONG WITH YOU?!
NOTHING. I JUST WANTED TO TELL YOU HOW I FELT...

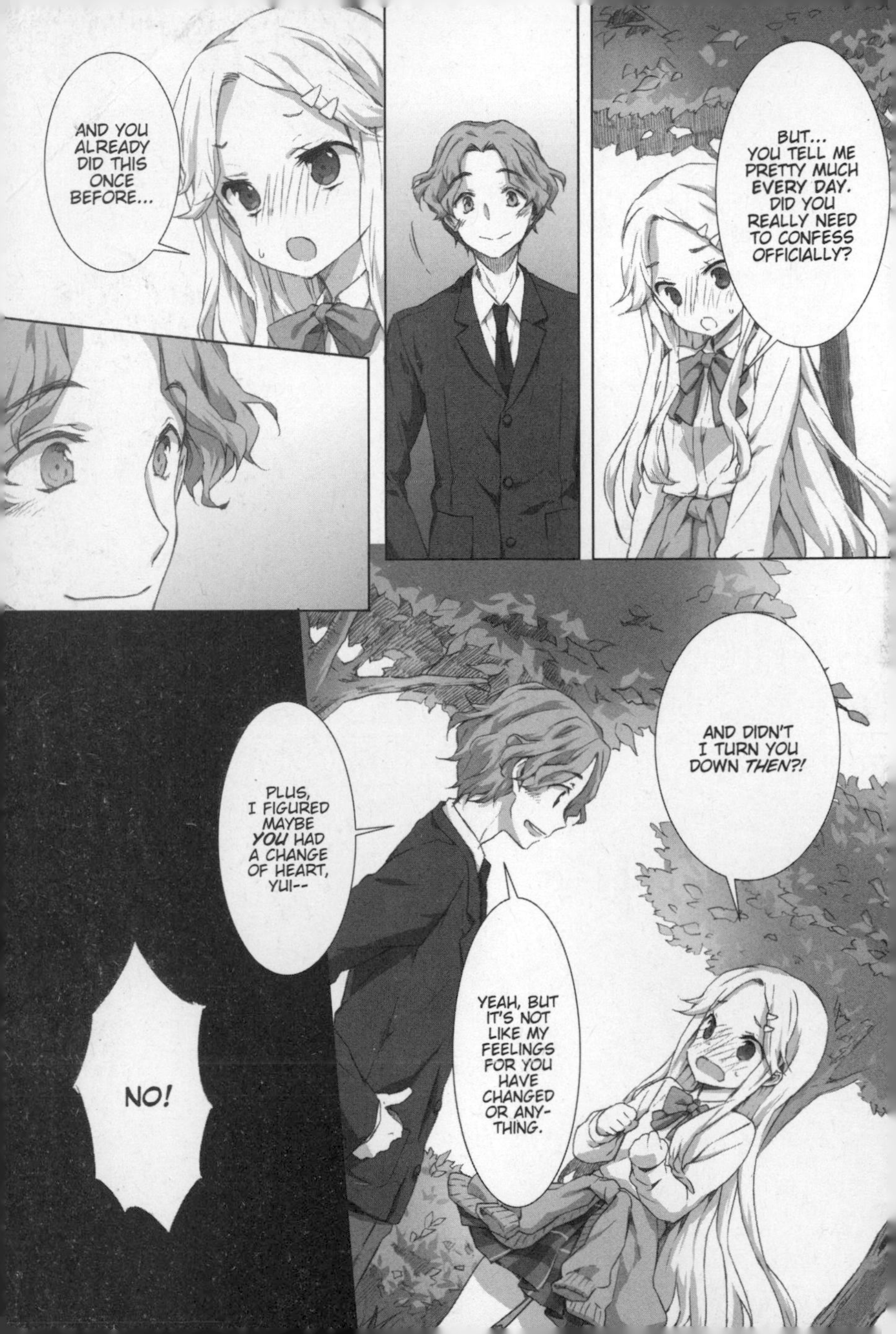
BUT... YOU TELL ME PRETTY MUCH EVERY DAY. DID YOU REALLY NEED TO CONFESS OFFICIALLY?
AND YOU ALREADY DID THIS ONCE BEFORE...
AND DIDN'T I TURN YOU DOWN *THEN*?!
YEAH, BUT IT'S NOT LIKE MY FEELINGS FOR YOU HAVE CHANGED OR ANY- THING.
PLUS, I FIGURED MAYBE ***YOU*** HAD A CHANGE OF HEART, YUI--
NO!

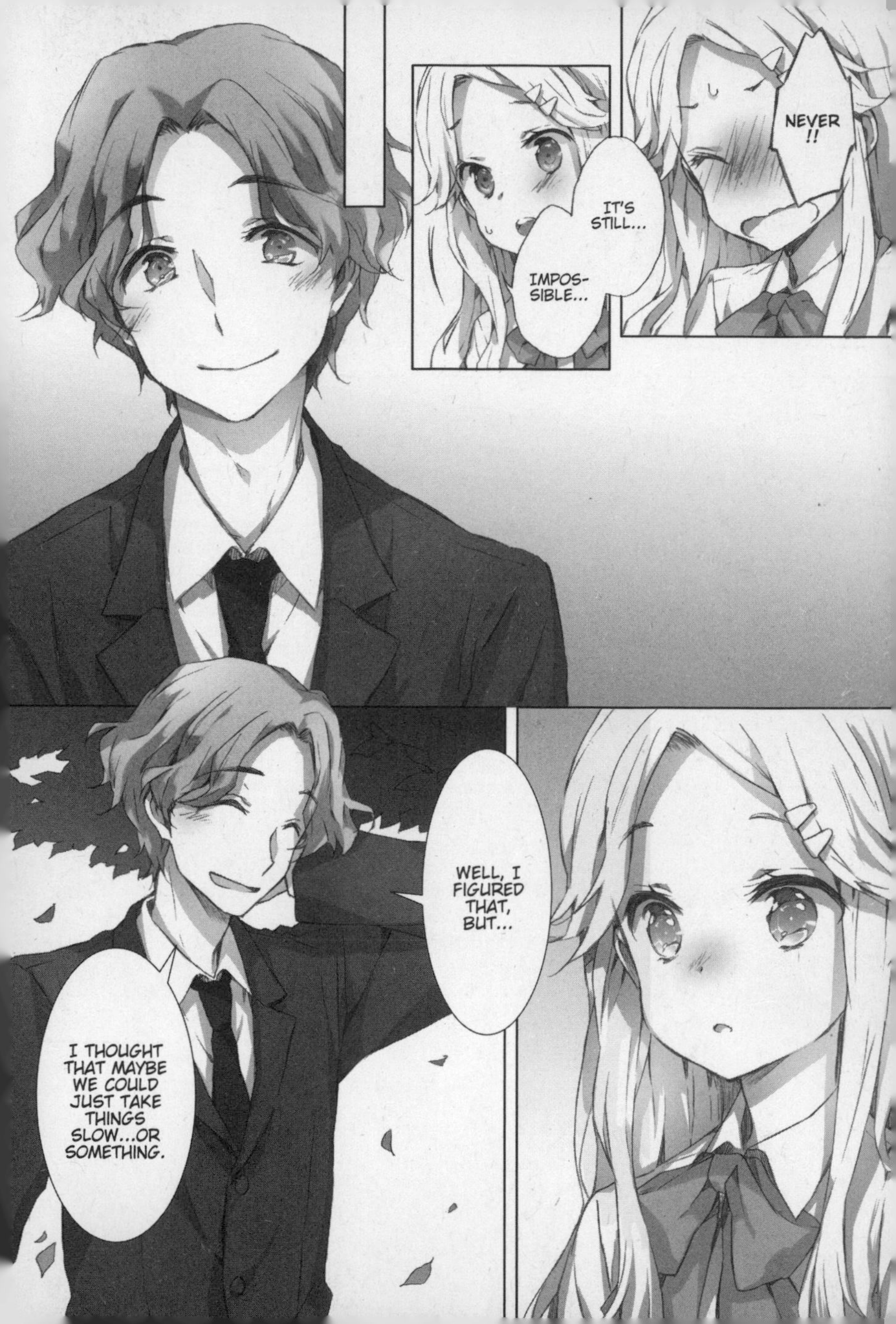
NEVER !!
IT'S STILL...
IMPOSSIBLE...
WELL, I FIGURED THAT, BUT...
I THOUGHT THAT MAYBE WE COULD JUST TAKE THINGS SLOW...OR SOMETHING.

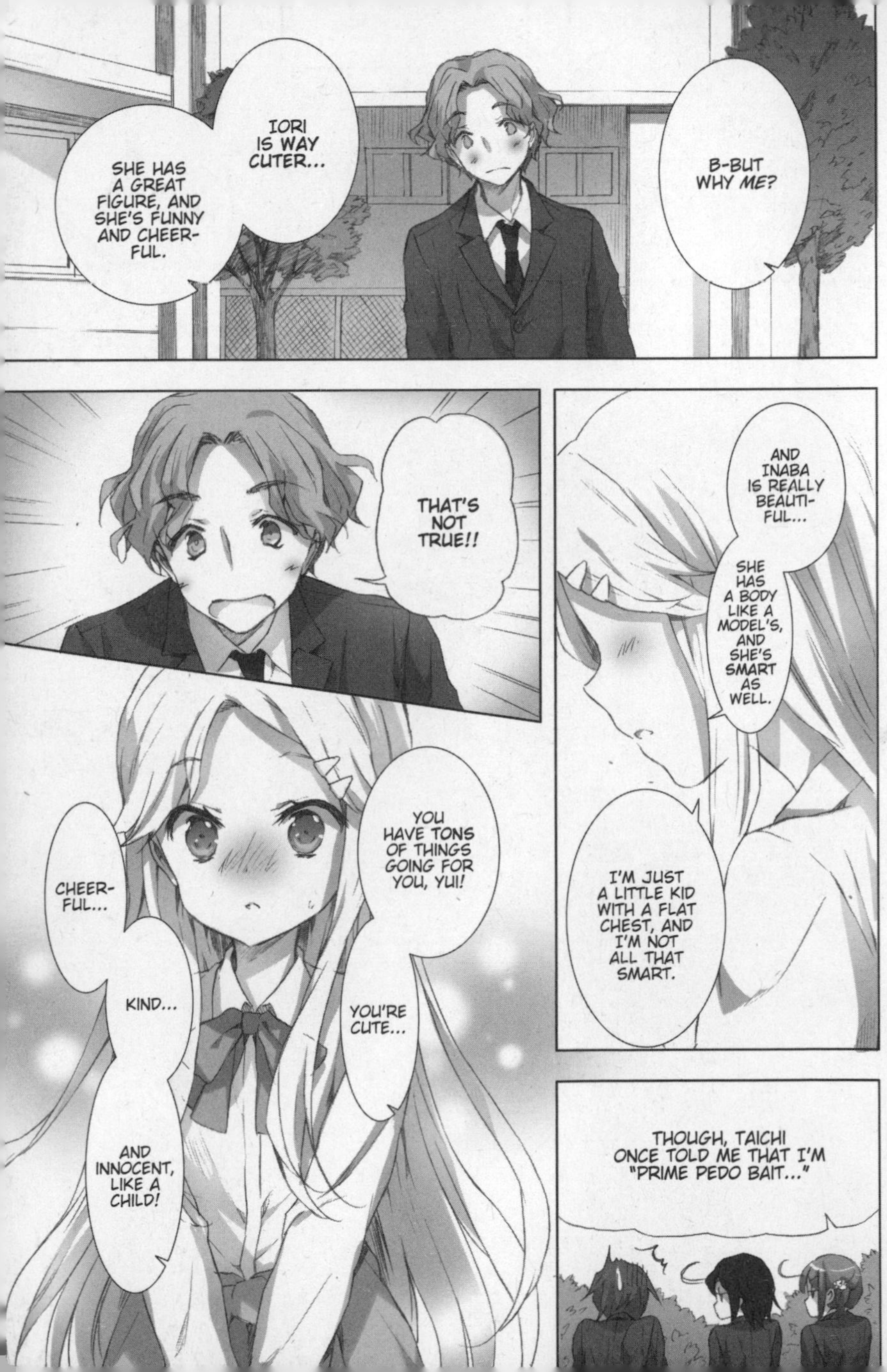
B-BUT WHY *ME*?
IORI IS WAY CUTER...
SHE HAS A GREAT FIGURE, AND SHE'S FUNNY AND CHEERFUL.
AND INABA IS REALLY BEAUTIFUL...
SHE HAS A BODY LIKE A MODEL'S, AND SHE'S SMART AS WELL.
I'M JUST A LITTLE KID WITH A FLAT CHEST, AND I'M NOT ALL THAT SMART.
THAT'S NOT TRUE!!
YOU HAVE TONS OF THINGS GOING FOR YOU, YUI!
YOU'RE CUTE...
CHEERFUL...
KIND...
AND INNOCENT, LIKE A CHILD!
THOUGH, TAICHI ONCE TOLD ME THAT I'M "PRIME PEDO BAIT..."

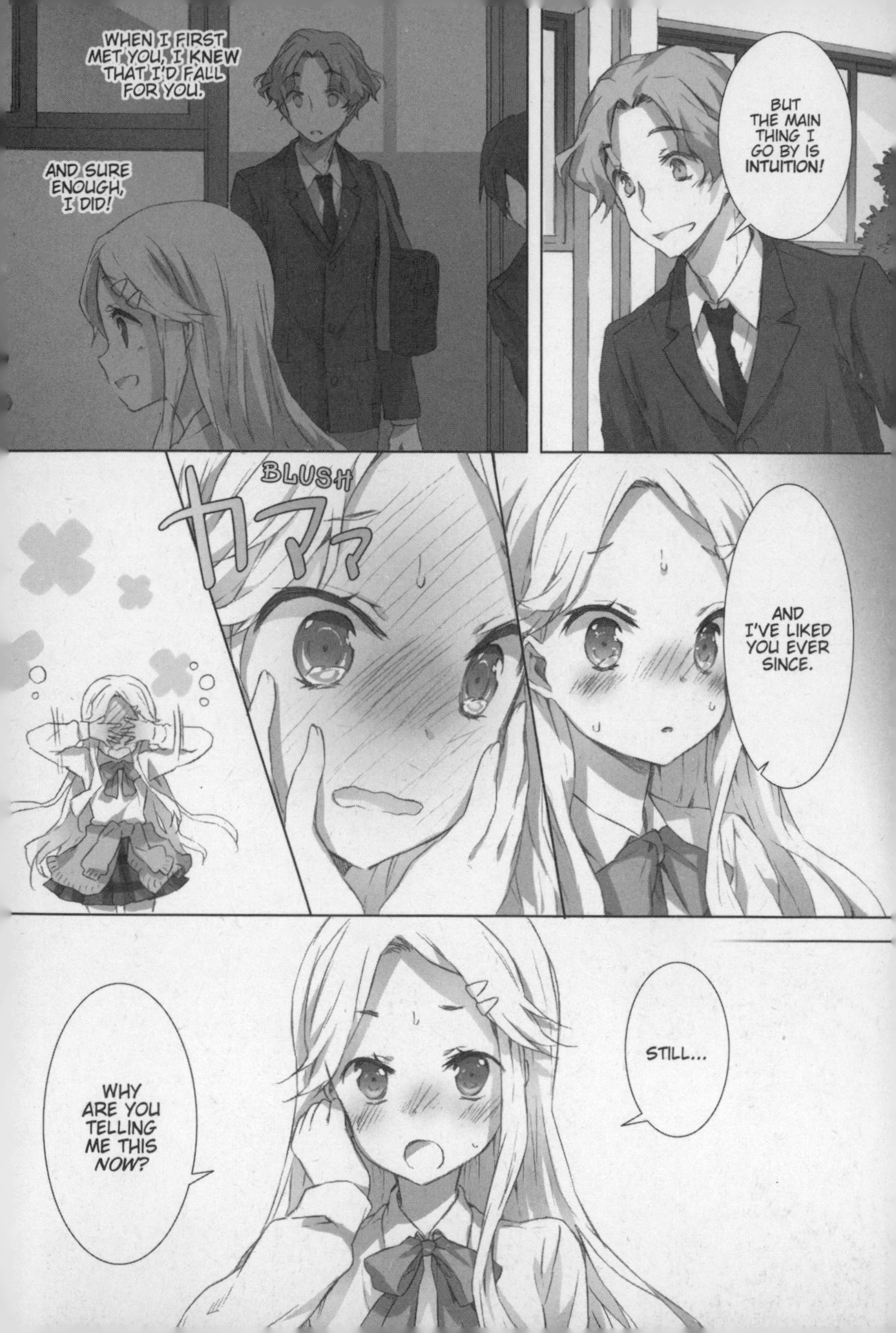
BUT THE MAIN THING I GO BY IS INTUITION!
WHEN I FIRST MET YOU, I KNEW THAT I'D FALL FOR YOU.
AND SURE ENOUGH, I DID!
AND I'VE LIKED YOU EVER SINCE.
BLUSH
STILL...
WHY ARE YOU TELLING ME THIS *NOW*?

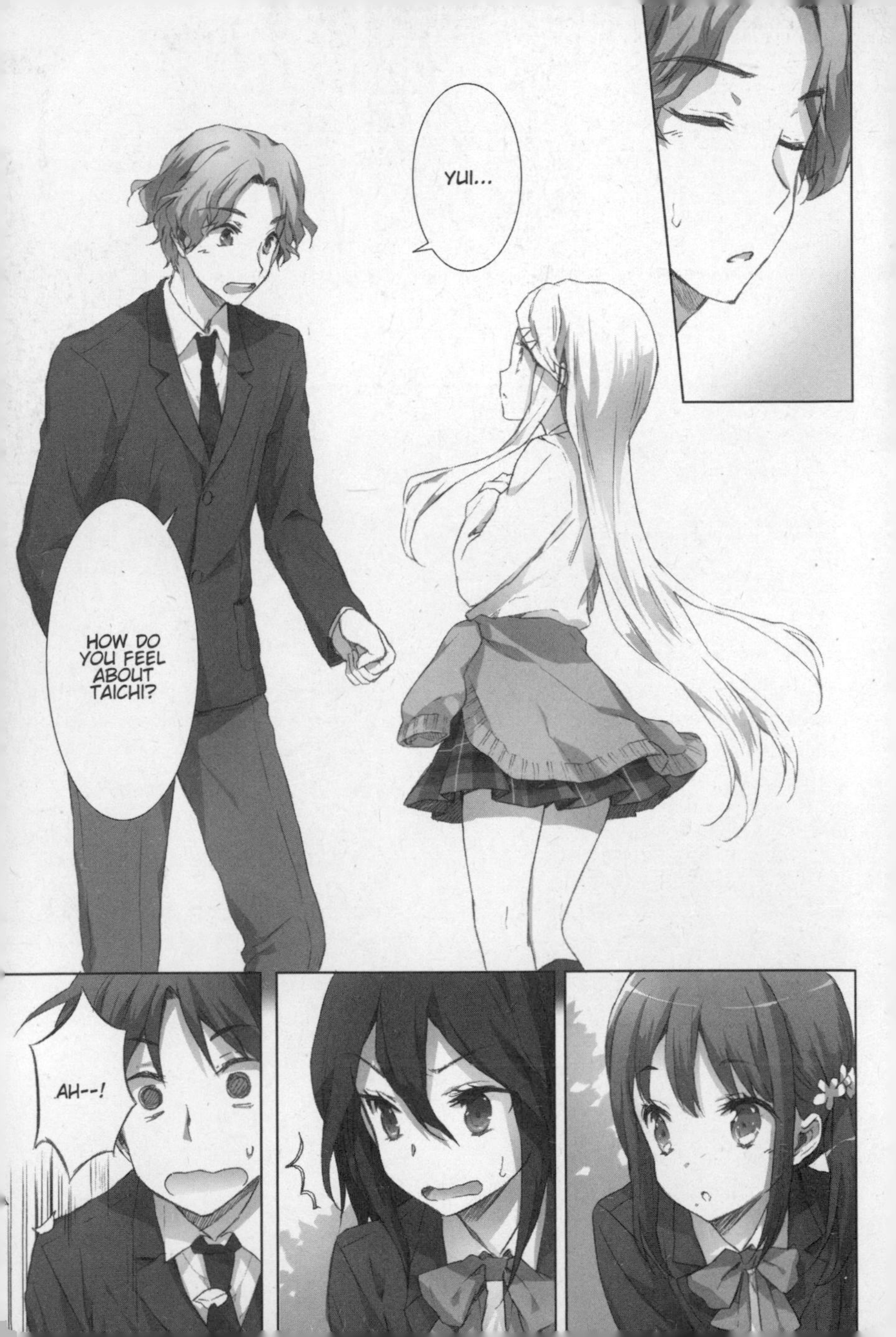
YUI...
HOW DO YOU FEEL ABOUT TAICHI?
AH--!

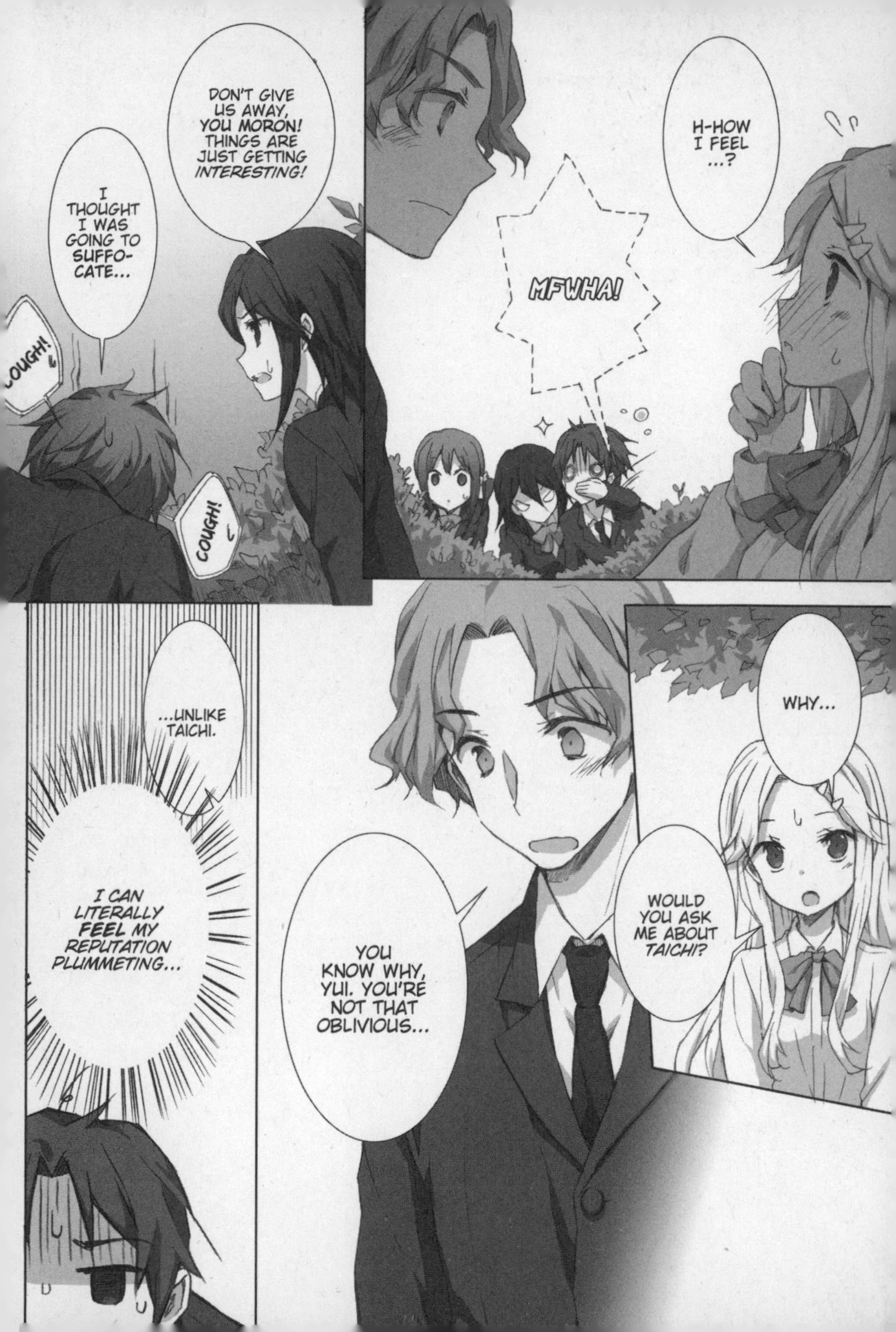
H-HOW I FEEL ...?
MFWHA!
DON'T GIVE US AWAY, YOU MORON! THINGS ARE JUST GETTING *INTERESTING!*
I THOUGHT I WAS GOING TO SUFFOCATE...
COUGH!
COUGH!
WHY...
WOULD YOU ASK ME ABOUT *TAICHI?*
YOU KNOW WHY, YUI. YOU'RE NOT THAT OBLIVIOUS...
...UNLIKE TAICHI.
I CAN LITERALLY **FEEL** *MY REPUTATION PLUMMETING...*

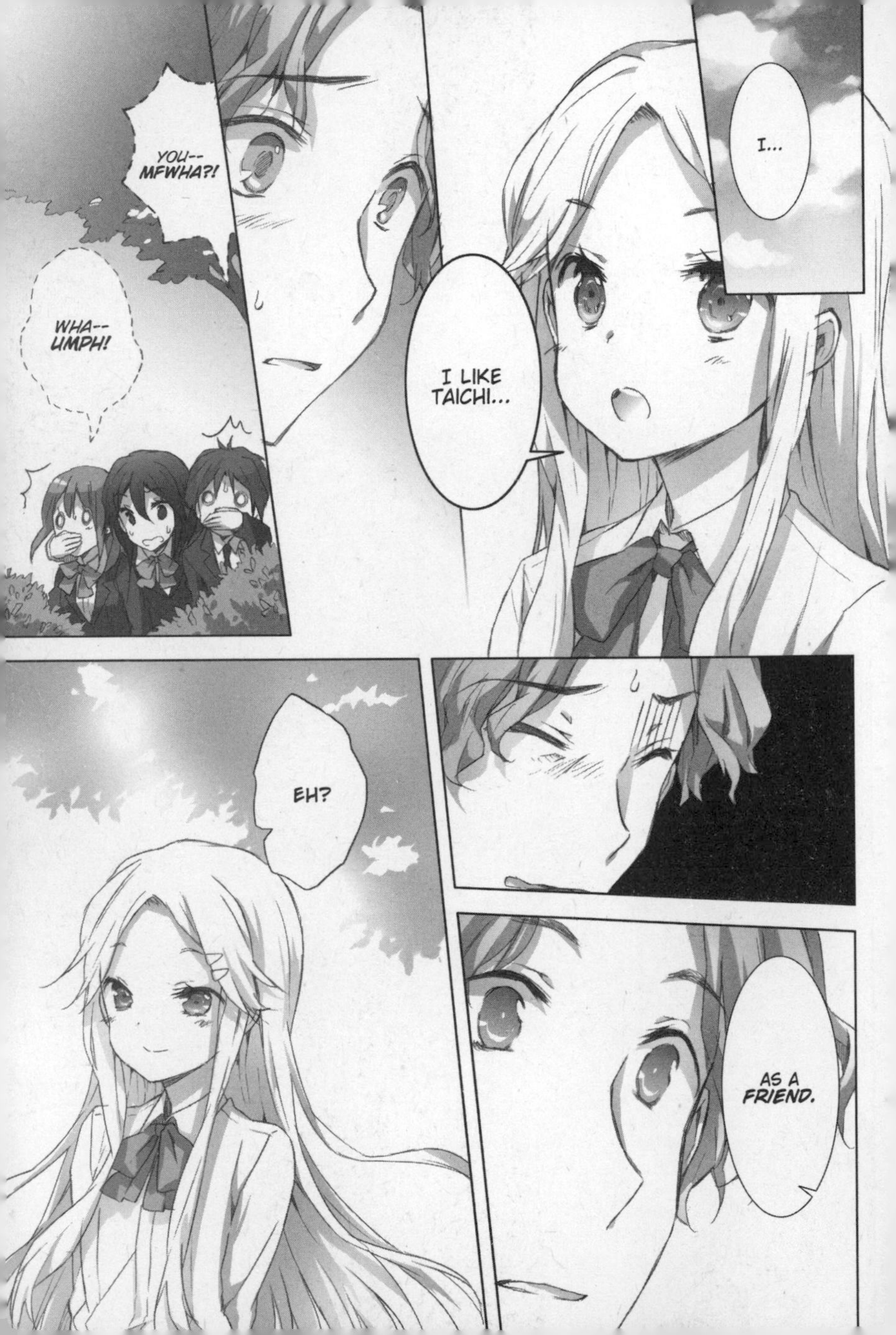
I...
I LIKE TAICHI...
YOU-- MFWHA?!
WHA-- UMPH!
AS A FRIEND.
EH?

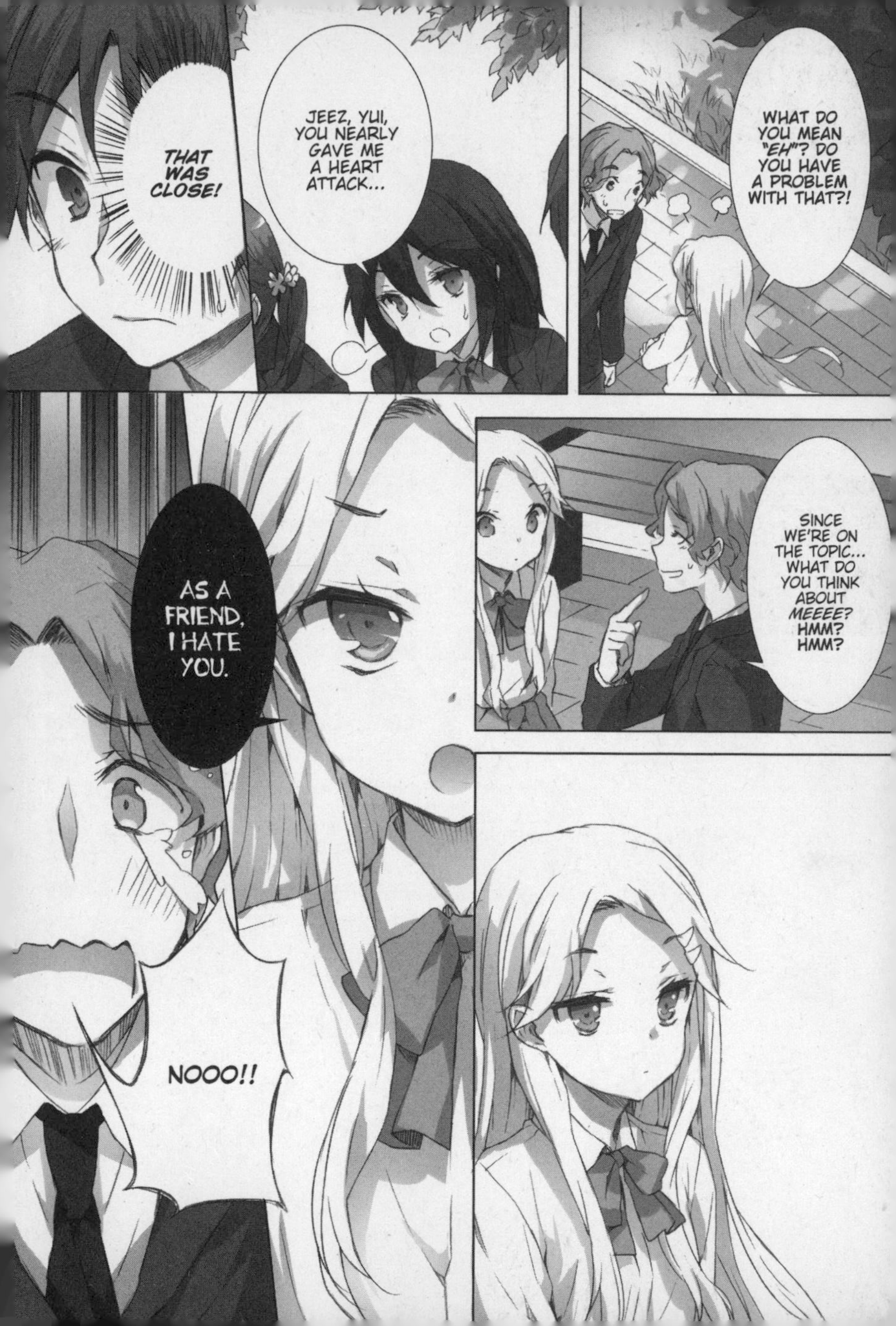
WHAT DO YOU MEAN "EH"? DO YOU HAVE A PROBLEM WITH THAT?!
JEEZ, YUI, YOU NEARLY GAVE ME A HEART ATTACK...
THAT WAS CLOSE!
SINCE WE'RE ON THE TOPIC... WHAT DO YOU THINK ABOUT MEEEE? HMM? HMM?
AS A FRIEND, I HATE YOU.
NOOO!!

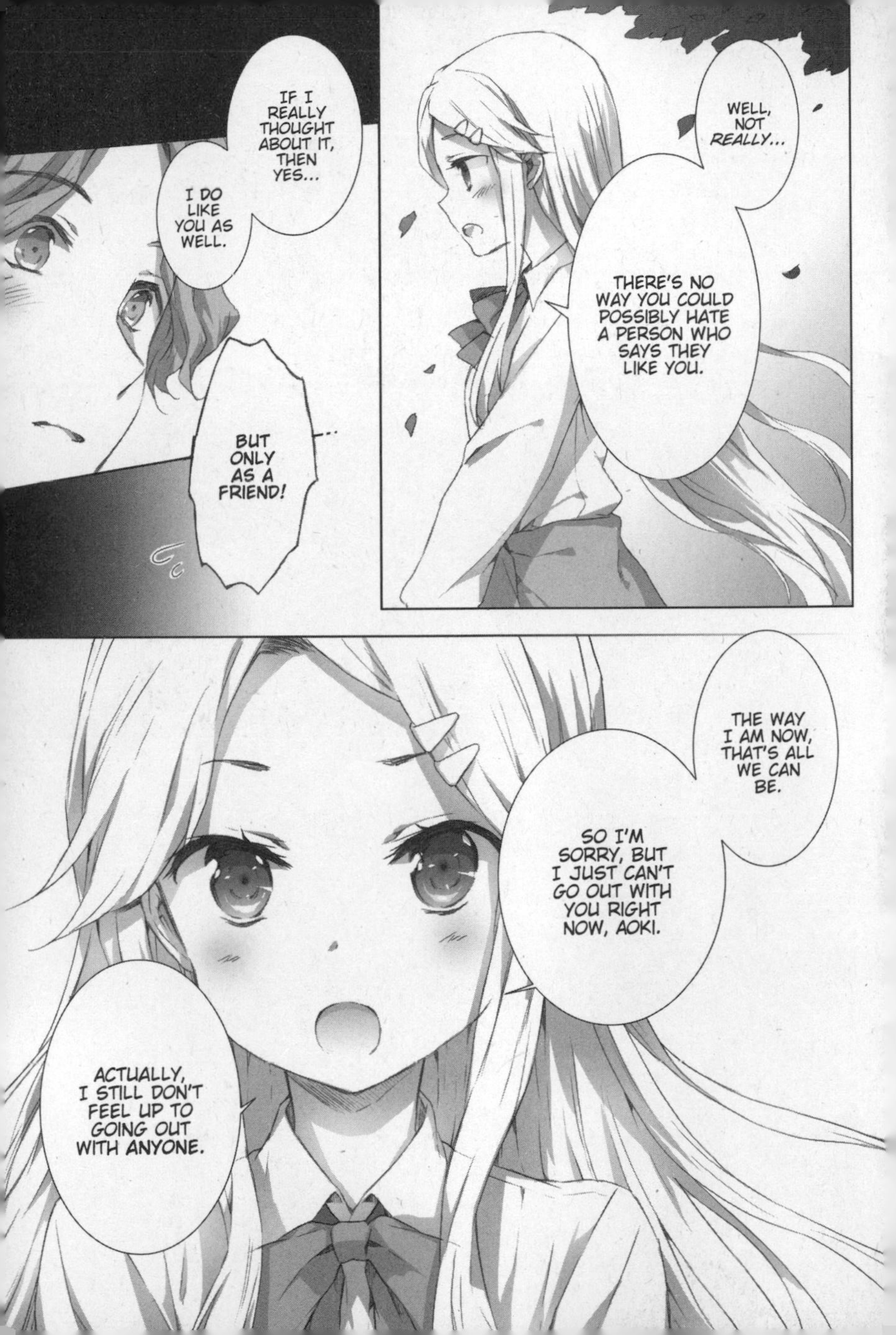
WELL, NOT *REALLY*...
THERE'S NO WAY YOU COULD POSSIBLY HATE A PERSON WHO SAYS THEY LIKE YOU.
IF I REALLY THOUGHT ABOUT IT, THEN YES...
I DO LIKE YOU AS WELL.
BUT ONLY AS A FRIEND!
THE WAY I AM NOW, THAT'S ALL WE CAN BE.
SO I'M SORRY, BUT I JUST CAN'T GO OUT WITH YOU RIGHT NOW, AOKI.
ACTUALLY, I STILL DON'T FEEL UP TO GOING OUT WITH ANYONE.

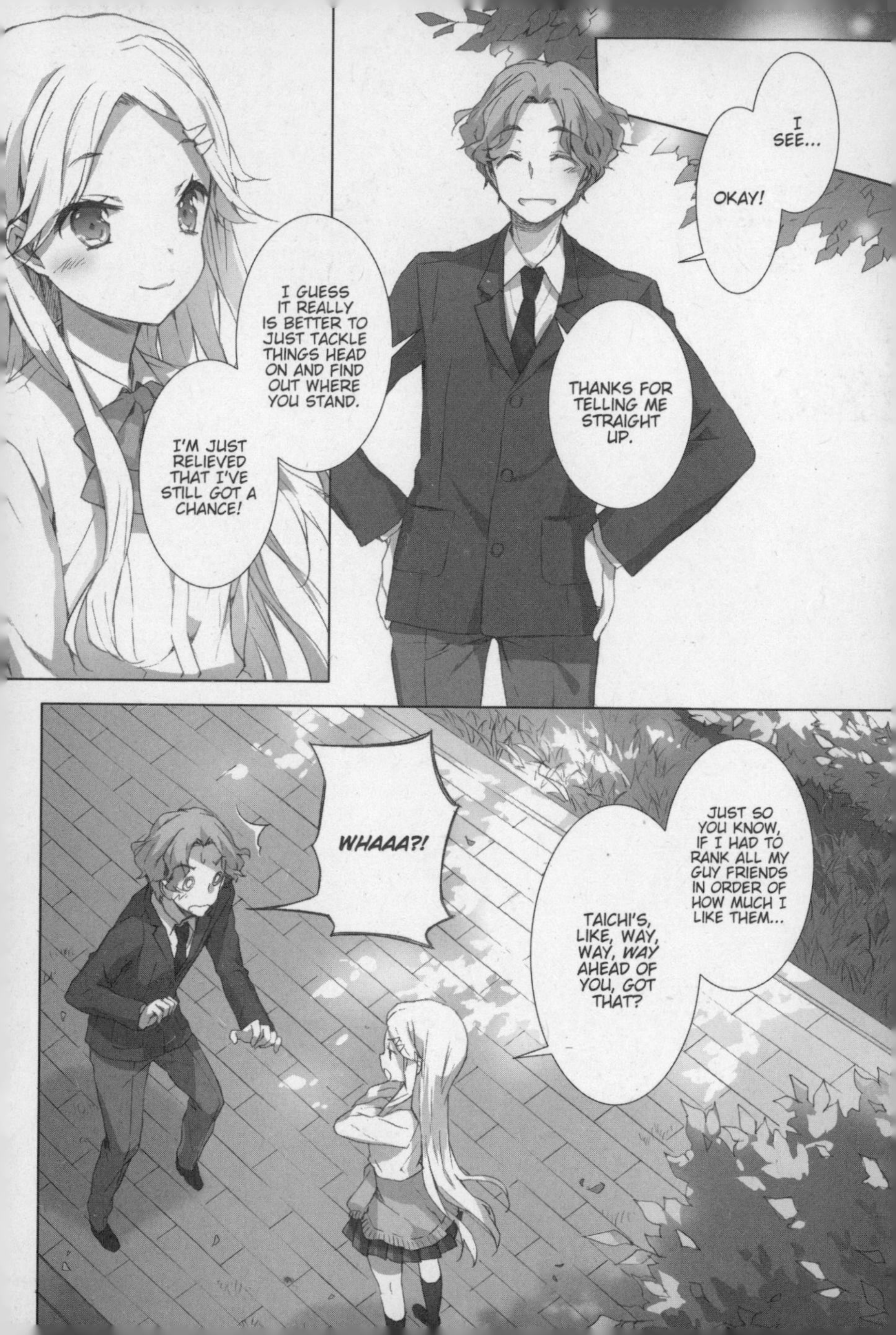
I SEE...
OKAY!
THANKS FOR TELLING ME STRAIGHT UP.
I GUESS IT REALLY IS BETTER TO JUST TACKLE THINGS HEAD ON AND FIND OUT WHERE YOU STAND.
I'M JUST RELIEVED THAT I'VE STILL GOT A CHANCE!
JUST SO YOU KNOW, IF I HAD TO RANK ALL MY GUY FRIENDS IN ORDER OF HOW MUCH I LIKE THEM...
TAICHI'S, LIKE, WAY, WAY, *WAY* AHEAD OF YOU, GOT THAT?
WHAAA?!

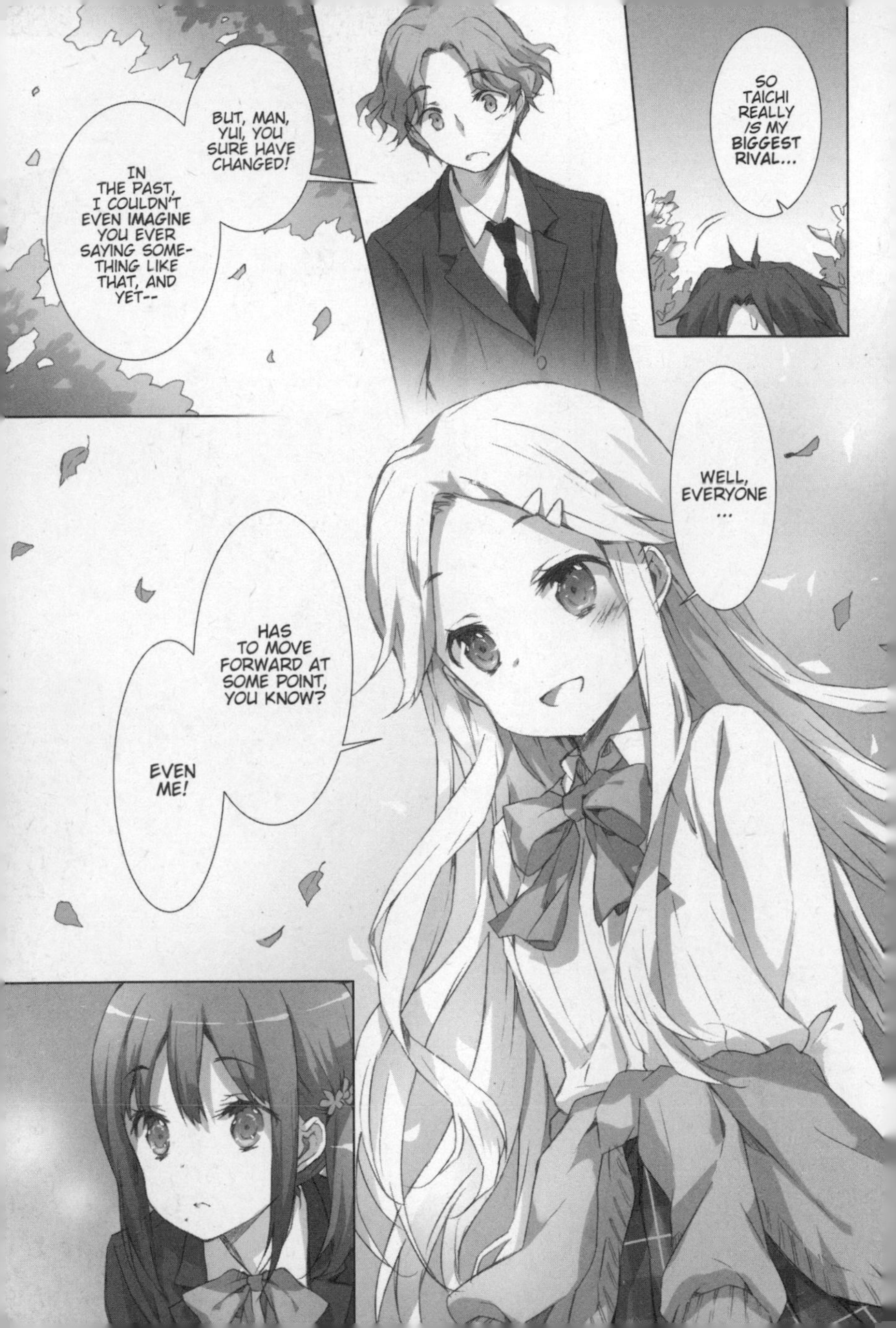
SO TAICHI REALLY IS MY BIGGEST RIVAL...
BUT, MAN, YUI, YOU SURE HAVE CHANGED!
IN THE PAST, I COULDN'T EVEN IMAGINE YOU EVER SAYING SOME-THING LIKE THAT, AND YET--
WELL, EVERYONE...
HAS TO MOVE FORWARD AT SOME POINT, YOU KNOW?
EVEN ME!

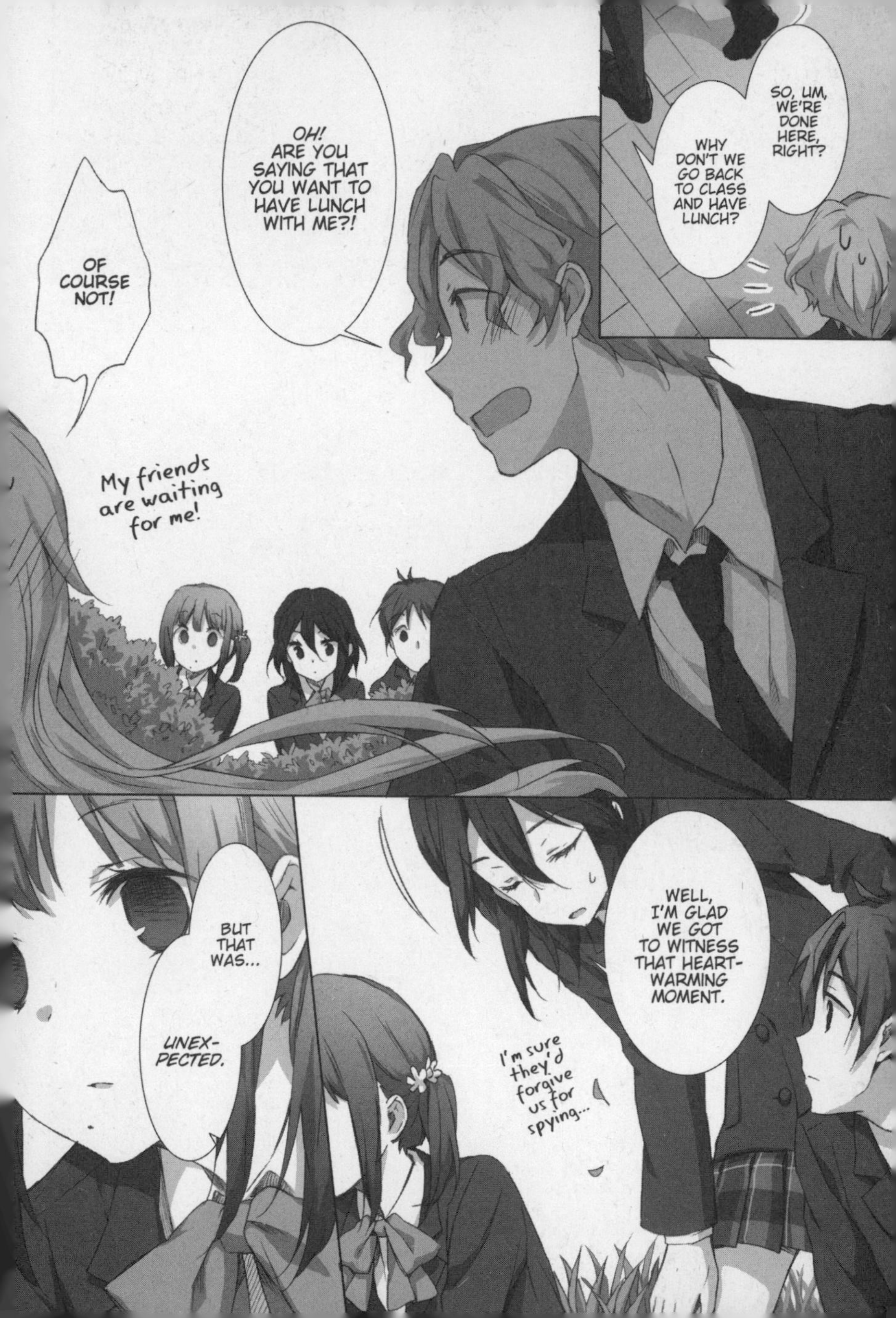
SO, UM, WE'RE DONE HERE, RIGHT?
WHY DON'T WE GO BACK TO CLASS AND HAVE LUNCH?
OH! ARE YOU SAYING THAT YOU WANT TO HAVE LUNCH WITH ME?!
OF COURSE NOT!
My friends are waiting for me!
WELL, I'M GLAD WE GOT TO WITNESS THAT HEART-WARMING MOMENT.
I'm sure they'd forgive us for spying...
BUT THAT WAS...
UNEXPECTED.

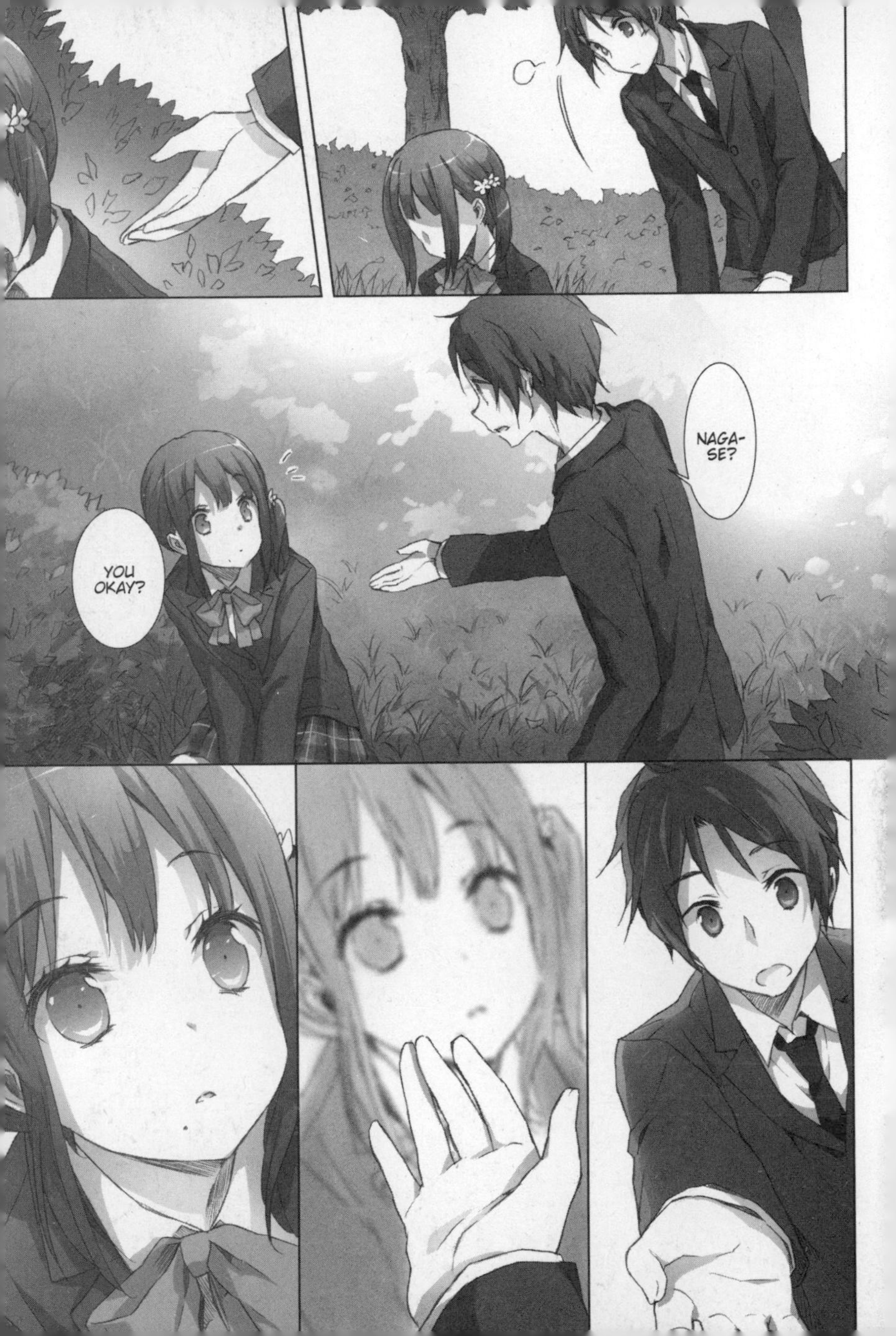
NAGA-SE?
YOU OKAY?

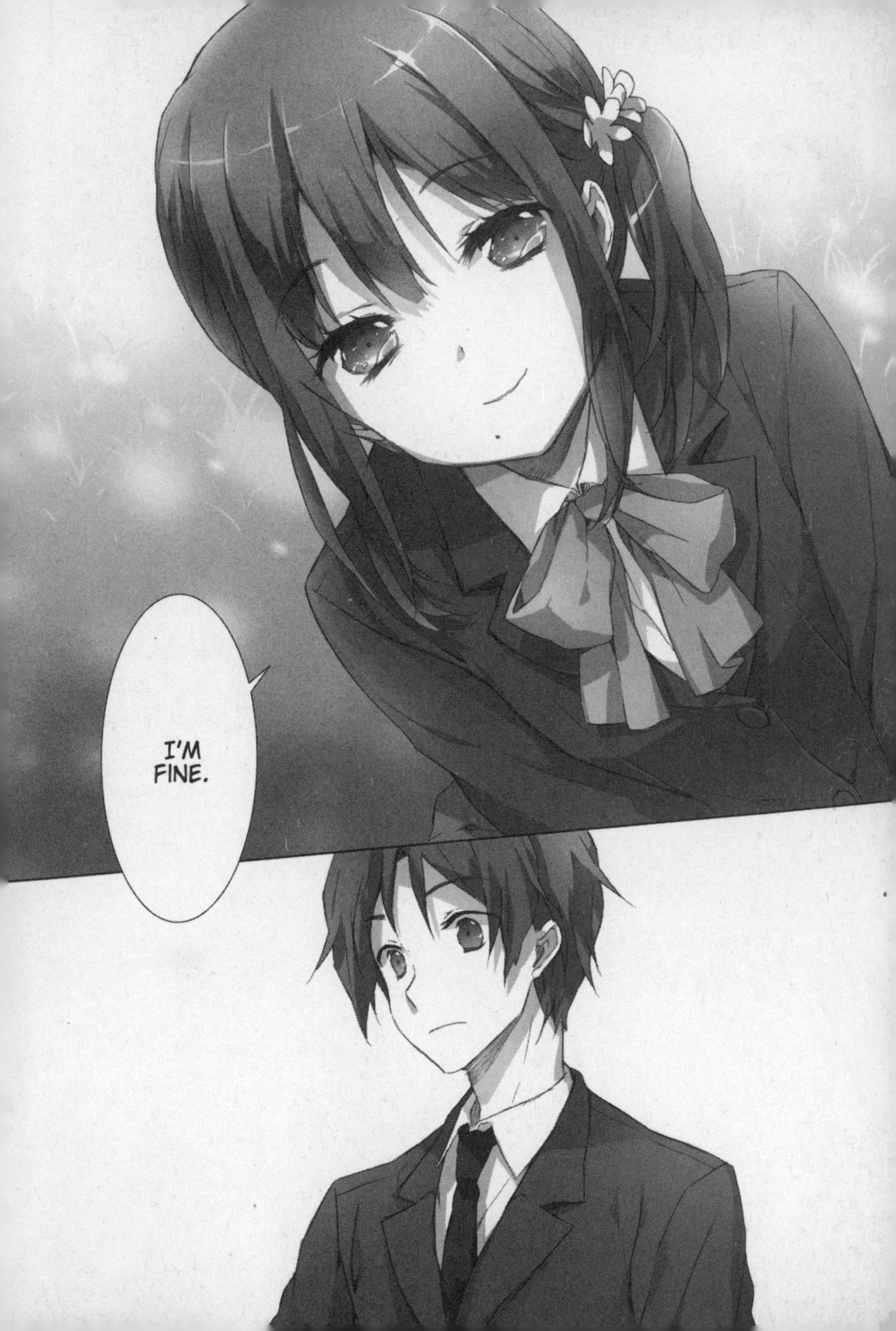
I'M FINE.

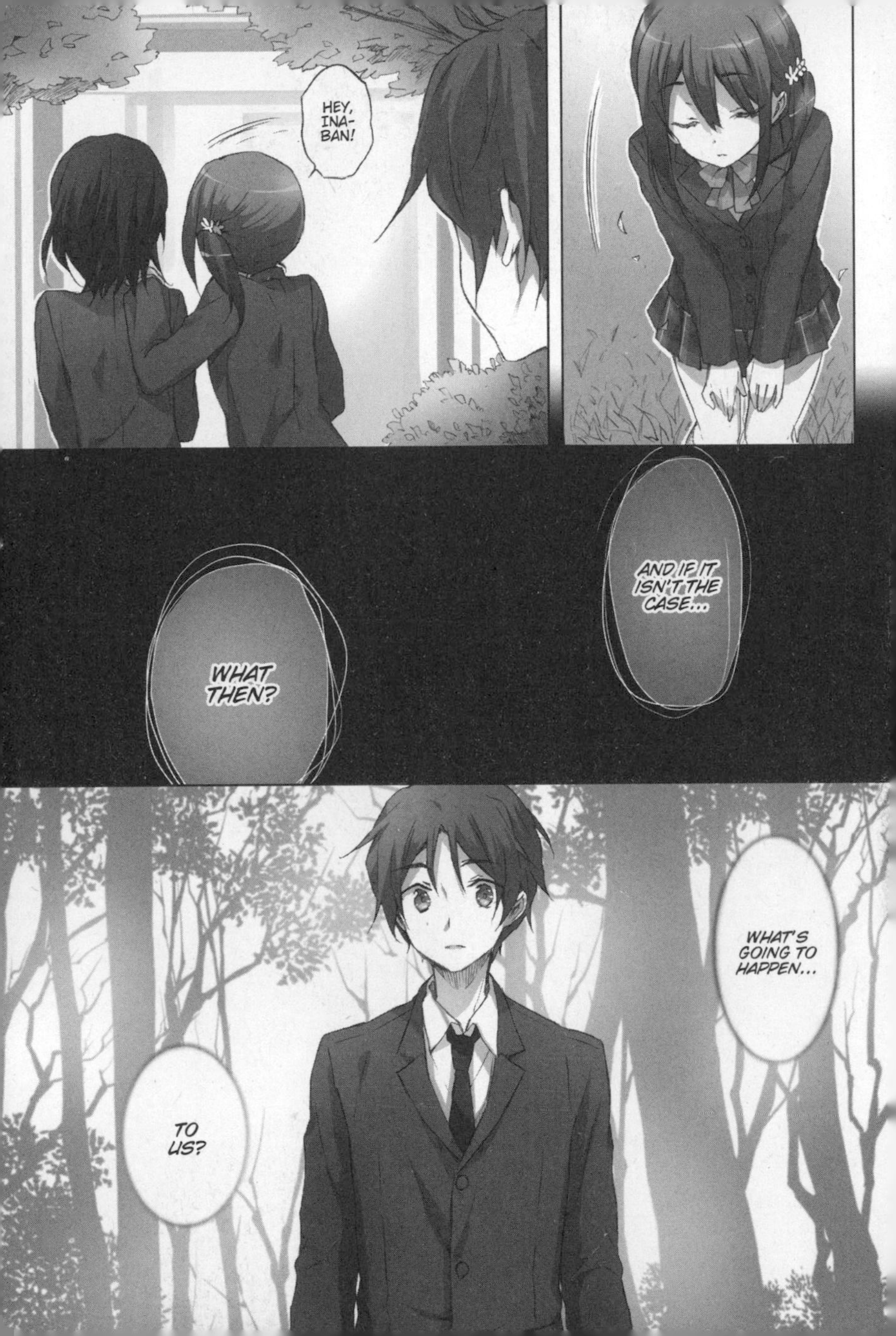
HEY, INA-BAN!
AND IF IT ISN'T THE CASE...
WHAT THEN?
WHAT'S GOING TO HAPPEN...
TO US?

KOKORO CONNECT

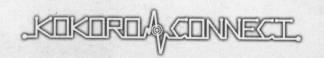

KOKORO CONNECT

Chapter 12

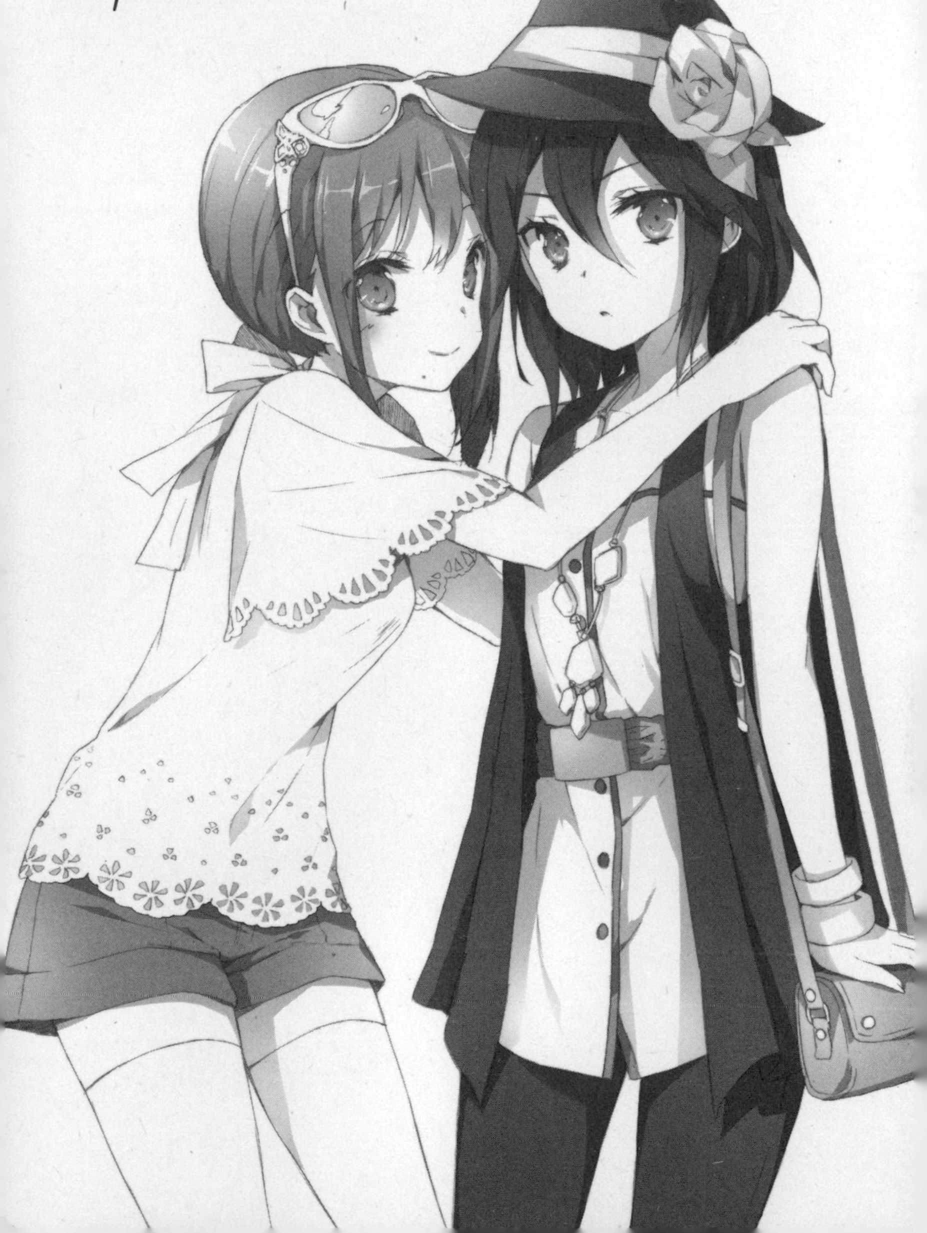

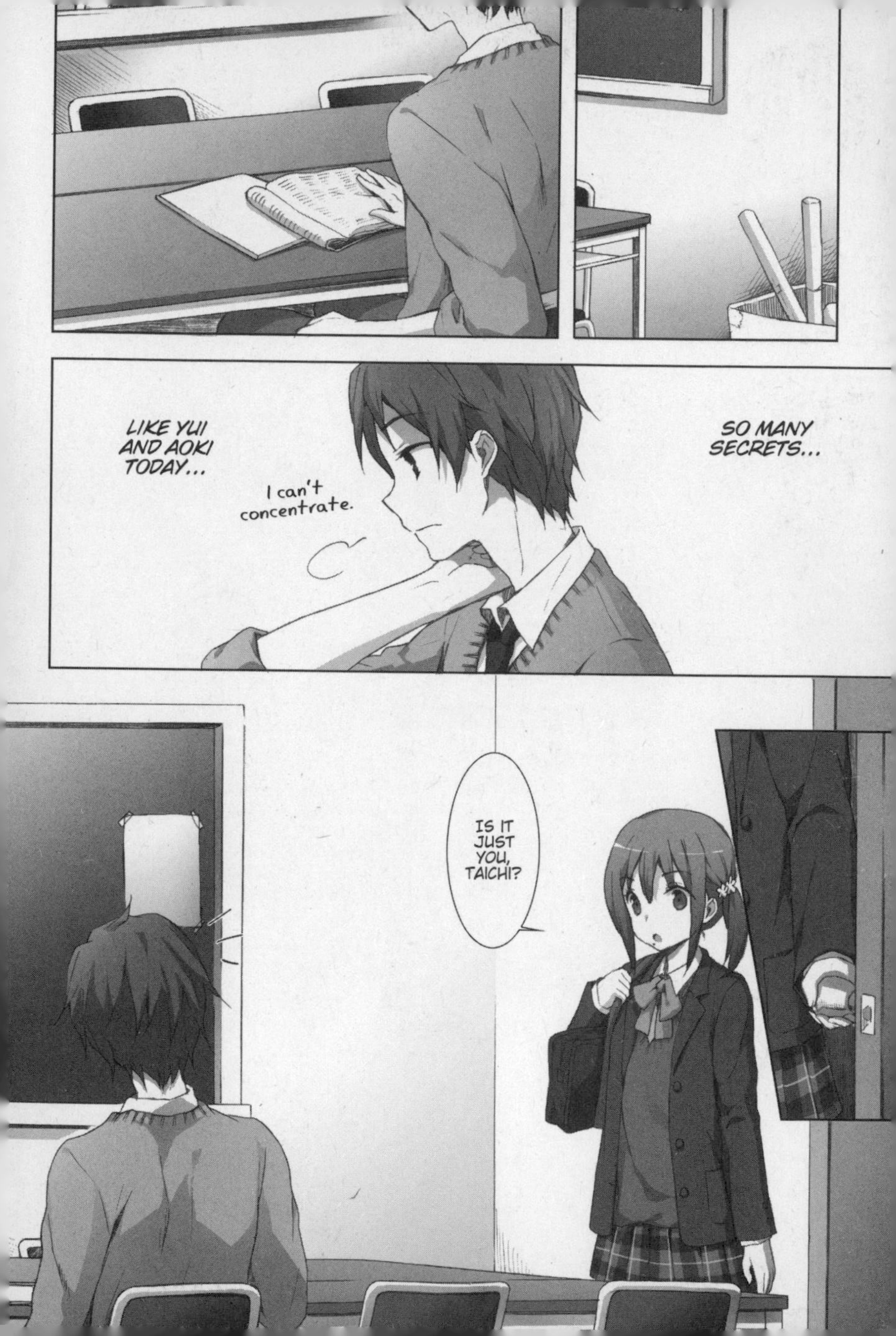
SO MANY SECRETS...
LIKE YUI AND AOKI TODAY...
I can't concentrate.
IS IT JUST YOU, TAICHI?

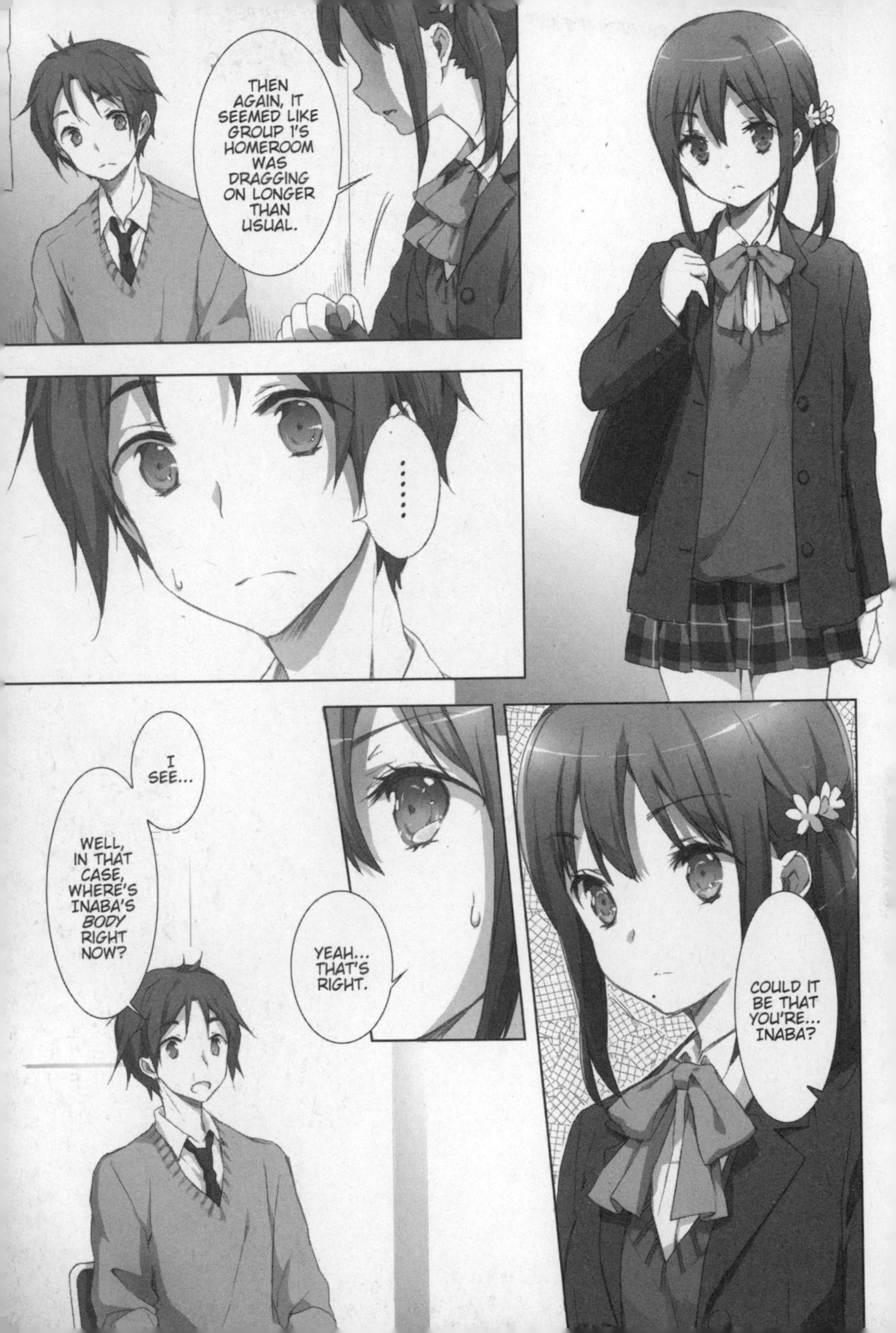
THEN AGAIN, IT SEEMED LIKE GROUP 1'S HOMEROOM WAS DRAGGING ON LONGER THAN USUAL.
......
COULD IT BE THAT YOU'RE... INABA?
YEAH... THAT'S RIGHT.
I SEE...
WELL, IN THAT CASE, WHERE'S INABA'S *BODY* RIGHT NOW?

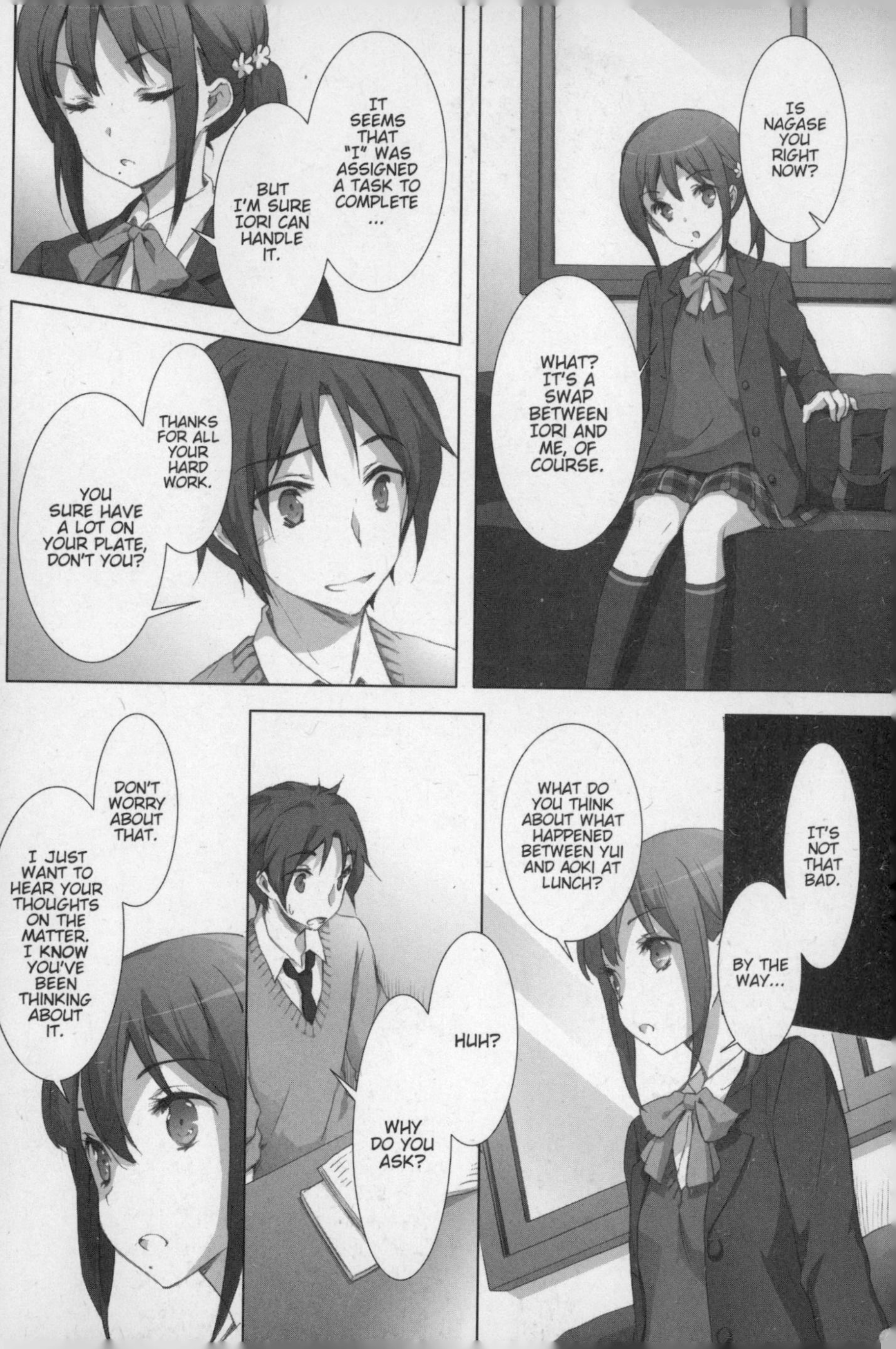
IS NAGASE YOU RIGHT NOW?
WHAT? IT'S A SWAP BETWEEN IORI AND ME, OF COURSE.
IT SEEMS THAT "I" WAS ASSIGNED A TASK TO COMPLETE...
BUT I'M SURE IORI CAN HANDLE IT.
THANKS FOR ALL YOUR HARD WORK.
YOU SURE HAVE A LOT ON YOUR PLATE, DON'T YOU?
IT'S NOT THAT BAD.
BY THE WAY...
WHAT DO YOU THINK ABOUT WHAT HAPPENED BETWEEN YUI AND AOKI AT LUNCH?
HUH?
WHY DO YOU ASK?
DON'T WORRY ABOUT THAT.
I JUST WANT TO HEAR YOUR THOUGHTS ON THE MATTER. I KNOW YOU'VE BEEN THINKING ABOUT IT.

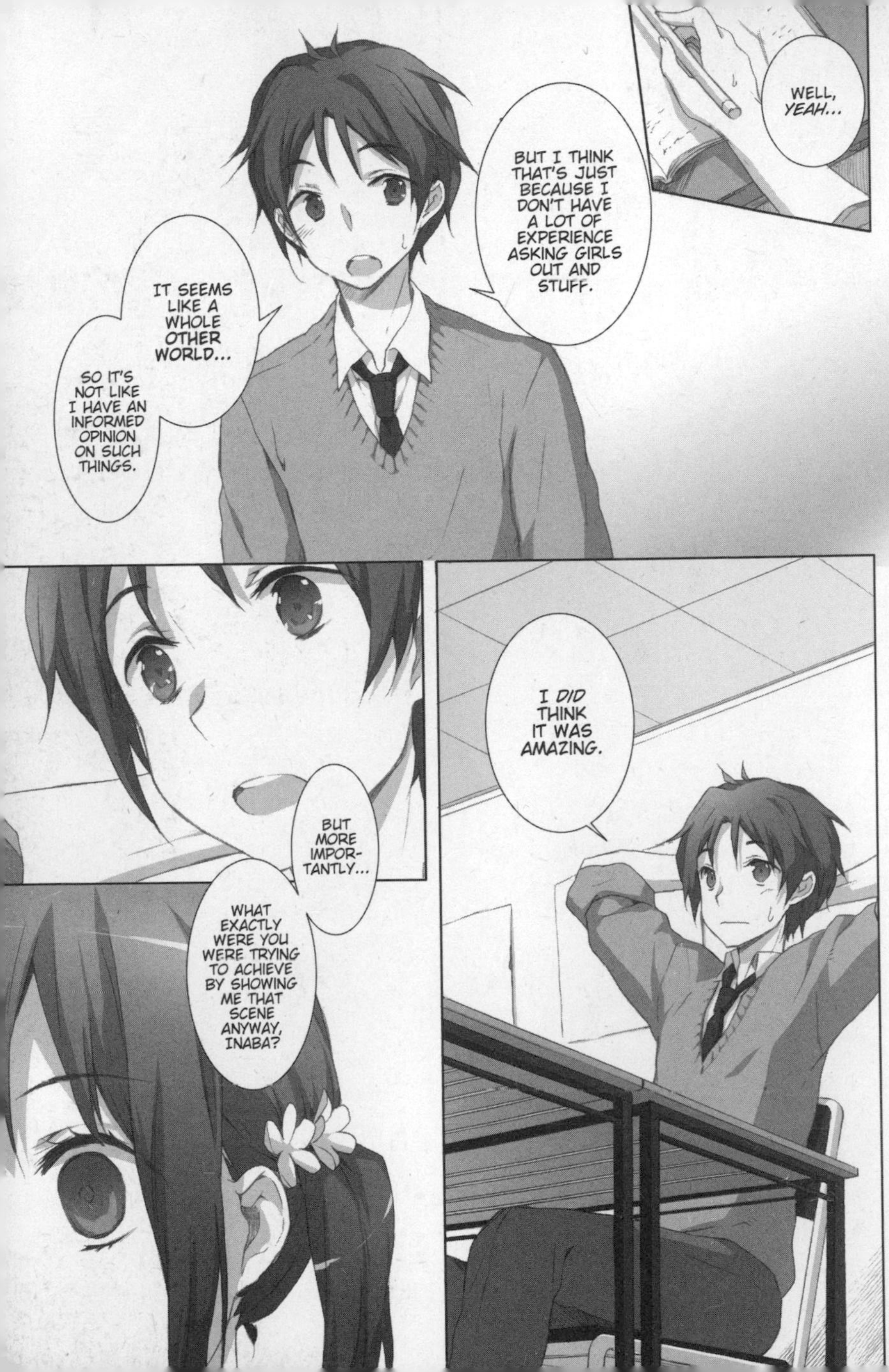
WELL, YEAH...
BUT I THINK THAT'S JUST BECAUSE I DON'T HAVE A LOT OF EXPERIENCE ASKING GIRLS OUT AND STUFF.
IT SEEMS LIKE A WHOLE OTHER WORLD...
SO IT'S NOT LIKE I HAVE AN INFORMED OPINION ON SUCH THINGS.
I *DID* THINK IT WAS AMAZING.
BUT MORE IMPOR-TANTLY...
WHAT EXACTLY WERE YOU WERE TRYING TO ACHIEVE BY SHOWING ME THAT SCENE ANYWAY, INABA?

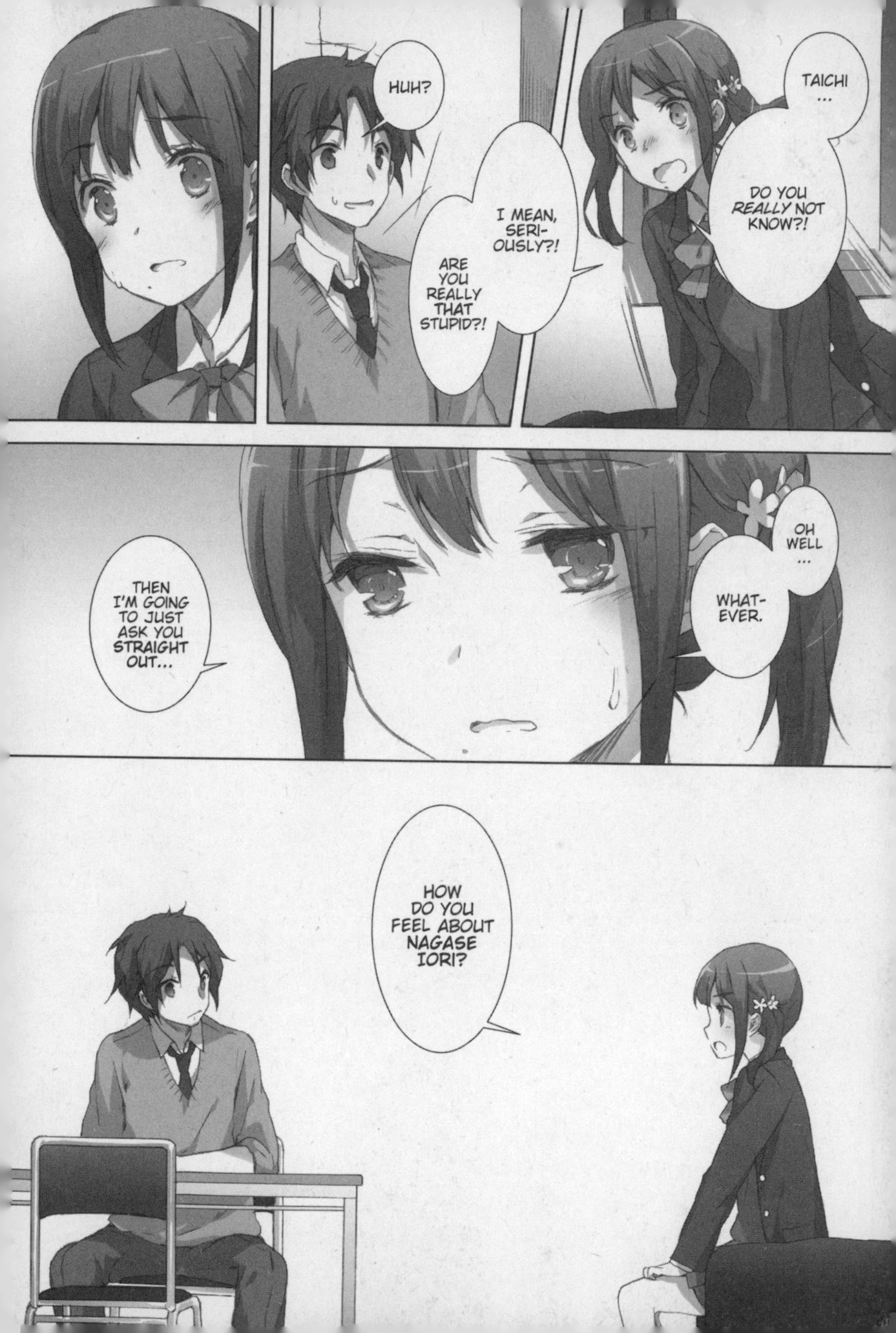
TAICHI ...
DO YOU REALLY NOT KNOW?!
HUH?
I MEAN, SERI-OUSLY?!
ARE YOU REALLY THAT STUPID?!
OH WELL ...
WHAT-EVER.
THEN I'M GOING TO JUST ASK YOU STRAIGHT OUT...
HOW DO YOU FEEL ABOUT NAGASE IORI?

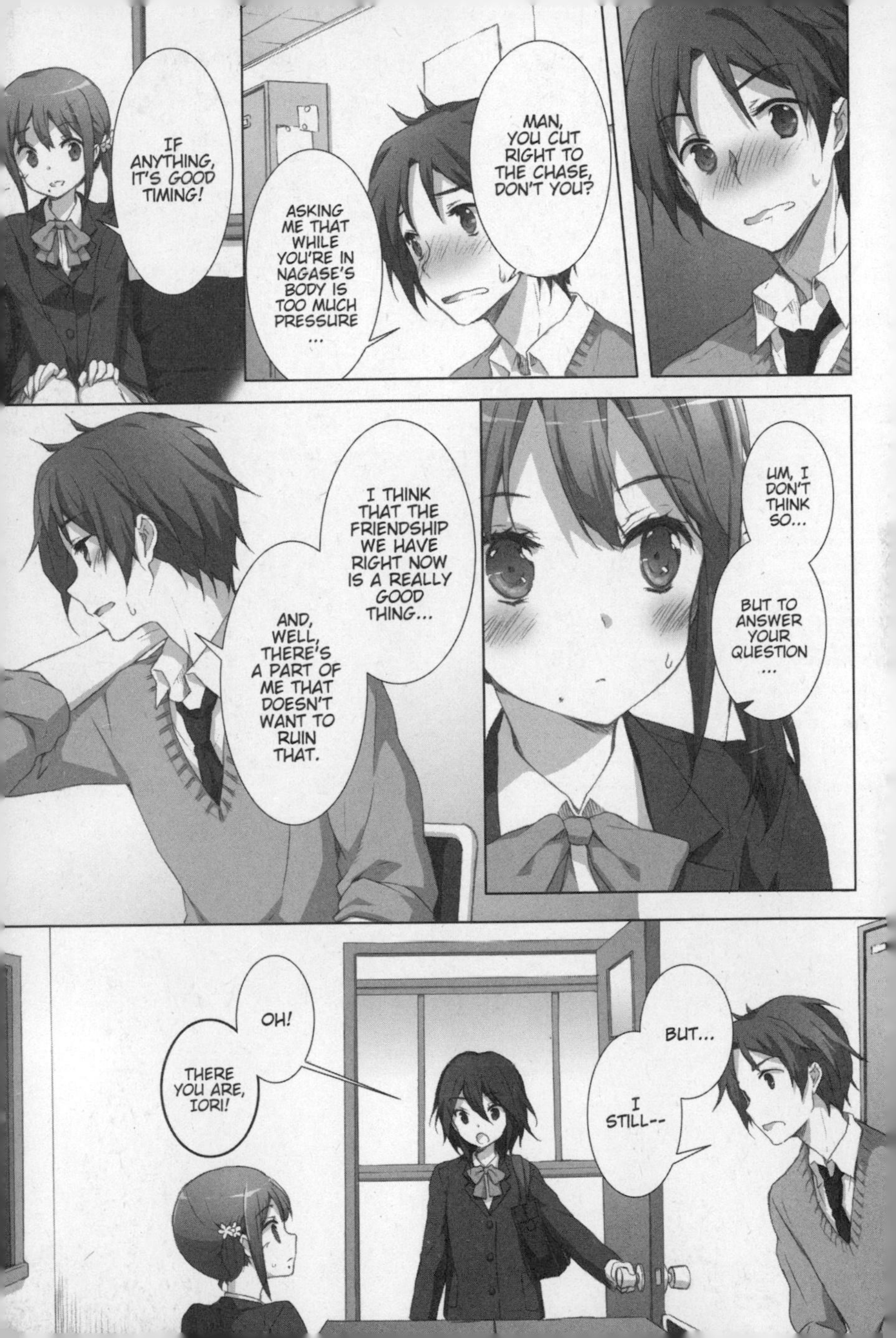
MAN, YOU CUT RIGHT TO THE CHASE, DON'T YOU?
ASKING ME THAT WHILE YOU'RE IN NAGASE'S BODY IS TOO MUCH PRESSURE...
IF ANYTHING, IT'S GOOD TIMING!
UM, I DON'T THINK SO...
BUT TO ANSWER YOUR QUESTION...
I THINK THAT THE FRIENDSHIP WE HAVE RIGHT NOW IS A REALLY GOOD THING...
AND, WELL, THERE'S A PART OF ME THAT DOESN'T WANT TO RUIN THAT.
BUT...
I STILL--
OH!
THERE YOU ARE, IORI!

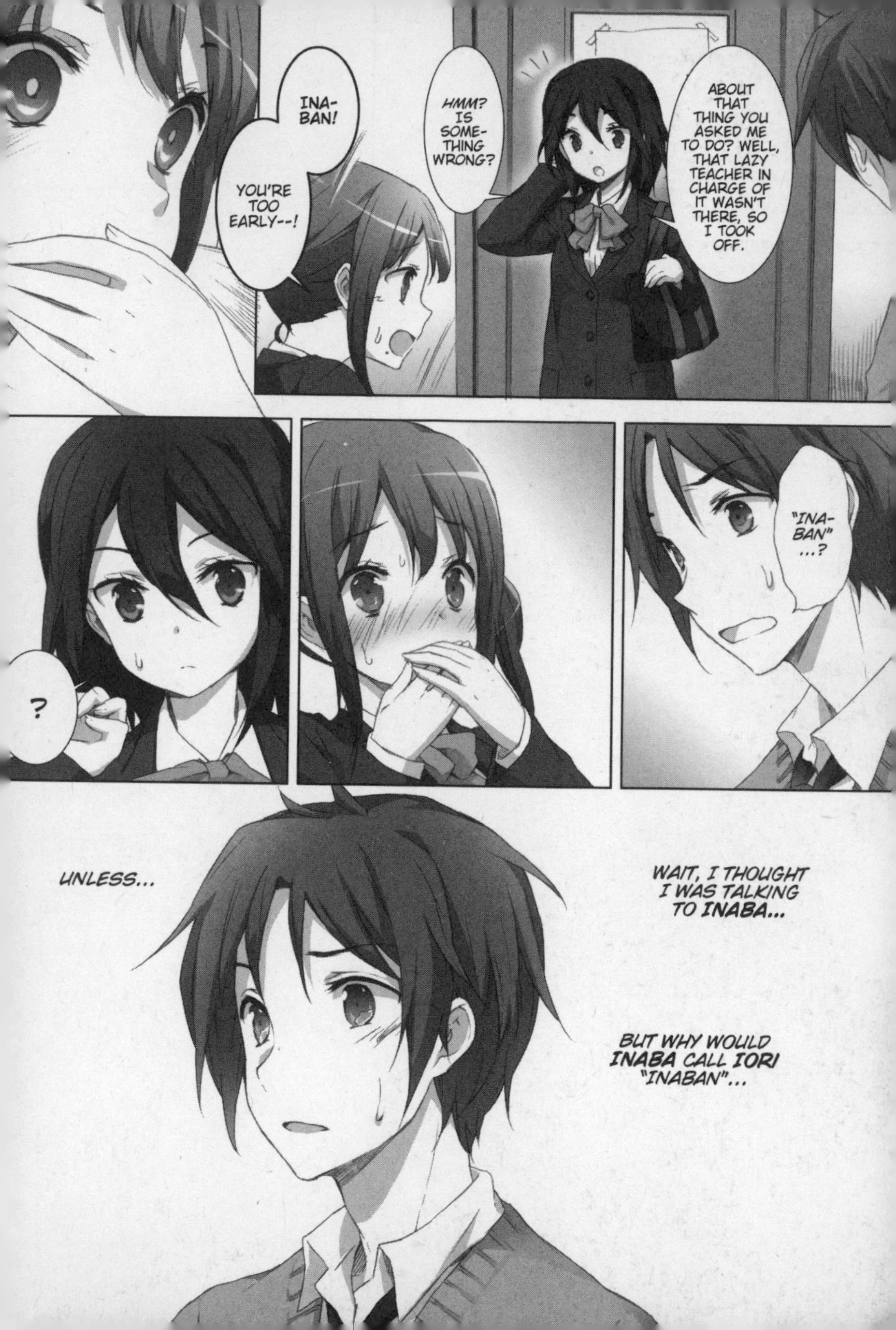
ABOUT THAT THING YOU ASKED ME TO DO? WELL, THAT LAZY TEACHER IN CHARGE OF IT WASN'T THERE, SO I TOOK OFF.
HMM? IS SOME-THING WRONG?
INA-BAN!
YOU'RE TOO EARLY--!
"INA-BAN" ...?
?
WAIT, I THOUGHT I WAS TALKING TO **INABA**...
BUT WHY WOULD **INABA** CALL **IORI** "**INABAN**"...
UNLESS...

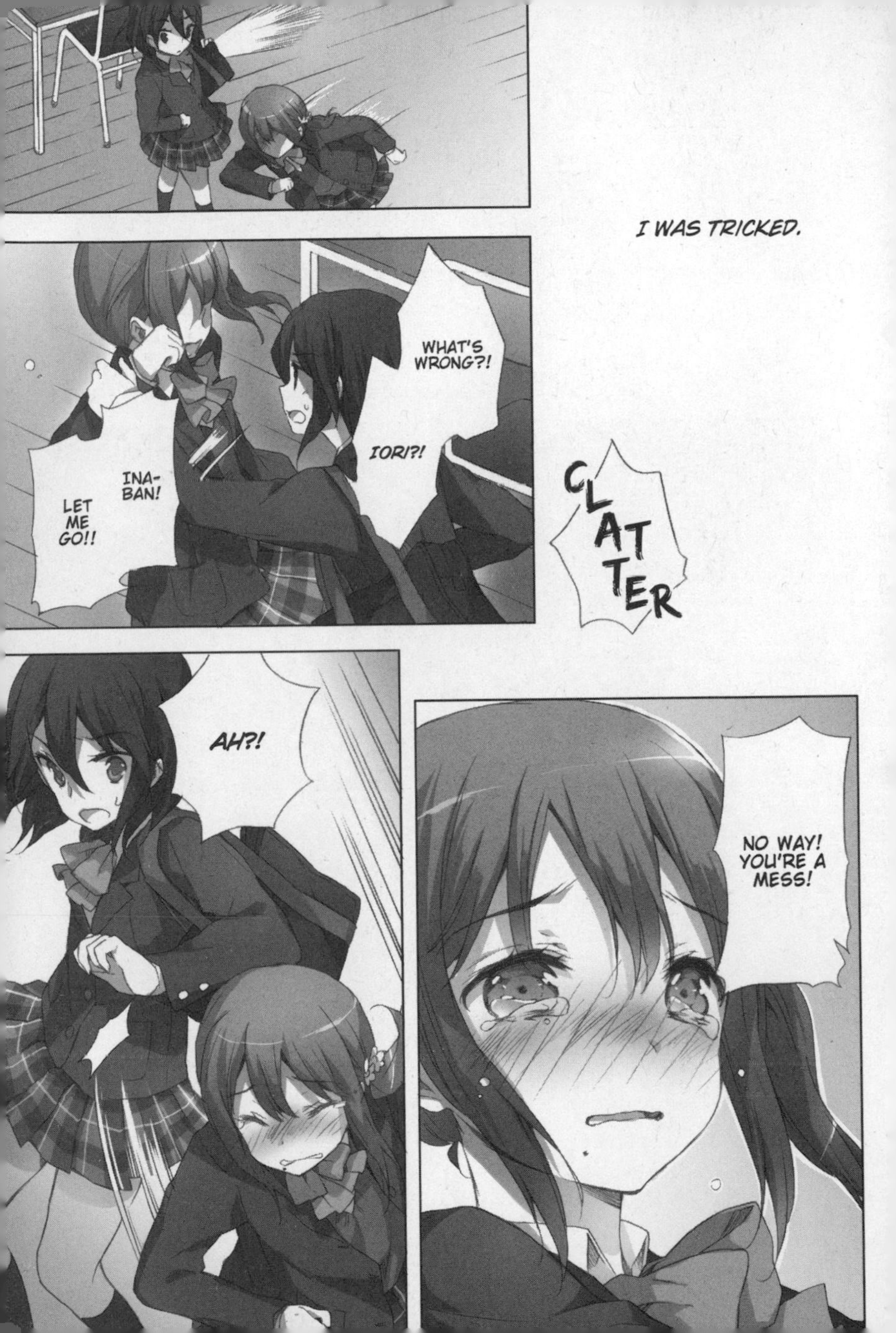
I WAS TRICKED.
CLATTER
WHAT'S WRONG?!
IORI?!
INA-BAN! LET ME GO!!
NO WAY! YOU'RE A MESS!
AH?!

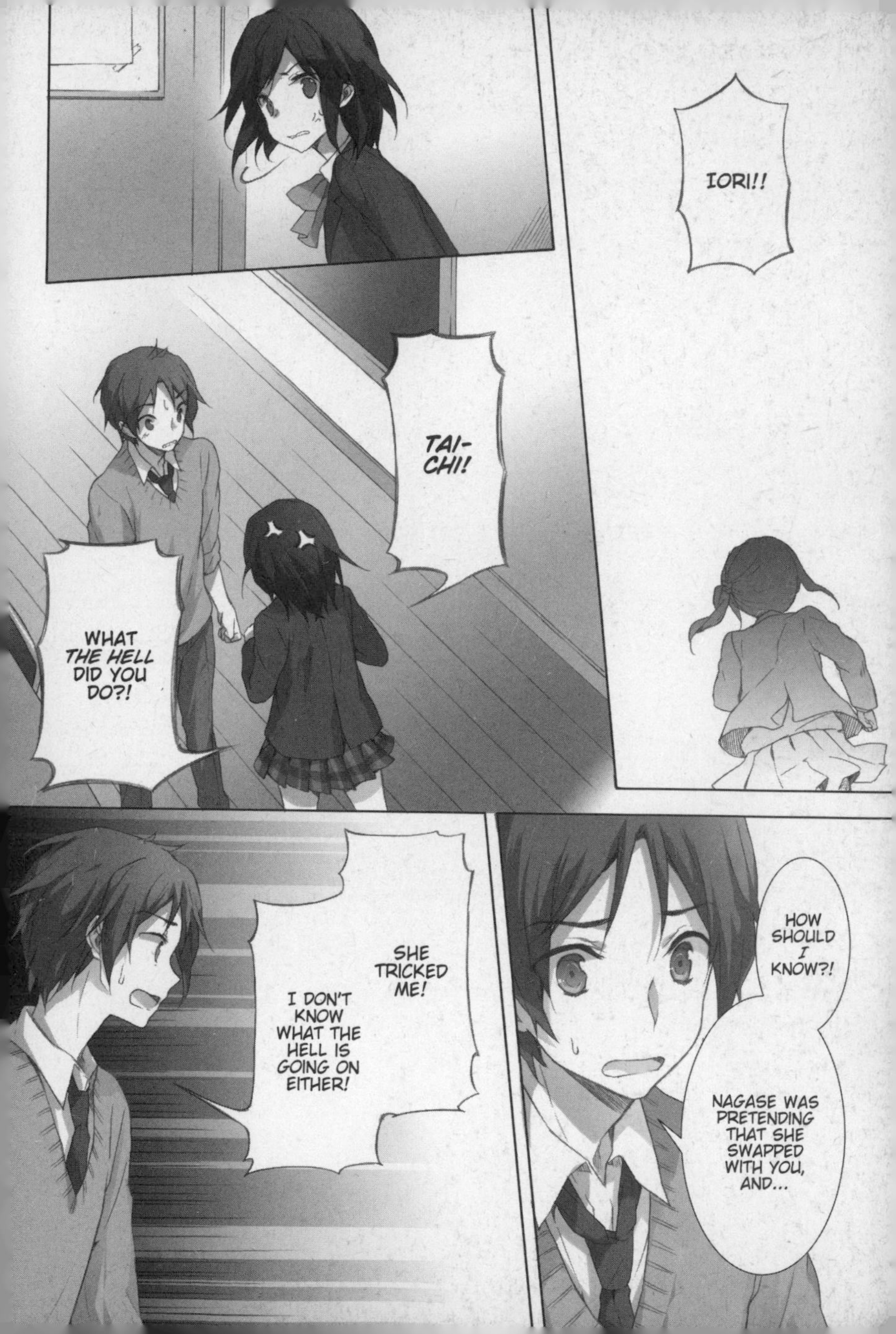
IORI!!
TAI-CHI!
WHAT THE HELL DID YOU DO?!
HOW SHOULD I KNOW?!
NAGASE WAS PRETENDING THAT SHE SWAPPED WITH YOU, AND...
SHE TRICKED ME!
I DON'T KNOW WHAT THE HELL IS GOING ON EITHER!

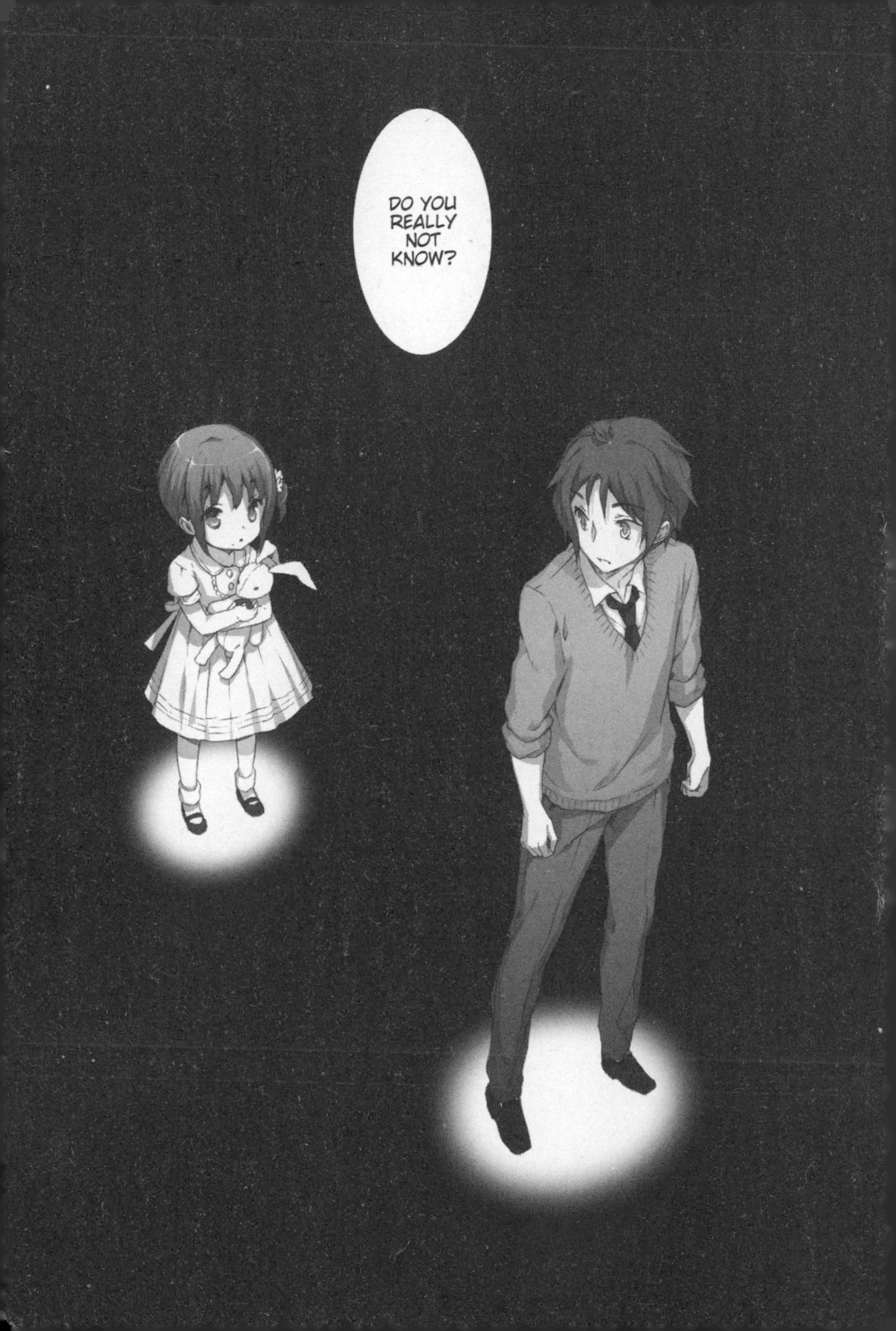
DO YOU REALLY NOT KNOW?

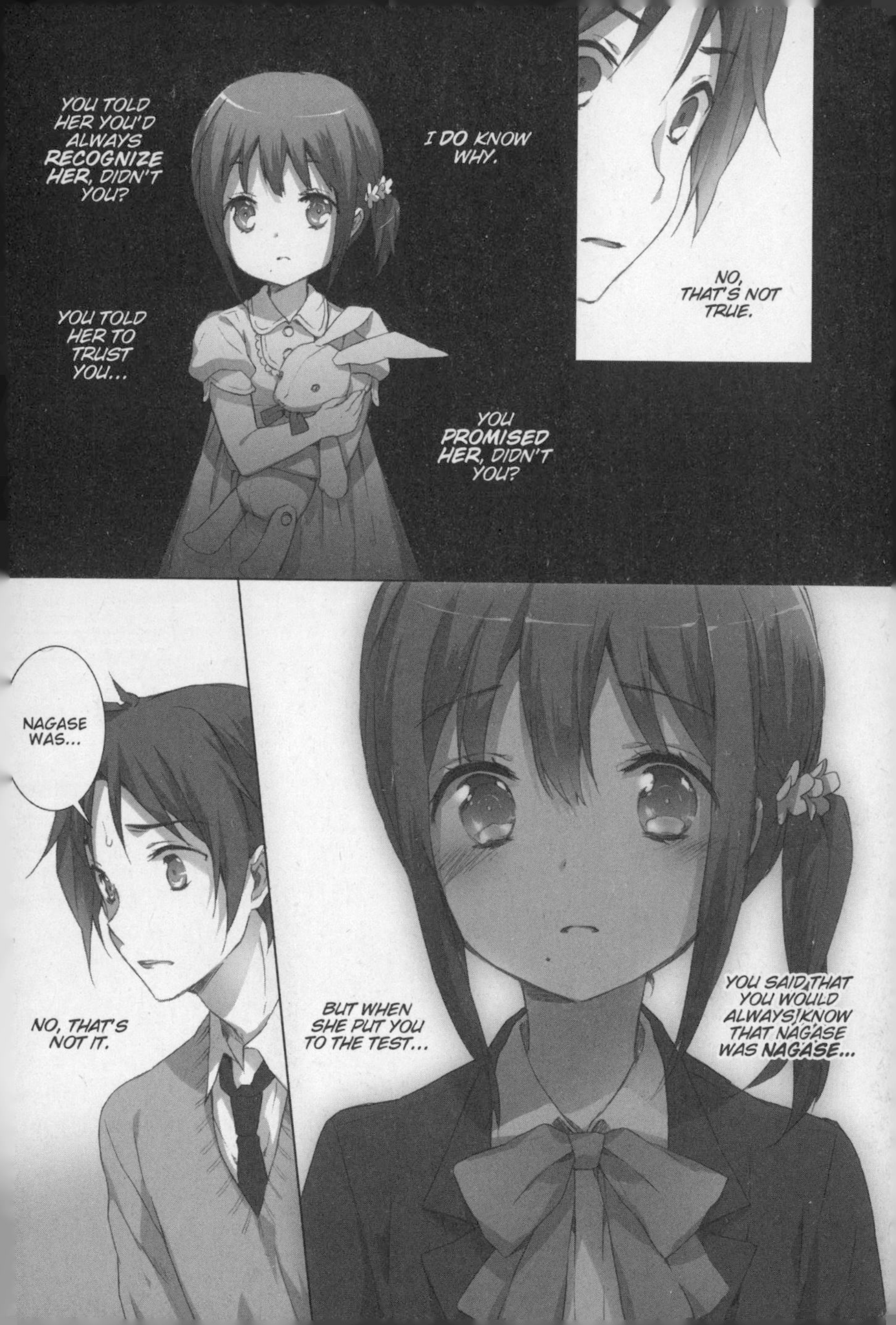
NO, THAT'S NOT TRUE.
I DO KNOW WHY.
YOU TOLD HER YOU'D ALWAYS RECOGNIZE HER, DIDN'T YOU?
YOU TOLD HER TO TRUST YOU...
YOU PROMISED HER, DIDN'T YOU?
YOU SAID THAT YOU WOULD ALWAYS KNOW THAT NAGASE WAS NAGASE...
BUT WHEN SHE PUT YOU TO THE TEST...
NAGASE WAS...
NO, THAT'S NOT IT.

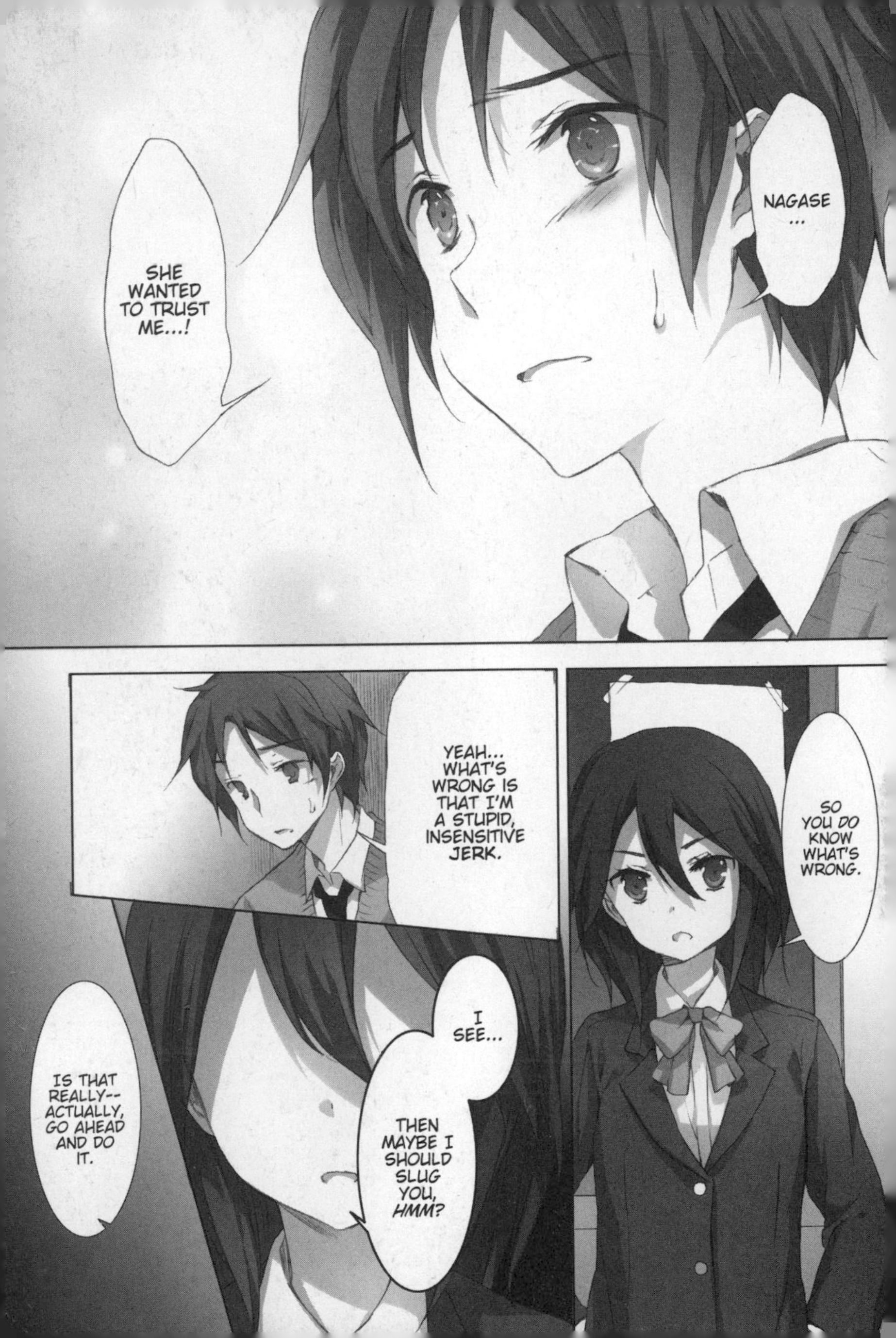
NAGASE ...
SHE WANTED TO TRUST ME...!
SO YOU *DO* KNOW WHAT'S WRONG.
YEAH... WHAT'S WRONG IS THAT I'M A STUPID, INSENSITIVE JERK.
I SEE...
THEN MAYBE I SHOULD SLUG YOU, *HMM?*
IS THAT REALLY-- ACTUALLY, GO AHEAD AND DO IT.

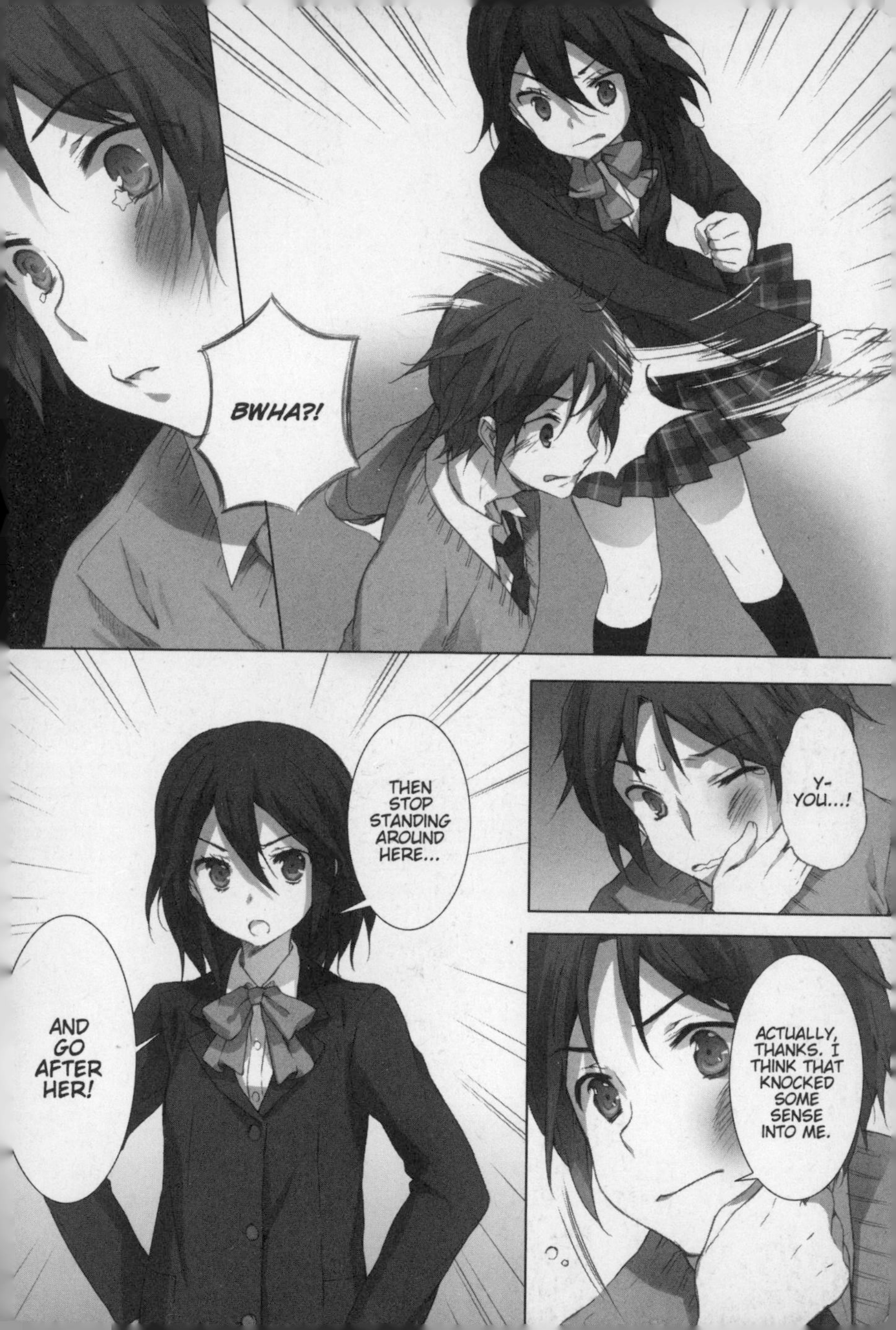
BWHA?!
Y-YOU...!
ACTUALLY, THANKS. I THINK THAT KNOCKED SOME SENSE INTO ME.
THEN STOP STANDING AROUND HERE...
AND GO AFTER HER!

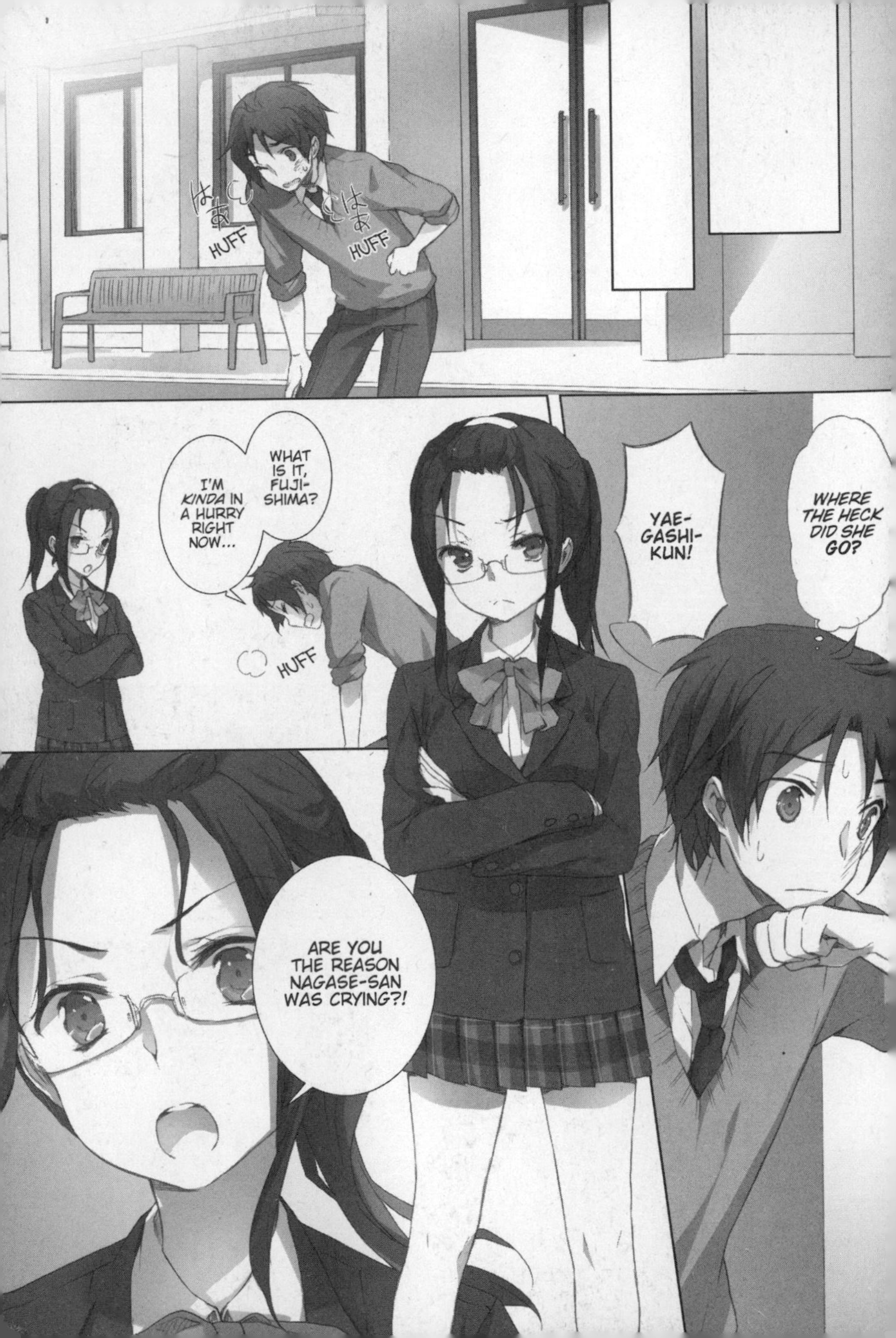
はぁ
HUFF
はぁ
HUFF
WHERE THE HECK DID SHE GO?
YAE-GASHI-KUN!
WHAT IS IT, FUJI-SHIMA?
I'M *KINDA* IN A HURRY RIGHT NOW...
HUFF
ARE YOU THE REASON NAGASE-SAN WAS CRYING?!

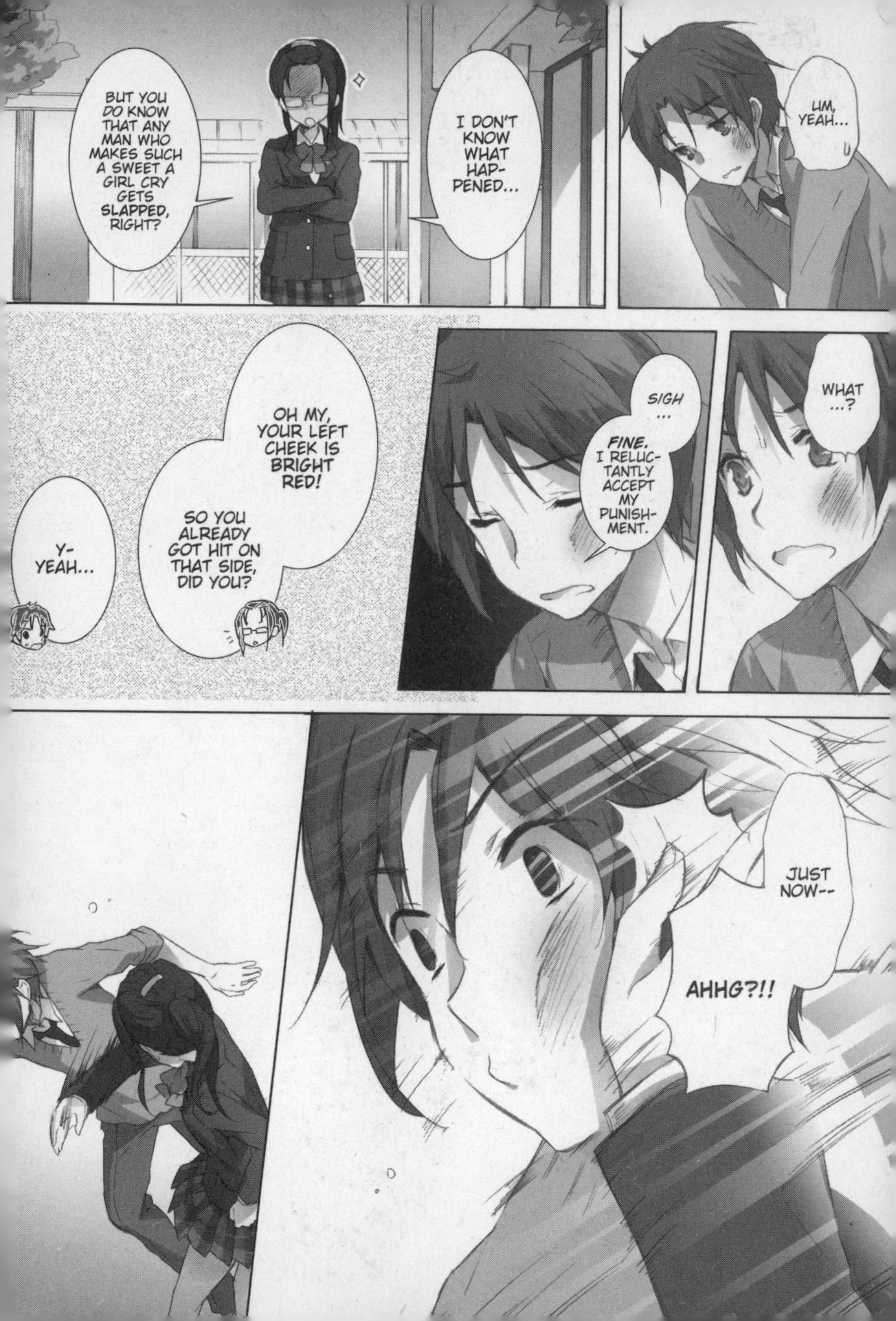
UM, YEAH...
I DON'T KNOW WHAT HAP-PENED...
BUT YOU DO KNOW THAT ANY MAN WHO MAKES SUCH A SWEET A GIRL CRY GETS SLAPPED, RIGHT?
WHAT ...?
SIGH ...
FINE. I RELUCTANTLY ACCEPT MY PUNISHMENT.
OH MY, YOUR LEFT CHEEK IS BRIGHT RED!
SO YOU ALREADY GOT HIT ON THAT SIDE, DID YOU?
Y-YEAH...
JUST NOW--
AHHG?!!

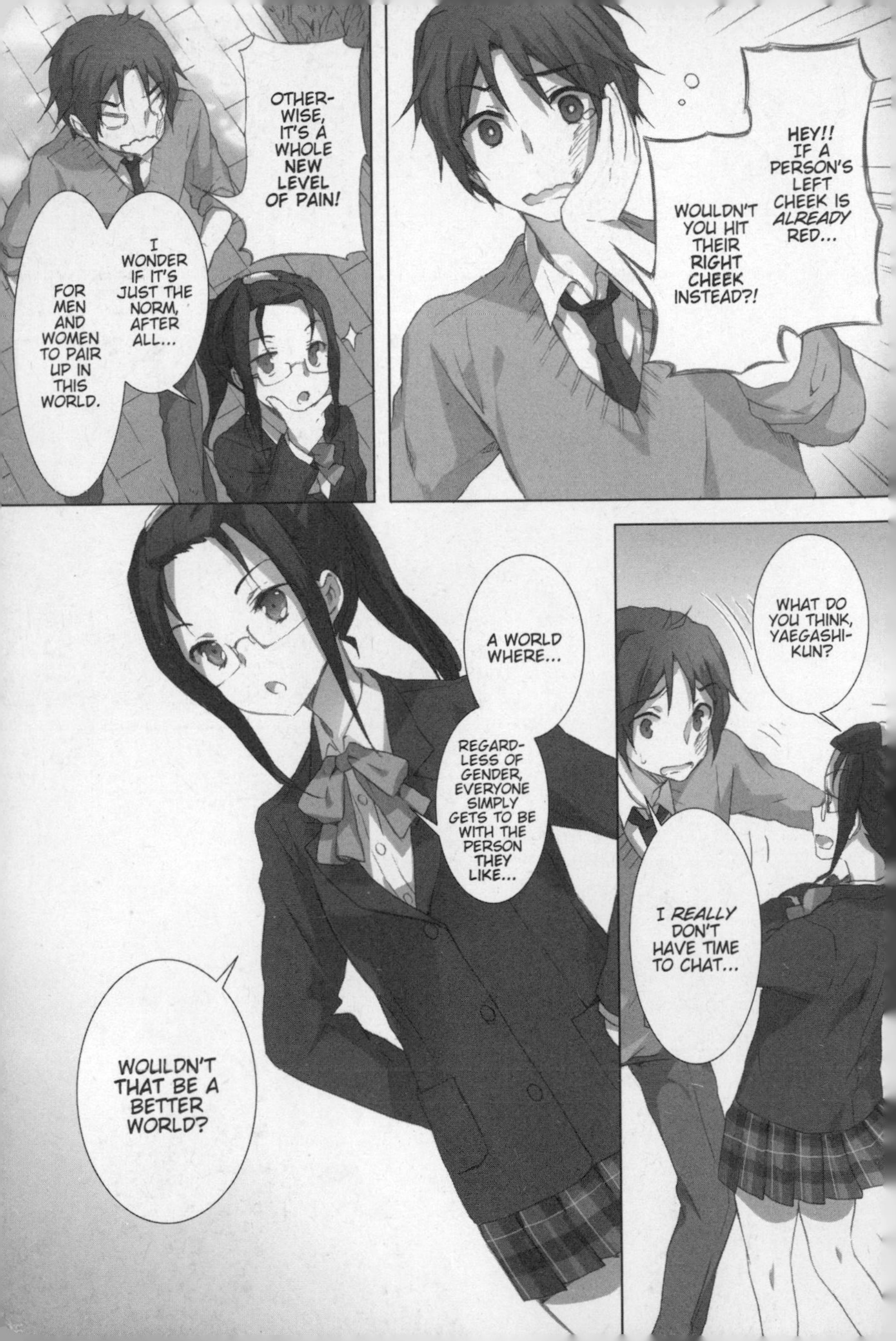
HEY!! IF A PERSON'S LEFT CHEEK IS *ALREADY* RED...
WOULDN'T YOU HIT THEIR RIGHT CHEEK INSTEAD?!
OTHER-WISE, IT'S A WHOLE NEW LEVEL OF PAIN!
I WONDER IF IT'S JUST THE NORM, AFTER ALL...
FOR MEN AND WOMEN TO PAIR UP IN THIS WORLD.
WHAT DO YOU THINK, YAEGASHI-KUN?
I *REALLY* DON'T HAVE TIME TO CHAT...
A WORLD WHERE...
REGARD-LESS OF GENDER, EVERYONE SIMPLY GETS TO BE WITH THE PERSON THEY LIKE...
WOULDN'T THAT BE A BETTER WORLD?

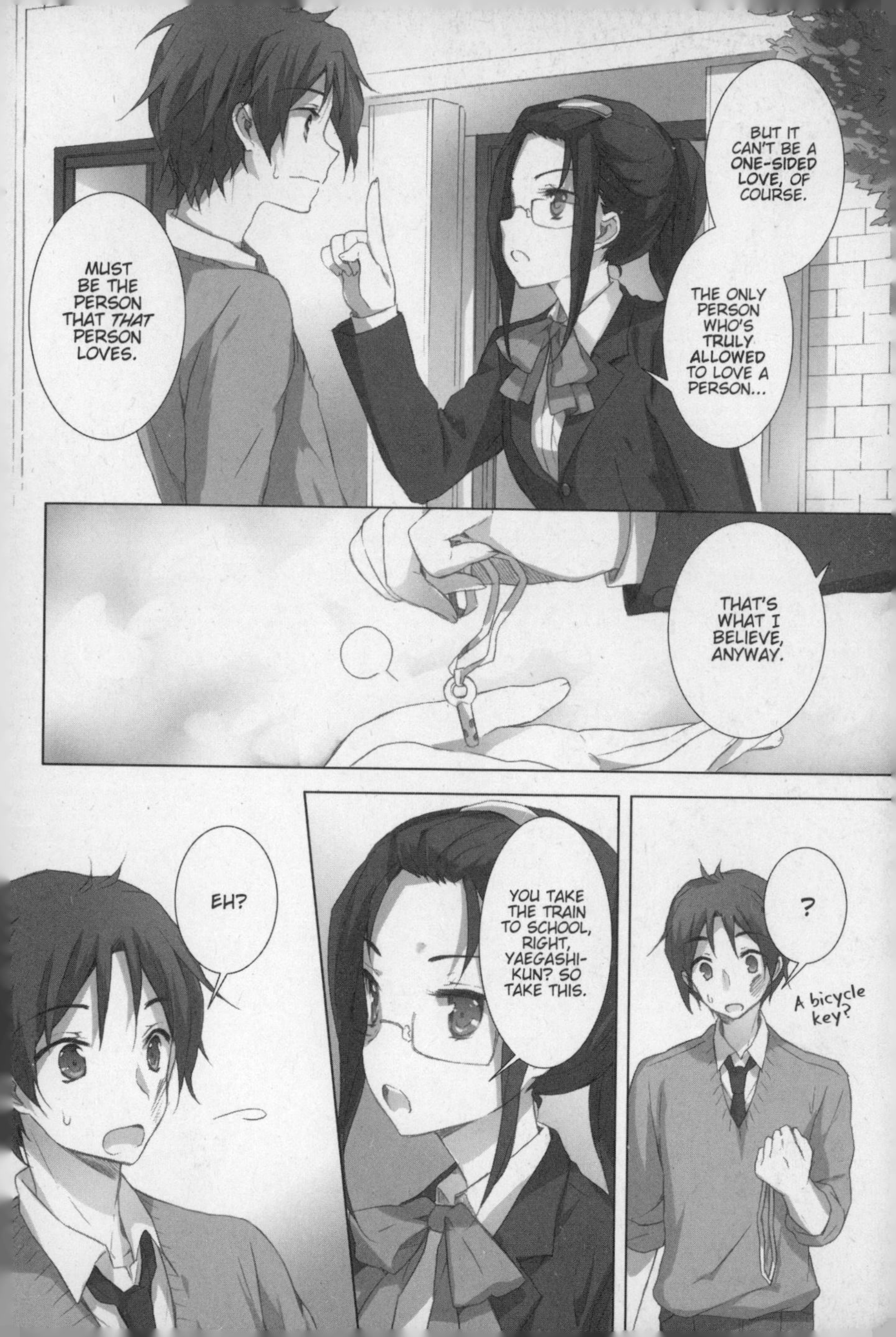
BUT IT CAN'T BE A ONE-SIDED LOVE, OF COURSE.
THE ONLY PERSON WHO'S TRULY ALLOWED TO LOVE A PERSON...
MUST BE THE PERSON THAT *THAT* PERSON LOVES.
THAT'S WHAT I BELIEVE, ANYWAY.
?
A bicycle key?
YOU TAKE THE TRAIN TO SCHOOL, RIGHT, YAEGASHI-KUN? SO TAKE THIS.
EH?

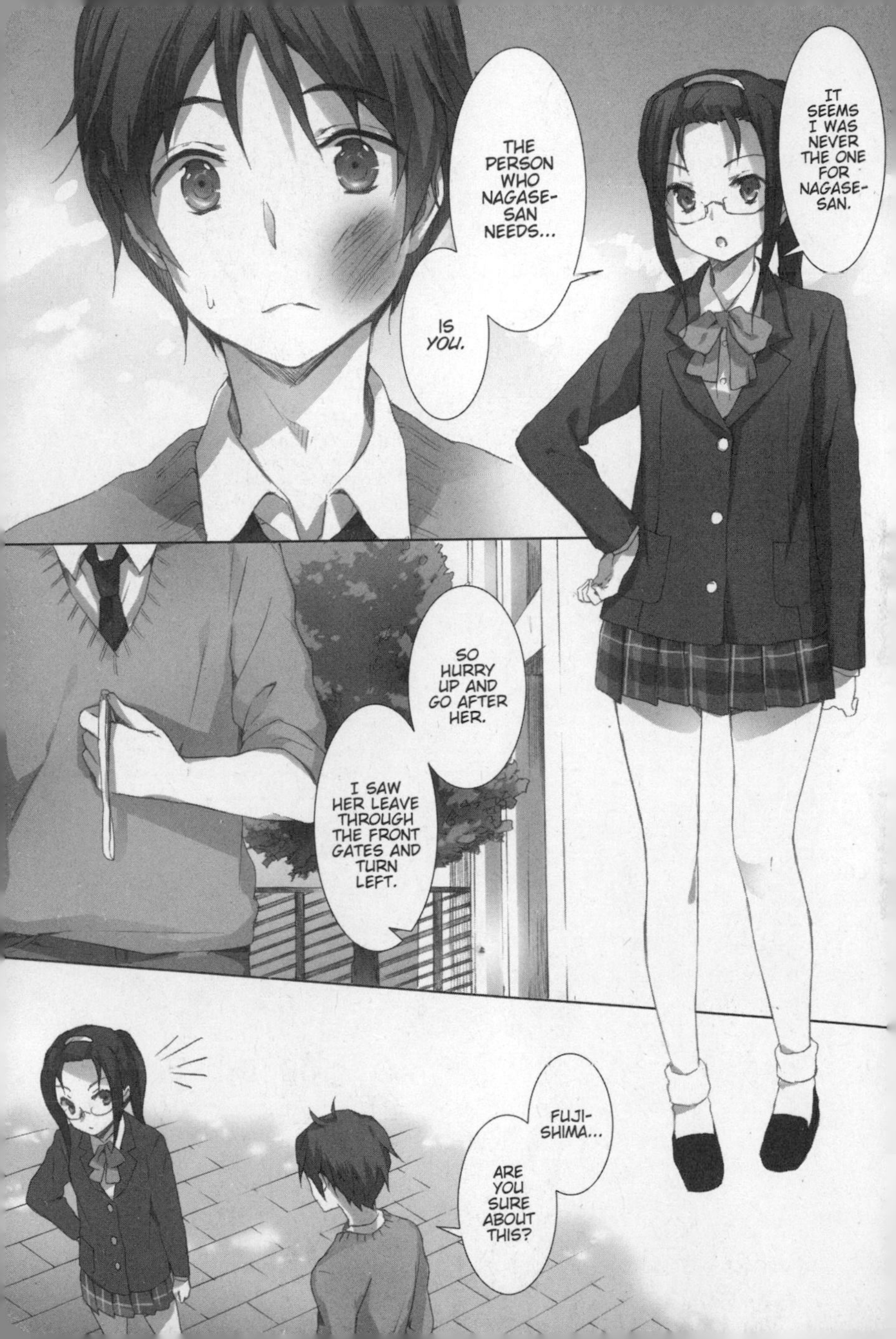
IT SEEMS I WAS NEVER THE ONE FOR NAGASE-SAN.
THE PERSON WHO NAGASE-SAN NEEDS...
IS YOU.
SO HURRY UP AND GO AFTER HER.
I SAW HER LEAVE THROUGH THE FRONT GATES AND TURN LEFT.
FUJI-SHIMA...
ARE YOU SURE ABOUT THIS?

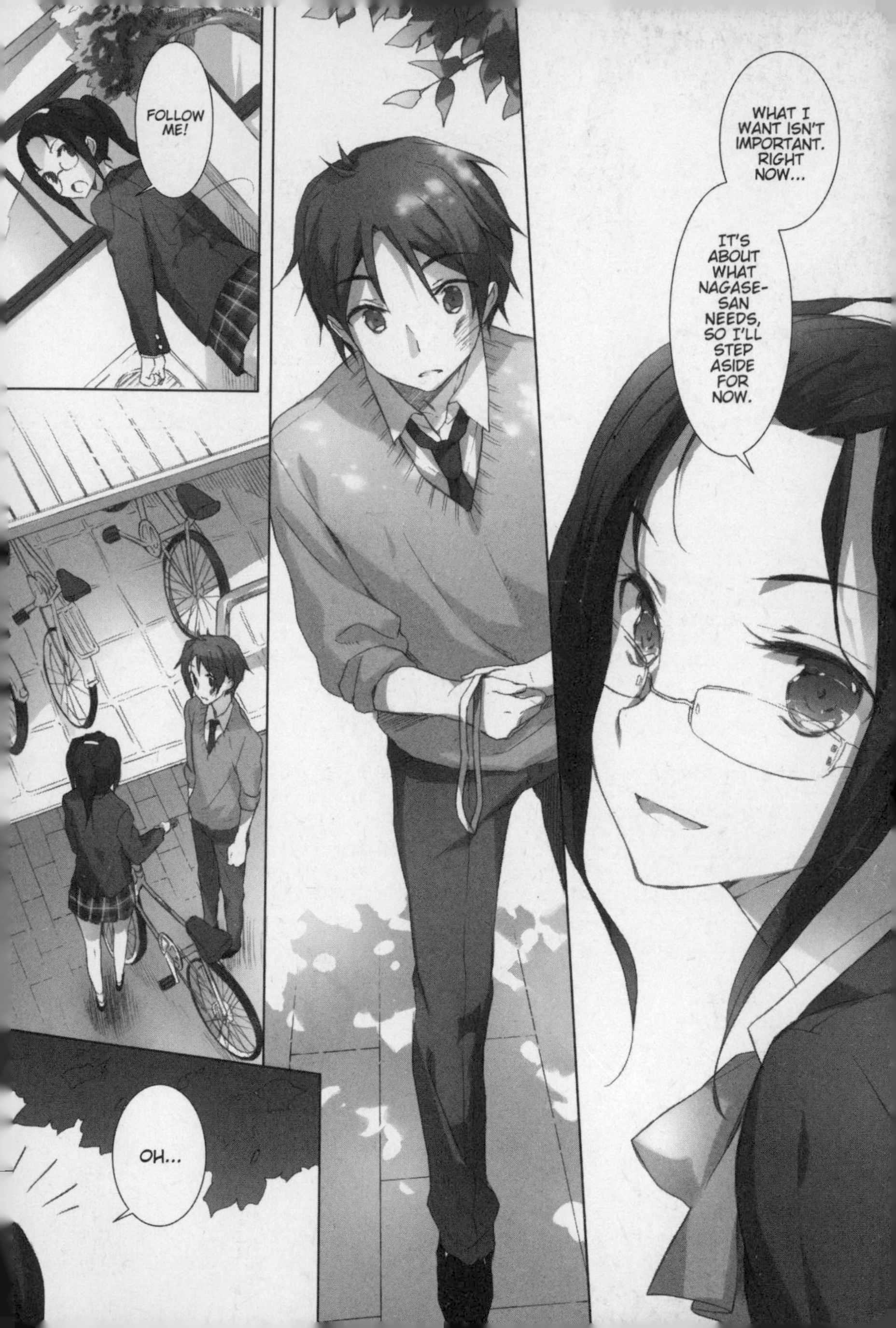
WHAT I WANT ISN'T IMPORTANT. RIGHT NOW...
IT'S ABOUT WHAT NAGASE-SAN NEEDS, SO I'LL STEP ASIDE FOR NOW.
FOLLOW ME!
OH...

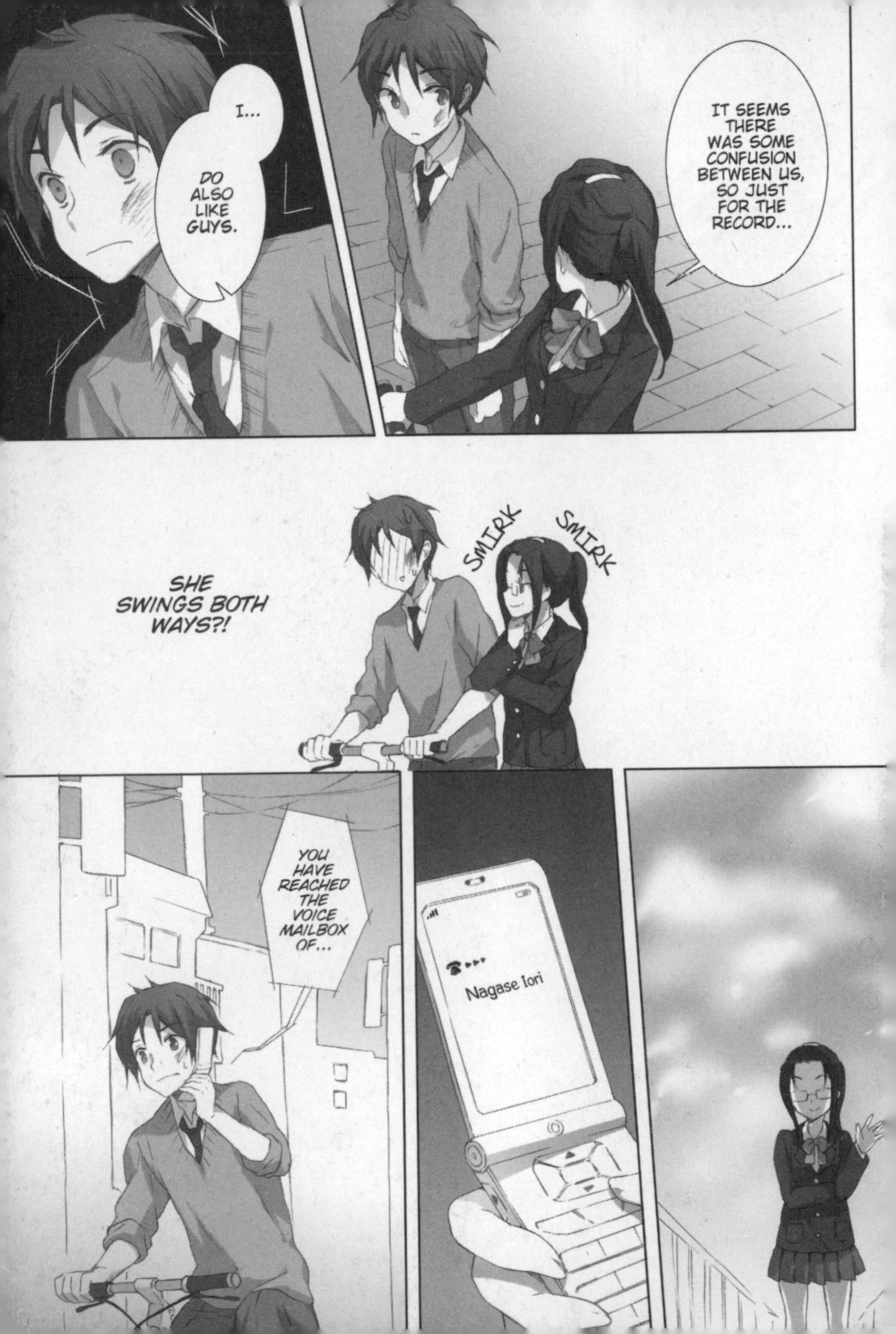
IT SEEMS THERE WAS SOME CONFUSION BETWEEN US, SO JUST FOR THE RECORD...
I...
DO ALSO LIKE GUYS.
SMIRK
SMIRK
SHE SWINGS BOTH WAYS?!
Nagase Iori
YOU HAVE REACHED THE VOICE MAILBOX OF...

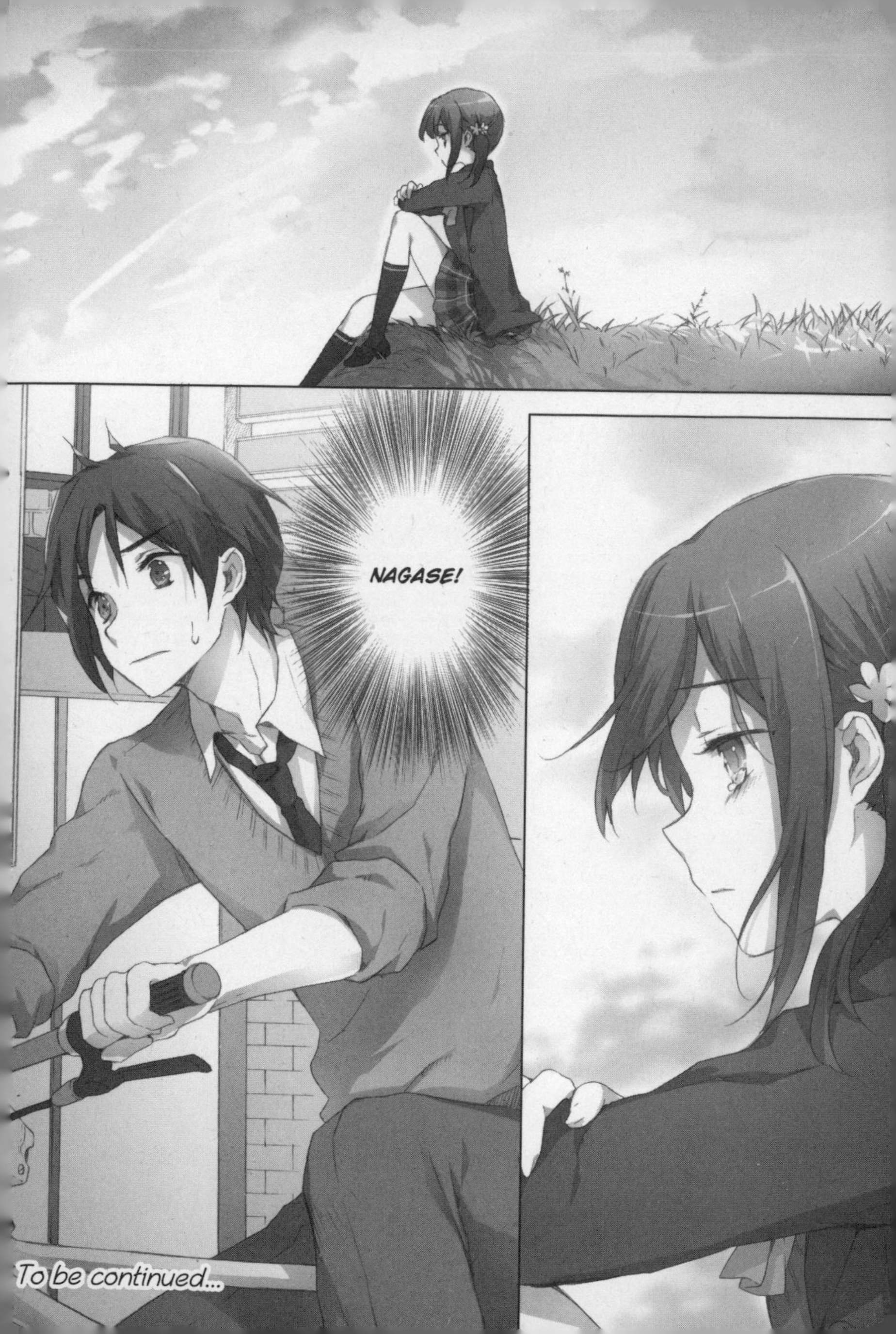
NAGASE!
To be continued...

KOKORO CONNECT

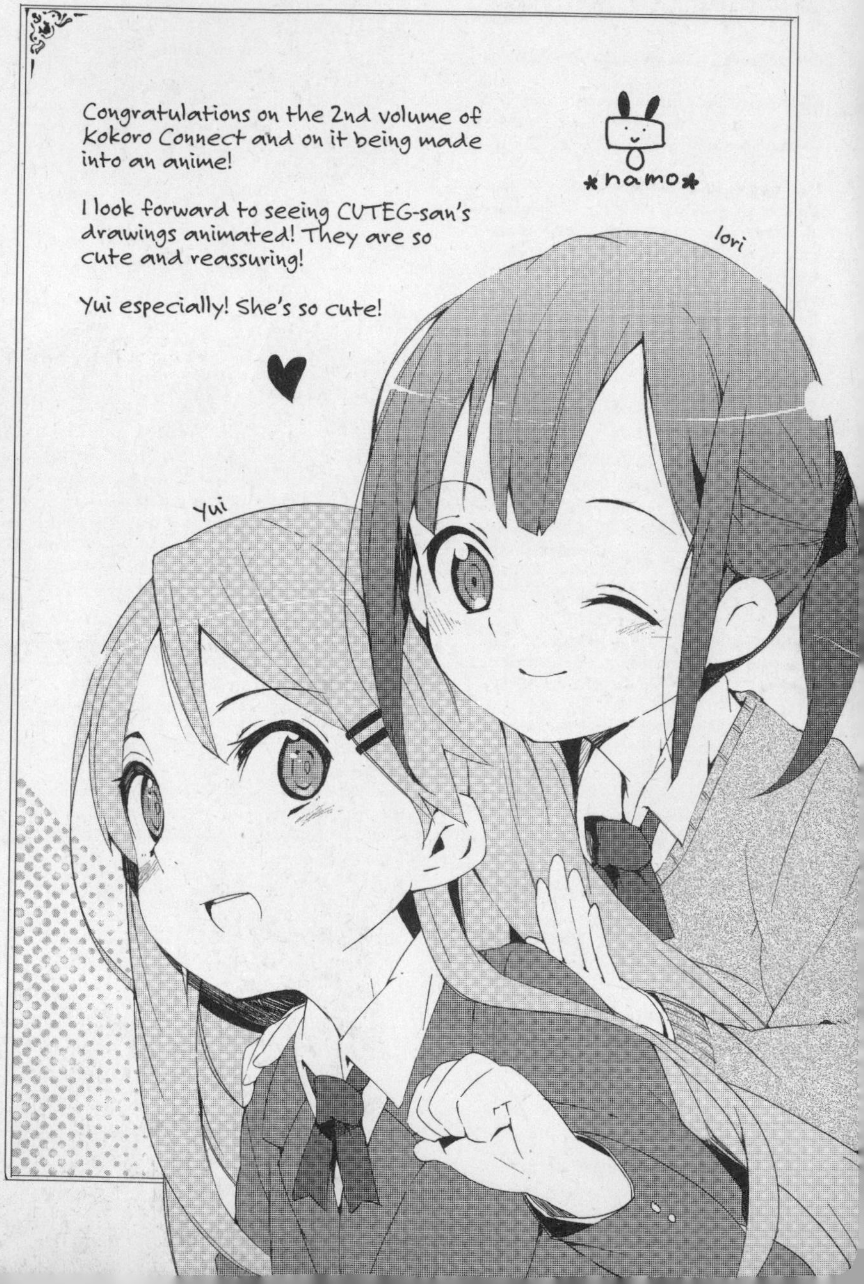
Congratulations on the 2nd volume of Kokoro Connect and on it being made into an anime!
I look forward to seeing CUTEG-san's drawings animated! They are so cute and reassuring!
Yui especially! She's so cute!
namo
Iori
Yui

AFTERWORD

It's volume 2! Thank you so much!!

Since Gossan didn't have a lot of appearances this time, I decided to draw him in this afterword. :D

I've been doing my best and drawing Kokoro Connect despite all the usual distractions and commotion around me. In fact, it's already been an entire year since I started to draw the manga adaptation of Kokoro Connect. I am always so surprised at how fast time goes by...

Now then,

ON BECOMING AN ANIME!

CONGRATULATIONS!
I am SO looking forward to it!

I can't help but feel excited when I think about getting to see everyone in action. Please, please, please continue to support Kokoro Connect from here on out!

+ Special thanks +

Sadanatsu Anda-san.
Shiromizakana-san
My handlers F-san and S-san
Mirin-chan Narin-chan
Pai-chan
Everyone who picked up this book!

CuteG
2011.12

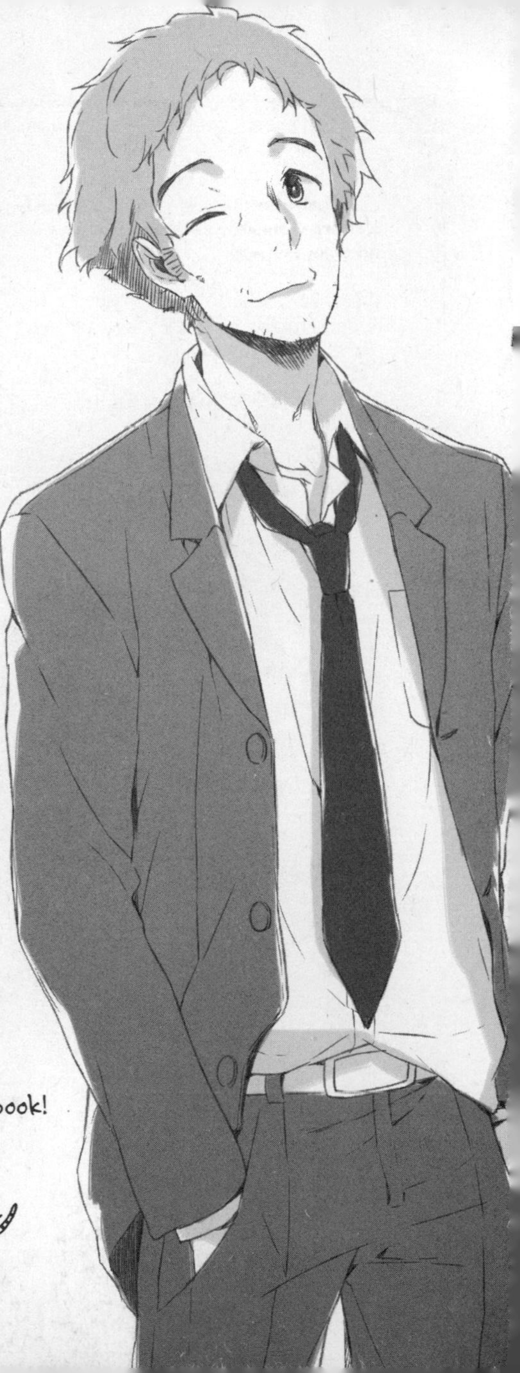

CUTEG COMMENT

MNCH

MNCH

This year, I think I'd like
to enjoy some winter sports...
like skiing or snowboarding
or what not.

CALGARY PUBLIC LIBRARY

NOV - - 2014